D1236317

Solitude and Compassion

Solitude and Compassion

The Path to the Heart of the Gospel

Gus Gordon

Maryknoll, New York 10545

Founded in 1970, Orbis Books endeavors to publish works that enlighten the mind, nourish the spirit, and challenge the conscience. The publishing arm of the Maryknoll Fathers and Brothers, Orbis seeks to explore the global dimensions of the Christian faith and mission, to invite dialogue with diverse cultures and religious traditions, and to serve the cause of reconciliation and peace. The books published reflect the opinions of their authors and are not meant to represent the official position of the Maryknoll Society. To obtain more information about Maryknoll and Orbis Books, please visit our website at www.maryknollsociety.org.

Copyright © 2009 by Gus Gordon.

Published by Orbis Books, Maryknoll, New York, U.S.A. All rights reserved.

No part of this publication may be reproduced or transmitted in any form or by any means, electronic or mechanical, including photocopying, recording, or any information storage or retrieval system, without prior permission in writing from the publishers. For permissions, write to Orbis Books, P. O. Box 308, Maryknoll NY 10545-0308, U.S.A.

Manufactured in the United States of America.

Manuscript editing and typesetting by Joan Weber Laflamme.

Library of Congress Cataloging-in-Publication Data

Gordon, Gus.
Solitude and compassion : the path to the heart of the gospel / Gus Gordon.
p. cm.
Includes index.
ISBN 978–1–57075–830–0
1. Solitude. 2. Compassion. 3. Spiritual life. I. Title.
BJ1499.S65G67 2008
204—dc22

2008035585

Contents

Part III
TOWARD A SPIRITUALITY OF INTEGRAL HUMANITY

Foreword

Richard Rohr

Why does religion not seem to be doing its job very well? Why are religious people too often the more greedy, the more security obsessed, the more likely to trust guns to protect themselves, and often the more racially bigoted, seemingly trapped inside of their own culture and nation? It does not speak of people who have met God or even met themselves. How could this happen on such a broad and now long-lasting scale, and among Christians of all stripes?

Jesus' most common and consistent self-naming was that he was a "son of the human" *(ben adan)* or, if you will, "a child of humanity"; he clearly saw himself as a member of the whole, the world beyond Judaism, one who was responsible for, and clearly in love with, *all* that God created. Jesus was very catholic, a universal man; it led him to point and move beyond the boundaries of his own nationality, religion, and social group. His highly transformed consciousness is rather clear and often scary to those of us who are not there yet. As his followers, we do not seem to be attaining anywhere near his level of transformation, which is exactly what he expected and offered: "I have given you an example, so that you may imitate what I have done" (Jn 13:15).

Gus Gordon has put his finger on the very heart of the problem. *We have gone neither deep nor broad.* We have emphasized neither solitude nor solidarity as essential to the spiritual journey. In fact, most of us are afraid of both and given little concrete training in either. Here is some training along with some fine sources and direction—with inspiration besides! You will be both deeper and broader by the time you finish this book.

World religion has largely been *follow the leader* and *belong to the group* up to now. This can get us only so far and is not very helpful when the more serious issues arise—like slavery, Nazism, racism, nationalism, social injustice, violence, earth care, and gross consumerism. Countries that self-identify as Christian have not been noteworthy in opposing or even recognizing most of these evils; in fact, they have often set the bar for history, and have set it very low. We who eat the body of Christ, and fight endlessly about how to do it, have not spent much time eating his actual message or method. One wonders after a while if it is an unconscious diversionary tactic whereby the ego can avoid actual conversion. If there is one thing the ego hates, it is to change. *We would rather keep rearranging the externals than change the internals.*

Jesus' relentless emphasis on interiority, undercutting of ego, and clarifying of intention ("shadow work") might make us think that Christianity would have moved the world to a higher level than mere external observances. But that did not happen. Why? I personally think because neither solitude nor solidarity is desired or possible in the first half of life, and we still live in a largely adolescent culture and church, where questions of identity, self-worth, status symbols, and security dominate.

Such wisdom as we find in the Gospels, the mystics, and the prophets, and in this book, will quickly send us on a path toward a "second half of life" spirituality, where we can ask the real questions of generativity, surrender, divine union, justice, and service, bridge building instead of boundary protecting, giving up control instead of trying to take control. *Solitude* and *solidarity* are perfect words to describe the real contents of religion instead of just more chatter about the container. *People who have met God can and will stand alone. People who have met God can and will stand together.*

Small "belonging systems," very passive attendance at religious services, ethnic groupings, often exclusionary at the core, largely became a substitute for any real personal or cultural transformation, much less any sense of mystical union, which is the ground for everything good and universal. "On that day you will know that I am in the Father, and you are in me, and I am in you" (Jn 14:20). We have ended up *worshiping* Jesus almost as a substitute for actually *following* him in either message or method. His life journey clearly exemplified a lot of chosen solitude, and a shocking-to-his-contemporaries solidarity—with outsiders, non-Jews, and even sinners. There was a clear connection between the two! He said "follow me," but he never once said "worship me."

Until we return to a practice-based spiritual life where people can know spiritual things to be true for themselves, as Jeremiah promised us (31:31–34) we will continue to:

1. Follow the leader as a substitute for the inner journey;
2. Belong to our groups, often defined by what we are against, and often passively attend their ceremonies as the very meaning of religion; and
3. Intellectually believe doctrines or moral positions to be true or not true.

We must be honest and admit that these three religious stances ask very little of us at all. It is a far cry from "leave all things and follow me" (Lk 14:33). As many have said, "If you want a prediction of the future, just keep repeating the past." And, "If you keep repeating the past, you will get the same future." These three church patterns are largely the ways that young people create identity, superiority, and security in the first half of life, but they are not very helpful in the second half of life. It is boundary keeping not bridge building. It is based on exclusion and not on inclusion. It is "group think," not God knowledge. *It is in true solitude that we find the wellsprings of God, self, and community, and it is in solidarity that we find the necessary outlets and cleansing for this bottomless well.*

Yes, we are largely an adolescent society, which I am sure God is patient with and still loves, but now I also know why Jesus wept (Lk 19:41). Two thousand years after the life-giving and explosive seed of the gospel, we have a right to hope for more from Christianity than mere "churchianity." At this point of immense global expansion and equally immense global devastation, we have no time for an infantile spirituality or a mere clerical reading of the Gospels. All of us are capable of drawing from that "inner spring inside, which wells up unto eternal life" (Jn 4:14). All of us are capable of loving beyond our own group, which alone deserves to be called love at all, according to Jesus (Mt 5:43–48).

We all know that God is very patient, but I am grateful that some of God's disciples are not, and that they share in the holy impatience of Job, Jesus, and the prophets. People like Gus Gordon are offering us adult religion and adult Christianity at a time when we cannot settle for anything less. *Those who are one inside will always create one world outside.* In fact, there is no other way.

Introduction

When I was a freshman at Villanova University in Pennsylvania, our religion professor challenged the class to read one religious book on sale at the university bookstore. I randomly chose *The Perfect Joy of St. Francis* by Felix Timmermans for no particular reason except maybe that attaining perfect joy did not sound like a bad idea. It turned out to be a providential choice because it so overwhelmed me that it set the ideals that have inspired and challenged me all my life. Francis's way of life was a wonderful and radical harmony between solitude and solidarity with the poor. He reflected the contemplative as well as the prophetic depths of Jesus in a most powerful and joyful way.

With this ideal burning in my heart and soul, I joined the Franciscan Order. As it turned out, I was privileged to meet the most marvelous individuals. But I soon discovered that the order had other priorities than either solitude or solidarity with the poor. The order was fundamentally committed to teaching at its various institutions. This basically meant that a member of the province needed to be dedicated to its institutional commitments. So I started to look elsewhere for communities that might have both solitude and solidarity as their fundamental priorities. I eventually concluded that I should attempt to live this vision on my own with a few companions. So for the past twenty years I have alternated my time between living in a hermitage atop a ridge in Middle Tennessee and going on the road to preach for the Food for the Poor ministry.

When you become accustomed to solitude and the world of nature, when you begin to relish the silence of the woods, the birds, the animals, the starry sky, when you cherish the simple warmth of loving relationships, you experience a gradual restoration of fundamental humanity. As a result you become increasingly sensitive to what is fake, vapid, and vacuous. It becomes harder and harder, for example, to watch TV, which seems to be more and more peopled by loud, jarring, glib, plastic, and even snide "personalities." And if you make the mistake of turning on one of the so-called Christian stations, you are often flabbergasted at what passes as religion. You witness audiences seemingly mesmerized by a steady stream of mindless, pietistic platitudes; audiences induced to jump and shout and flail their arms about "for Jesus." It's hard to tell the difference between this and audiences jumping up and down on "The Price Is Right" in the hope of winning a refrigerator. Then there is the Mother Angelica phenomenon, where Mother presides over what could be described in polite terms as a romper-room religion. It seems we are incredibly sophisticated in our society when it comes to finances, new technologies, smart bombs, sports, cars, entertainment, but all of a sudden revert to infancy when it comes to religion or spirituality. As one biblical scholar commented: "It's OK to have a fifth grade understanding of God and the scriptures—as long as you're in the fifth grade!" Or in the words of Saint Paul: "Everyone who lives on milk . . . is a child. But solid food is for the mature. . . . Leave behind the basic teaching about Christ and advance to maturity" (Heb 5:13—6:1). And, of course, there are the ever-present capitalist propagandists who wrap themselves up in self-serving moralities, passing themselves off as spokespeople for Christianity! What you discover is that the whole inner world is increasingly being hijacked and colonized by vulgar and specious pseudo-spiritualities. So it is back to solitude, silence, simplicity, and solicitude.

When visiting Christian parishes in the United States on behalf of Food for the Poor, you encounter another form of distorted spirituality. On the one hand, you are continually overwhelmed by the incredible people you meet who anonymously yet powerfully witness in their own unique way to Jesus and his radical gospel. So it is a "heart-full" journey, but it is also a disturbing one, because you are confronted with the pervasive and seemingly impregnable dichotomy between a highly privatized spirituality and any sense of responsibility for the suffering peoples of the world. Solitude spirituality has become radically dissociated from solidarity spirituality. Francis's vision of the gospel life has become a highly elusive reality.

In our information age it is almost culpable ignorance not to know what the world situation is, but what you discover is that most Americans have absolutely no idea of what is going on in the world. Perhaps the simplest way of describing the world situation is the following: On the planet today there are about 6.6 billion people. If we were to divide the world up into fifths according to standard of living, every person in the United States lives a lifestyle in the top fifth of this world. In other words, if all economic factors are considered, the poorest person in the United States lives materially better than four-fifths of humanity. At the bottom fifth, there are 1.3 billion people. Every one of them tonight will go to bed hungry and every one of them will have to try to survive on less than $370 a year! What we have, Pope John Paul II said, is the story of the rich man and Lazarus writ large, that is, globally.

Simone Weil, one of the great religious figures of the twentieth century, became convinced that Catholicism was not really Christian, even though she had a Dominican priest as her confessor. One day during the Second World War, when she and her companions were helping children made homeless when their orphanage was bombed, Simone decided to rest a while in quiet prayer at a nearby Catholic church. Much to her surprise the church was packed with people praising and thanking God that they were spared the bombing. But not one of them lent a hand in helping the homeless children. It was because of this experience that she never became a Catholic. If our churches are packed with people thanking God for their blessings and good fortune while remaining totally oblivious to and taking no responsibility for the suffering peoples of the world, then perhaps Simone Weil's conclusion is also true today.

Each year, the United States government allocates less than 0.2 percent of its vast wealth to the poorest billion of our brothers and sisters of this world. Although this is truly scandalous in itself, even more scandalous is that of all the funds gathered in a given year in the Christian churches of the United States, less than 0.2 percent are allocated to the poorest billion people living literally in the ditches of the world. Listening to Jesus' parable of the good Samaritan, could we not conclude that the Christian churches have in fact institutionalized the approach of the priest and Levite who walk past the man in the ditch?

The question that concerns me most is this: where are those voices, those communities, those visions that hold together that profound vision of Saint Francis of Assisi: solitude and solidarity? This question is the basis for this book.

The following are the teachers who have guided me most in this exploration:

- Thomas Merton, a Catholic Trappist monk who wrote extensively on both contemplative and social issues. Theologian David Tracy ranks Merton as "perhaps the most significant Christian figure in twentieth-century America." As Clifford Stevens puts the matter: "The men of the twenty-fifth and fiftieth centuries, when they read the spiritual literature of the twentieth century, will judge the age by Merton." I am indebted to no one more than Merton for witnessing to and delving deeply into the life of solitude as well as turning his most penetrating insights onto the great problems of the world.
- Raimon Panikkar, a Catholic priest, born in Spain, citizen of India, and long-time resident of the United States. He holds doctorates in chemistry, philosophy, and theology. He speaks a dozen languages and writes in six of them. His contributions to comparative religions and Christian theology have made him a foremost pioneer in East-West interreligious dialogue. He is one of the leading religious thinkers of our time. I have found his insights profound, challenging, brilliant, and inspirational.
- Martin Buber, a Jewish philosopher who may be the greatest religious thinker of the twentieth century. He proposed a religious philosophy of dialogue as well as a "horizontal" mysticism that radically confronts the privatization of religion as well as the reduction of personal life to psychologism. As great as Buber's books are, he was greater still as a man, especially at the time of his people's most terrible agony. On the occasion of Buber's eightieth birthday, the eminent theologian H. Richard Niebuhr wrote: "More than any other person in the modern world, more even than Kierkegaard, Martin Buber has been for me, and for many of my companions, the prophet of the world and the witness to that truth which is required of the soul not as solitary but as companionable being."

Abraham Joshua Heschel told a *Newsweek* reporter when Buber died: "I know of no one with a life as rich with intellectual adventures or who so strongly responded to their challenges as Martin Buber. His greatest contribution was himself, his very being."

- Chogyam Trungpa, a Buddhist scholar and teacher following the Tantric tradition. He was an abbot in a monastery in Tibet until Tibet was invaded by the Chinese communists. When he migrated to America, he founded the Naropa Institute in Boulder, Colorado. He became possibly the greatest expositor of Tibetan Buddhism of the twentieth century. He is certainly the most brilliant and insightful Buddhist teacher I have ever come across.
- Emmanuel Levinas, one of the most acclaimed philosophers of our time. Pope John Paul II once said in Paris: "There are two great philosophers in the religious sphere: Levinas and Ricoeur." For Jean Luc-Marion, Levinas, "along with Bergson, were the greatest French philosophers of the twentieth century." Levinas spoke out of both the Jewish and the Greek traditions. Levinas insisted on the primacy of ethics and on an exorbitant and infinite responsibility for other human beings.
- Joseph Campbell, a preeminent scholar, writer, and teacher who was the world's foremost authority on mythology as well as a brilliant interpreter of our most sacred traditions. His religious insights are at once provocative, profound, creative, and unique. He often challenged the religious presumptions of our times.
- Johann Baptist Metz, a Catholic priest who is one of the greatest and most influential European theologians of our time. He is most widely known for his development of what he calls political theology, which radically challenges the individualistic and privatizing tendencies of today's religious life.
- Pedro Casaldaliga, Catholic bishop of Sao Felix, Brazil. One of the greatest living Christians whose courage, compassion, and fierce pursuit of justice have led him to be unceasing in his struggle for the poor and to be on their side in solidarity. His writings are profoundly sharp, insightful, and radically challenging.
- Ibn Al Arabi (1165–1240), a spiritual genius who is one of the greatest mystics of all time. He is known in Islam as al-Shaykh al-Akbar, the Greatest Spiritual Master, and has been the most influential thinker in Islam over the past seven hundred years. Through the richness of his personal experience and the constructive power of his intellect, he made a unique contribution to Sufism.
- Aloysius Pieris, SJ, a leading Sri Lanken liberation theologian, founder and director of the Tulana Research Center in Kelaniyu, Sri Lanka. He is the first non-Buddhist to receive a doctorate in Buddhism from the University of Sri Lanka. In his writings he presents a profound, creative, unique, and challenging integration of the solitude/solidarity dynamic.

PART I

SOLITUDE

1

The Solitude/Solidarity Dynamic

One of the fundamental dynamics we discover in human existence is the interplay and sometimes tension between solitude and solidarity. This core human dynamic is a challenge and dilemma not only to one's personal life but also is found in one of society's basic socio/political tensions, that is, between individual liberty and collective responsibility. This dialectic of two fundamental human categories has been alternately characterized as withdrawal/engagement, personhood/community, autonomy/relationship, the kingdom within/without, contemplation/action, gnosis/agape, East/West, and so on. If the Eastern world unfolds its energy inwardly, emphasizing silence and withdrawal, the Western world demonstrates its dynamism outwardly, emphasizing communication and engagement. If the East accepts and endures, the West conquers and transforms. If the Easterner is serene, the Westerner is always struggling. If the Easterner is homeward bound, the Westerner is always on the go.

This dynamic is reflected in each person's unique constitutive essence and psychological makeup. On the psychological level, Carl Jung contrasts introverted people, who find their center of energy within, with extroverts, who are energized primarily from without. Jung believed that

> the introverted nature is Platonic in that it is mystical, spiritualized, and perceives in symbolic forms, while the extraverted nature is Aristotelian in that it is practical, a builder of a solid system from the Platonic ideal. The introvert is directed primarily toward an understanding of what he perceives, while the extravert naturally seeks means of expression and communication.[1]

If the solitary, contemplative, introverted type leans toward the internal, idealistic, theoretical, abstract, intuitive, a-historical, the active, extroverted person moves more towards the outward, realistic, practical, existential, historical. This fundamental dialectic raises a question: If solitude and solidarity are two primordial modes of human existence, how do we hold both together all the while faithful to our unique personhood as well as our responsibility to the world?

What we find historically is that there has been a continual debate concerning the merits of solitude and solidarity. There have always been those who have been so dedicated to one part of the polarity that they have minimized, ignored, or even denigrated the other. If, for example, one experiences the human person as fundamentally alone, then the emphasis will be on the need for solitude. But if one sees a person as basically a social being, then the call will be for solidarity in relationships. The philosopher John Cowper Powys maintains in *A Philosophy of Solitude* that "the conscious 'I am I' within us is absolutely alone. It is alone from the first moment of its awareness of life to its last moment on the threshold of what may be its final extinction."[2] He therefore concludes that "the drifting, brainless, gregariousness of so many human beings, competing for, tormenting one another, is an attempt to escape from this inherent loneliness of the self."[3] So, for him, social relationships are an escape, not a fulfillment. He agrees with Jean Rostand, who said, "To be adult is to be alone";[4] or as the Hindus traditionally believe, all human beings ideally mature into hermits. Carl Jung, who traveled a lonely route, maintained in *Psychology and Alchemy* that for a man, "the highest and most decisive experience of all . . . is to be alone with his own self."[5] Therefore, someone like Thoreau, living alone on Walden Pond, demonstrated an exemplary way of living an authentic existence. Thoreau once said: "I find it wholesome to be alone the greater part of the time. To be in company, even with the best, is soon wearisome and dissipating."[6]

On the other hand, as Paul Tillich notes, the first thing the God of the Bible deemed not good was that Adam was alone. Or, as it is written in Ecclesiastes: "It is better that two be together than one. . . . Woe to him that is alone" (Eccl 4:9, 10). Archbishop Desmond Tutu explains: "In our African idiom we say a person is a person through other persons; that the solitary, totally self-sufficient person is a contradiction in terms; such a person is really subhuman."[7] D. H. Lawrence insisted on much the same point:

> Everything, even individuality itself, depends on relationship. . . . The light shines only when the circuit is complete. . . . In absolute isolation, I doubt if any individual amounts to much; or any soul is worth saving, or even having. My individualism is really an illusion. I am part of the great whole, and I can never escape. But I can deny my connections, break them . . . and become a fragment. Then I am wretched.[8]

Perhaps Sartre stated the case most starkly: "We are . . . delivered from the 'internal life' . . . in that everything is finally outside, everything, even ourselves . . . outside, in the world, among others."[9] From this perspective, living a life in solitude would be a totally inauthentic mode of existence, since sociality defines true humanity.

In seeking to find the deepest possible roots of this primordial dialectic of solitude/solidarity and their integration, I believe it is necessary to begin exploring reality from a mystical/metaphysical point of view. Without a mystical/

metaphysical approach, any further analysis will surely lack any ontological depth. It is important here to concede that any understanding of the Divine can never fully correspond to the divine mystery. There is always the danger of creating a conceptual idol. But with this proviso, it is not necessary to conclude that nothing conceptual should be attempted. I believe David Steindl-Rast is right when he says, "Our theoretical understanding of spirituality is just as important as our actual experiences of God, or Buddha, or spirit of any name."[10]

We can discover in the mystics from all the different traditions (both East and West) that this within/without or alone/together polarity is intuited in the ontological depths of reality. God (or Reality) has been revealed (unveiled) as at once God unmanifest (the within of God) and God manifest (God without); as both self-sufficient and self-diffusive; as both alone and relational. If the East emphasizes God "unmanifest" (emptiness, *sunyata*, and so on), the West has emphasized God manifest (creation, revelation, logos).

The God unmanifest is the unknowable God—the *Theos agnostos*, Nothing, Mystery, *Sunyata*, God beyond God, the Unnameable, the God beyond qualities, the Tao that cannot be spoken, the silent, hidden, solitary, supra-personal God. Out of this unknowable divine essence comes forth the God manifest or *Deus revelatus—Tathata*, Yahweh, Christ, Logos, Allah. Using Teilhardian terms, we could say that there was a "flaring forth of the primordial energy." Raimon Panikkar writes:

> An undifferentiated Unity, a mysterious Principle, moved itself from solitude, freed itself from inactivity, created, produced, gave birth to existence, to time, to space and all that moves in-between. There was, or rather there is, a first originating moment, a Source, a One, a God, a Matter, a Seed.[11]

The unmanifest God, in a way of speaking, did not wish to remain alone without offspring, barren in itself. From infinity all things, all latent individualities, called divine Names by such mystics as the Christian Dionysius the Aeropagite and the Sufi philosopher Ibn al Arabi, have yearned to be revealed. They have sought to be emancipated from their virtuality, freed from their inactivity. "God wanted to know himself, hence creation," says the Buddhist scholar D. T. Suzuki. The divine Essence out of a deep yearning to become manifest liberated the divine Names from the solitude of their unknowness. It is as if the psychogenesis of creation is the Divinity's need for self-reflection, self-enjoyment, self-giving, and self-relating; as if creation is a mirror in which the Divine essence beholds Itself, shares Itself, and becomes Itself.

Plato understood God unmanifest as the Good "beyond being" that actually transcends existence but this "self-sufficing Perfection" is also, at the same time, a "self-emptying Fecundity" that is the source and origin of all manifest creation. Arthur Lovejoy summarizes Plato's insight: "A timeless and incorporeal One became the ground as well as the dynamic source of the existence of a temporal and material and extremely variegated universe." Plato called this entire manifest creation a "visible, sensible God."[12]

A further understanding of this divine dynamic, which emerges especially in our time because of such visionaries as Pierre Teilhard de Chardin, is to see this divine self-expressing and self-realizing emerging in a constant state of becoming. This divine primordial energy is, as it were, in a constant state of urgency to give, to share, to grow, to expand, to become new and renewed. In the words of Beatrice Bruteau: "The natural pressure of Being [is] to expand, to be more and to give Being, to be in every possible way."[13]

If we turn our attention to the Buddhist perspective, we find that when Buddhists speak of emptiness (the unmanifest), they are not talking of simple nothingness in a nihilistic sense. Rather, the Buddhist *sunyata* (emptiness) is alternately translated as both "emptiness" and "bursting with fullness." That is why Chogyam Trungpa refers to it as "fertile emptiness, pregnant emptiness."[14] Or, as Ram Dass explains: "Emptiness is really not empty; emptiness is full of *everything*. The 'everything' is just not manifest."[15] Adding further insight to this emptiness, the ancient Cabbalists taught that the one characteristic that could be attributed to an otherwise indefinable "infinite nothingness" was that it was a bestower, a giver. A corresponding insight can be found in the thought of the Christian Franciscan, Saint Bonaventure. In his *Itinerarium* he agrees with Plato that the first and highest principle of Reality is the Good. And, as he sees it, the primary quality of this Good is that it is self-diffusive. Hence, Bonaventure intuits that the highest Good is the most self-diffusive. Creation can then be seen as a "sacrifice, a giving of oneself, a creative immolation."[16] We could further note that in our time Heidegger insisted on translating *Es Gibt* not in the usual way, "It is," but more primordially as "It gives." The ultimate term is never the subject, nor the object, nor even Being, but givenness. This has in some sense led theologians, especially Jean-Luc Marion, to rethink God not through the heavy metaphysical language of Being, substance, or essence, but instead in terms of love, gift, excess.

The central Christian biblical metaphor for understanding this divinity is to see the divine intention to share its being as *agape*. *God is Love* is the central Christian intuition about the great mystery. Passionate, overflowing, infinitely giving love is the essence of divine Being. Dionysius the Areopagite adapts the Christian experience that God is love to the Greek notion of *eros* or yearning. If God unmanifest (understood as without qualities) has any qualities at all, then it is an abyss of love. This love is ecstatic and creative, so it draws God out of hiddenness and leads the divine energy to center its being on the object of divine love: creation. As he understands it, the eternal, passionate God is "beguiled by goodness, by love, and by yearning and is enticed away from his transcendent dwelling and comes to abide within all things."[17]

This insight finds its Christian foundation in the Christian intuition that this divine within/without or emptiness/form is seen as not so much dialectical as trinitarian or tri-alectical, hence personal and relational, as we shall see. The divine mystery (Karl Rahner comments: "The Mystery we call God") is intuited as at once supra-personal and personal; eternal transcendence and infinite communion. The unmanifest (Father) and the manifest (Son) and the eternal love between them (Spirit) are seen as three distinct modes (divine persons) of the Real, and therefore the Real, or ultimate mystery, is always supra-personal and personal at the same time. The Alone is always engaged. The supra-personal is never impersonal. What we have, on the one hand, is the insistence that "as the Father has life in himself, so he has granted the Son also to have life in himself" (Jn 5:26). In other words, we are pointing to the unique, solitary identity of each person or the person's *entasy*. Yet, on the other hand, each of these personal modes is intuited as being in one another *(ecstasy)*, living and dwelling in one another, where each is not static but a living process of self-donation, so eagerly giving itself to the other that their acts of loving life-exchange set up an unceasing circulation of self-energy and self-gift. In the words of Raimon Panikkar: "A current of love circulates throughout the three worlds [theos/cosmos/anthropos]. Love, to be sure, is no mere feeling; it is, rather, the dynamism itself of the real, the force that moves the universe."[18] Therefore, the self-giving of divinity is at once a relating, in a relationship with, in a process of communing, a communion, and a community. As Martin Buber believed, "In the beginning is the relation, and in the relation is the power which creates the world, through us and with us and by us, you and I, you and we, and none of us alone."[19]

I would like to introduce here the understanding that what we say of divinity is also at the same time a saying about humanity. As Karl Rahner taught, all theology must also be anthropology. Every statement about God must also be a statement about humanity. In light of this, Raimon Panikkar makes an important point: "Everything that exists, any real being, presents this triune constitution expressed in three dimensions."[20] There is a threefold core of all that exists insofar as it is. Or to put it in Beatrice Bruteau's words: "We are not merely made in the image of God but we are made in the image of Trinity."[21] A person, therefore, cannot be conceived of simply in the singular alone (entasy), but also in the plural (ecstasy). "It may not be possible (has no meaning,)" concludes Bruteau, "to find the image of God in *myself*, singular. Just as God does not (cannot) exist as only one Person, so we are the image not as singulars alone but as the community. As images of the Holy Trinity, we are, in our deepest reality, the Holy Communion."[22] Panikkar concludes in a very similar way: "Person is relation because Being is relation. Being is a verb, a communitarian—that is, personalist . . . and to-be-together is the act of being.'"[23] Hence, one of the key understandings of ourselves as persons is that we are at once solitary (identity/entasy) and relational (communion/ecstasy), and we participate fully in the divine nature when we enter into communion with reality from our own ground, with others who are also in the deepest dimension *themselves*, as well as an essential dimension of *ourselves*.

To conclude, therefore, through the many spiritual and philosophical traditions the depths of the Real are discovered as at once emptiness and form, unmanifest and manifest, alone and relational, supra-personal and personal, self-sufficient and infinite giving, being and becoming, solitary and in solidarity with all creation. We could also extend this dia- or tria-lectic further, seeing *Spirit* as the third term, or the energy field that potentiates and integrates both poles. For a more inclusive vision we find that the Real embraces stability and flexibility; self and the other, inside and outside, exclusive and inclusive; determinism and freedom; predictability and unpredictability; order and randomness; self-protection and self-sacrifice or self-giving. It is central to this study to understand that all these intermingling primordial realities are found in the depths of human nature. We are all made in the image of the great Mystery. We are all, in a sense, mini-expressions of the divine Energy. We could even say that it is because we discover these dynamics within our human nature that we intuit (some would say "reify these insights to conclude") that this is the nature of the Real.

Ken Wilber makes the point that there are two primary ways in our spiritual traditions that we respond to this fundamental dynamic between emptiness and form, aloneness and relationship, between being and becoming. Wilber posits that we are either *ascenders* or *descenders*.[24] Carl Jung made a similar distinction between mystics who either deny or embrace.

Plato and much of the early Buddhist tradition would be examples of ascenders. One first ascends to the Absolute (emptiness) by denying or detaching oneself from the visible world (flux) only to return and embrace the world. Ascenders are those who seek to remove themselves from or transcend the world of rational thinking, the senses, and relationships to refine their perceptions and go in search of the One, beyond the many and form altogether. They seek, in Plotinus's phrase, to be "alone with the Alone."

It is with Saint Augustine that we find the Christian basis for Western spirituality. His concentration on "God and soul" devalued both the human body and the sensuous experience of sociality and nature. Rather, he zeroed in on inward, direct, self-experience as *the* way to God. So Saint Augustine, for example, desired to know "God and the soul." "Nothing else?" "No, nothing else!" Those who want to know God must forget the world, close the door on all their senses, and withdraw themselves through contemplation. Then they will simultaneously come to know both themselves and God. Hence Saint Augustine counseled: "Do not wish to go out; go back into yourself. Truth dwells in the inner man."[25] Or as Thomas Merton, early in his life as a monk, describes such an approach: "How simple it is to find God in solitude. There is no one else, nothing else. He is all there is to find. Everything is in Him. And what could be more pleasing to Him than we should leave all things and all company to be with Him and think only of Him and know Him alone, in order to give Him our love."[26]

The descenders take a radically different approach. It is not out of participation in a solitary relationship with the great Mystery that one comes to know creation but rather through creation one comes to know the great Mystery. Teilhard de Chardin expresses it, "Purity does not lie in separation from, but in a more profound penetration of the Universe."[27] Martin Buber's thought would be a prime example of a descender spirituality. For Buber, God is not only "wholly Other" but at one and the same time the "wholly Same," the mystery of the self-evident, nearer to me than my I. Thus, for an authentic relationship with the Real or "Thou," we are not called to be lost in an ecstasy in which we no longer hear the call of the immediate hour. Nor will we find meaning in the world yonder, but here and now, demanding confirmation in this life and in relation to this world.

Buber teaches that mysticism need not lead us outside the world; rather, he directs us to this concrete world so that we can see the seen and taste the tasted with the strength of our lives. We come to know the holiness of the world "by bending over the experienced thing with fervor and power, until the confronting, the shaping, the bestowing side of things spring up to meet me and embrace me."[28] Relationship to the eternal Thou is not separate from the inter-human, the communal or the social but rather is the radical center of them all. There is no such thing, therefore, as an I-Thou relationship with God that comes when one turns away from neighbor and world. Buber's asceticism is not giving up relationships and the things of this world but rather turning one's whole existence to the meeting with reality of this world and not apart from it. As Buber explains: "I have given up the 'religious' which is nothing but the exception, extraction, exaltation, ecstasy. . . . I possess nothing but the everyday out of which I am never taken. . . . I know no fullness but each mortal hour's fullness of claim and responsibility."[29]

In contrasting the ascender spirituality with descender spirituality we come to see that we are, in fact, dealing with two distinct forms of mysticism. We may say that both the solitary life and a life of solidarity have their own unique mysticisms. *Mysticism* is not a univocal term and thus can be seen and experienced in many different modes. If we could come up with at least a tentative understanding of mysticism, we could say that it points to the experiential and transformative union of a person with the ultimate Mystery of life, where the veils of illusion and egotism give way to the heart of the Real. Or we could tentatively appropriate Leonardo Boff's compelling outlook:

> Mysticism is life itself apprehended in its radicalism and extreme density. Existence is endowed with gravity, buoyancy, and depth. . . . Mysticism always leads to the transcendence of all limits.[30]

Working out of this proposition, we discover that *solitary* mysticism seeks, in a primarily private, interior experience and expression, union with God, the Real, or Emptiness. It can take either an intellective or affective approach, but the constant is the solitary experience.

One of the main forms of solitary mysticism found in the East, as well as in a few Western mystics like Meister Eckhart, is what Huston Smith calls "intellective mysticism." By *intellection* he means that there is something in the soul that is so intrinsic to God that it is one with God. That something is "the pure intellect itself." This is how he describes it: "When we turn inward and brush aside the contents of consciousness to get at the pure awareness that underlies it, we realize we *are* that awareness, which, as intellection, is the Godhead. Not the fullness of the Godhead, but the Godhead all the same."[31] Intellective mysticism places the emphasis on the intellect and thus instinctively positions knowing above loving, wisdom above compassion, truth above the good, and unity above the union of communion. According to Saint Augustine, if we trace the intellect to its ground, we discover God as truth or wisdom.

Intellective mysticism involves a mental or conscious transformation where knowledge itself, according to Proclus, "is a kind of conversion." A person is called, not to ecstasy or relational love, but to insight or enlightenment. Enlightenment, which is the goal, has no personal note in it. Satori remains thoroughly impersonal. From this perspective all things of the universe are seen as the essence of the Mind itself. But this knowledge of intellective mysticism is beyond that of the discursive intellect. Rather, it employs the intellect to transcend the intellect. By a renunciation of all knowledge, one reaches an unknowing, a knowledge (gnosis) that exceeds one's understanding. This contemplative journey leads the aspirant to a supra-intelligible source, merging consciousness into the divine darkness (emptiness), which is at the same time absolute supra-sensible Light (enlightenment).

Solitary mysticism can also take an affective turn and be expressed as a love affair between the soul and God. This type of mysticism is prominent, for example, in Christian spirituality. This love mysticism, however, is specifically about the love relationship of the alone with the Alone. A love directed to the neighbor might be an overflow of this relationship but would not in itself be a direct encounter with God as we will see it is with *solidarity* mysticism. Here, the presence of God is seen as hungry to enter into an intimate, loving, and ecstatic communion with the individual soul. The awe and adoration that such an experience of love brings forth is the foundation of this form of mysticism. In Hinduism this is called Bhakti Yoga. The fundamental praxis of the initiate, it could be finally noted, is meditation or contemplation in both intellective and affective solitary mysticism. We will see later that this is *not* the primary praxis of solidarity mysticism.

Perhaps the most prominent form of *solidarity* mysticism is found in the Judeo-Christian biblical tradition. This form of mysticism is at the opposite end of the mystical polarity. For this tradition, the highest divine manifestation is not primarily experienced in solitude but rather or more directly through solidarity with the human community. If solitary mysticism is characterized by a vertical relationship with transcendence, solidarity mysticism is characterized by a horizontal relationship or what Leonardo Boff calls "trans-descendence," where transcendence does not get lost in or is not reduced to transcendence.[32] Or to press this point even further, since in solidarity mysticism the divine Presence is passionately identified with the world's castoffs and those who cry out for justice, we could speak even more pointedly of the divine "in-scendence" or an incendiary trans-descendence. "I have come to cast fire upon the earth" (Lk 12:49). Or, in the words of Teilhard de Chardin,

"Someday, after mastering the winds, the waves, the tides, and gravity, we shall harness for God the energies of love, and then, for a second time in the history of the world, man will have discovered fire."[33]

According to Huston Smith's evaluation, representing solitary mysticism, "of the two dimensions [vertical and horizontal], the vertical relationship is the more important."[34] But for solidarity mysticism the vertical is not higher or more important than the horizontal. The within is not superior to the without. Both the vertical and the horizontal, the within and the without, interpenetrate each other in a totally reciprocal way. If there is a priority at all from the perspective of the solidarity tradition, it is that in the final analysis solidarity mysticism judges the authenticity of a solitary praxis. This conclusion is derived from the principle that there can be wisdom without compassion, but there cannot be compassion without wisdom. Arnold Toynbee indicates this priority, "A transformation in solitude can have no purpose, perhaps no meaning, except as a prelude to the return of the transfigured personality into the social milieu out of which he had originally come."[35] Anthony Claret describes a true Christian missionary as "a man on fire with love, who sets its fire wherever he goes."

Solidarity mysticism understands God not primarily as supreme intelligence/wisdom/truth, but rather as the supreme Good. As Martin Buber exclaims: "The Good towers above being in dignity and power."[36] If intellective mysticism places the emphasis on the intellect, solidarity mysticism places the emphasis on the will. Returning to Saint Augustine, he noted that if we retrace the will to its ground, we discover God as goodness. The Christian tradition calls this goodness, love. "God is love" is the ultimate that can be revealed about the divine dimension. As Teilhard de Chardin expressed it: "Love is the most universal, the most tremendous, and the most mysterious of the cosmic forces."[37] From this perspective love is greater than knowledge, the heart is more central than the mind; the good is higher than the true, or Plotinus's "One," or Saint Thomas Aquinas's "Being." If intellective mysticism focuses on "Big Mind," solidarity mysticism primarily moves in the direction of "Big Heart." The true spiritual maturity of a human person is not found exclusively in one's state of consciousness but rather in the integrative wholeness realized by a person fully engaged in the world.

If much of the Western spiritual tradition, especially of the institutional church, is a will to absolute truth, solidarity mysticism discerns above the will to truth the call of goodness. What is good is better than what is true or beautiful, or better still, the great challenge is to raise the true and beautiful to the good. Of all the saints, Saint Francis of Assisi has often been proclaimed as the perfect mirror of Jesus. And it is noteworthy that we discover in the writings of Saint Francis the word *heart* forty-two times, while the word *intelligence* appears only once; *love* twenty-three times, while twelve times for *truth; mercy* twenty-six times, while once for *intellect; doing* one hundred seventy times, while *understanding* only five times.

But ultimately this approach, which emphasizes the priority of love, does not pit love against knowledge but sees love to be of the very essence of true knowledge. *Ama ut intelligas*, or "love that you may understand." Love is not a mere affection but is a form of knowledge. It is a "loving knowledge" since we can only truly know what we love. Therefore, the only knowledge worth anything is love. As Saint Augustine describes the path of love: "In my case, love is the weight by which I act. To whatever place I go, I am drawn to it by love" (*Confessions*, 13. ix.10).

In the Judeo-Christian tradition, one knows reality best when one is acting in it. Understanding reality (the noetic moment) demands that one take responsibility for reality (the ethical moment) and even more important, take charge of reality through action (the praxic moment).[38] In biblical terms, one knows God when one does justice (Jeremiah, Hosea); one knows by loving. God is not a theoretical problem that we are called upon to solve but rather a mystery we participate in. The divine reality is experienced as "enacted," and it is in the enactment of love that one comes to know God. Jesus taught: "You will know them by their deeds" (Mt 7:16). It was not Marx but Saint Francis of Assisi who insisted: "One knows as much as one does."[39] As Emmanuel Levinas puts it in philosophical terms: ethics precedes ontology; metaphysics is enacted in ethical relations. If Socrates says that "one must know the good to do the good," this tradition insists that "one must do the good to know the good." Truth is verified not primarily in thought but in one's living. As Rabbi Haninah ben Dosa used to say: "Anyone whose deeds surpass his wisdom—his wisdom will endure; anyone whose wisdom surpasses his deeds—his wisdom will not endure" (Avnot 3:12).[40] This is why Levinas insisted: "One does not know ethics, one undergoes it. It is in the undergoing of ethics that one comes to know."[41] From this perspective, believing and doing are not two different things. "What is faith made of?" asks Levinas. "Words? Ideas? Convictions? What do we believe with? 'With every bone. Ps 35:10.' . . . Doing what is right is the very act of belief."[42] If the solitary approach ascends in silence, interior intimacy, and contemplation, this tradition's praxis descends or trans-descends into the human community as enacted love and justice. In Aloysius Piersis's words, we are drawn between "a knowledge that directs us to nirvana and the compassion that pins us down to the world."[43] Or in the words of Bishop Mendez de Almeida, we are drawn into a compassion that puts our finger "into the wound of reality."[44]

Both solitary and solidarity mysticisms are fundamental and integral movements of spiritual life. Although both dimensions are ultimately incomprehensible, they nevertheless impel us at times to fall silent in contemplation and awe but also to respond to the needs of others in love and responsibility. Any union with the Real will necessarily have both solitary and social dimensions. Buber describes a person who has attempted to hold these two polarities together: "Mixing with all and untouched by all, devoted to the multitude and collected in his uniqueness, fulfilling on the rocky summits of solitude the bond with the infinite and in the valley of life the bond with the earthly . . . he knows that all is God."[45]

2

Buddhist and Judeo-Christian Approaches

In seeking to unite and integrate the dual dynamics of solitude and solidarity, we find among the many religious paths of the world those that emphasize the solitary and those that emphasize the social. For the purposes of simplicity and personal inclination, I am choosing to contrast the path of Buddhism with that of the biblical Judeo-Christian tradition in order to point to their different paths and praxes as well as finding fundamental elements in both that can be the basis of an integral humanity. We first point to their decidedly different priorities, perspectives, and praxes.

If Buddhism seeks a direct non-dual experience of Emptiness *first* and out of that experience relates to *tathata* or the manifest world, the Judeo-Christian approach is incarnational, going through the manifest creation to encounter the unmanifest/Emptiness/Father. If, in confrontation with the absolute mystery, the Buddhist's approach is more intellective, seeking realization through insight/wisdom/gnosis, the Judeo-Christian approach is more affective, personal, and communal, moving the will to compassion and the doing of justice. If Buddhism talks about consciousness and the levels of consciousness, the Judeo-Christian tradition speaks of conscience and a change of heart. Whereas for Buddhism wisdom is sought primarily through contemplative experience, for the Judeo-Christian it emerges primarily through the experience of radical solidarity with our neighbor. If the Buddhist hero is the "enlightened one," the Judeo-Christian hero is the servant. To put it in the starkest terms at the outset: when Buddha "calls" a disciple, meditation is the praxis. As Chogyam Trungpa once said: "You might be fat, thin, big, small, intelligent, stupid—whatever you are, there is only one way, unconditionally, and this is to begin with the practice of meditation. The practice of meditation is THE and ONLY way."[1] When Jesus calls a disciple, service in unconditional love of one's neighbor is the praxis. Jesus told his disciples: "Whoever wants to be greatest among you must be your servant, and whoever wants to hold the first place among you must be everybody's slave. For the Son of Man himself has not come to be waited on, but to wait on other people, and to give his life to free many others" (Mk 10:43–45).

If Buddhism calls us to go within, the Judeo-Christian tradition sends us forth. If the Buddhist is counseled to withdraw from society, the Judeo-Christian path immerses us in society. The highest form of life for the Buddhist is the monastic. As Aloysius Pieris, SJ, points out: "Monastic life constitutes the 'institutional center' as well as the 'spiritual apex' of a Buddhist Community."[2] For the Judeo-Christian tradition, the highest form of life is the responsible participation in the human community. If Buddhists withdraw at least temporarily from the world to gain the spiritual enlightenment required to help others, the Judeo-Christian path engages its followers in service to make sure their contemplation is rooted in the real world. If Buddhism is the way of wisdom that opens up the heart to compassion (a compassion that is all the more powerful in that it is born from wisdom), the Judeo-Christian path is the way of compassion and justice that initiates the person into wisdom. Emmanuel Levinas points out that "the love of wisdom is spurred by the wisdom of love."[3] Or, as William Johnston describes this tradition, one becomes "wealthy in a wisdom that comes from love."[4] The goal of the Buddhist is not to transform the external world by acting personally or physically upon it, but to seek a transformation by producing better human beings. The Judeo-Christian tradition has always believed that transformation of individuals goes hand in hand with transformation of the "outer" world and its social structures.

The ideal path for Buddhists, therefore, is to *first* attain non-dual enlightenment, a non-dual union with Emptiness/*Sunyata*/God unmanifest and *then*, after realizing this enlightenment, to bring their vast experience and knowledge to help others reach the same reality. Their teachings are the direct expression of what they have learned in their solitary search (albeit in the *sangha* community). They subsequently work to help others travel the same path to realization that they have traveled. If a prisoner wants to free his companions from misfortune, he must first break out of his own chains. The spiritual path, therefore, begins with a period of retreat from the social world, like a wounded deer looking for a solitary, peaceful spot to heal her wounds. A beginner might feel an immense desire to help others but generally does not have sufficient spiritual maturity to be able to do so.

If the priority of the Buddhist approach is first to discover our enlightened state by going "within," the Judeo-Christian biblical approach is decidedly different in emphasis. (I mention "biblical approach" because at least within the Christian tradition Jesus' praxis is rarely prioritized historically.) The interrelationship of withdrawal into solitude and service in solidarity is not necessarily *first* to discover God or to find enlightenment by going within and *then* to go into the world of our brothers and sisters and help them discover what we have discovered. Nor is it the point that we first find God or enlightenment in solitary meditation and then as an overflow or a result of this experience we seek to serve our neighbor. From the Judeo-Christian perspective, service does not receive its value only secondarily or indirectly from our solitary experience of God. Rather, the experience of God is every bit as real and central in service as in solitary contemplation. Meister Eckhart articulated a spirituality of the active life "which does not see the active life as a preliminary stage of, or an overflow from, contemplative union with God, but as type of loving union with God in its own right."[5] When Saint Francis was undergoing his transformation, he began to spend a lot of time in solitude, but he came to realize that, until he could embrace one of the suffering lepers whom he often met on the roads, his conversion would not be real or complete.

The experience of God in solitude is not something we bring back into our personal and social world in order to invest it with a meaning it did not previously have. It is not as if God only arose in meditation and not in the whole of the world. Martin Buber explains, "Whoever goes forth to meet the world goes forth to meet God." Elsewhere he says, "In truth, there is no God-seeking because there is nothing where one could not find him."[6] The divine reality is everywhere, and it is only the dimness of our vision or our ego-fixation that keeps us from awareness. And what dispels this veil over reality is not only Gnostic insight, but more radically, the almost violent tearing away from our self-absorption by having our hands and faces and hearts and souls rubbed in the pain of suffering people. This is what Pope Paul VI called the "spirituality of the good Samaritan."[7]

Nor is it the point that our relationship with God/Emptiness is one of contemplation while our relationship to the world is one of action. First of all, from the Judeo-Christian perspective, God is not only contemplated but also *practiced* or *enacted* in the world. God is something we do; we do God. The God-experience is, therefore, both passive and active. Second, the world is not only the object of action but also of contemplation. We learn to see the world through the eyes of the divine dimension, to "look around us with loving eyes; discovering the deepest and most urgent needs with the eyes of the heart allowing our hearts to be touched and moved."[8] Both God and the world are the locus of contemplation and action.

Therefore, discovering God or recovering our enlightened state occurs both in solitude and solidarity. It is not only an ascending and a descending, but at the same time transcendence in descendence or trans-descendence. God is not only discovered vertically but horizontally; there is for the Judeo-Christian a horizontal transcendence, an active or outward mysticism.

Mysticism can be approached with eyes closed, shutting out the outside world, or eyes wide open to the other, to all creation. If Buddhism draws one into a mysticism with one's eyes closed, Christianity, in the words of Johann Baptist Metz, is a "mysticism of suffering with the eyes open."[9] If the Buddhist tendency is to look within, with eyes either closed or cast down, and to rest in emptiness, the Judeo-Christian path is to behold the other and engage in service. From the Hebrew tradition, Emmanuel Levinas, a Jewish philosopher, illustrates this approach when he writes:

> The response to the love of God, the response to the Revelation, cannot be effected in an act that simply goes in an opposite direction, but on the

> same route opened up by the love of God for Man; the response to the love of God for Man is the love of my neighbor.[10]

From a Christian perspective, Johann Baptist Metz explains this biblical approach in much the same way:

> Christian mysticism finds . . . that immediate experience of God which it seeks precisely in daring to imitate the unconditional involvement of the divine love for persons, in letting oneself be drawn into the descent of God's love to the least of our brothers and sisters. Only in these moments do we find the supreme nearness, the supreme immediacy of God . . . and that is why mysticism, which seeks this nearness, has its place not outside of, beside, or above responsibility for the world of our brothers and sisters but in the center of it.[11]

A crucial point for this study is being made by both these statements. The dynamic expressed is not as is so often assumed in spiritual teaching, namely, that as God loves me so I must return that love in an interior private love affair with God. Rather, as God loves us so we must love as God loves. God loves by going forth from the God-Self into a total gift to the other. The process of human divination is through a radical identification with this divine kenosis in the selfless gift of self to our neighbor, to the suffering other. Instead of a regression into an interior/private experience of a kind of sublime "shut-upness," we are called into the egress out of ourselves into the world.

In this context it is important to note that in the dual love commandment of Jesus—to love God with all our mind, heart, and strength, and to love our neighbor as ourselves—love of neighbor is placed on the same level as love of God. Love of neighbor is not a second commandment, subordinate to the first, but is equal in importance to the first. Ceslas Spicq, in his monumental study *Agape in the New Testament*, states: "To love one's neighbor is a commandment equal to the precept to love God."[12] In fact, the Synoptics stress love of neighbor more than they do the love of God. Love of God is seldom urged in the New Testament whereas the whole New Testament spills forth with endlessly repeated exhortations to love one's neighbor. Jesus brings these two exhortations of love, that is, love of God and love of neighbor, together in such a tight bond that they mutually interpret one another. In fact, in the Gospel of John the two commandments seem to merge to form one single one. In John 13:34 Jesus refers to his "new commandment": "This is my commandment, that you love one another as I have loved you." As Michael Amaladoss comments: "The newness may be precisely in the fact that he drops the first commandment about loving God. The reason is that it is in the neighbor that we love God."[13]

If Buddhism tends to draw the person into the state of *atarxia* or the state of being unperturbed by what goes on in the world, the Judeo-Christian tradition seeks to perturb and disturb complacent consciences. If Buddhism stresses that ultimately all is right with the world and therefore serenity is blessed, the Judeo-Christian view emphasizes that all is not right with the world and calls those blessed who "hunger and thirst after justice." It is interesting, for example, that for some Buddhists the person of Jesus who weeps and gets angry and who is finally executed because of his confrontation with the powers can actually be a disturbing figure. The Buddhist monk Thich Nhat Hahn remarked about the figure of the crucified Jesus: "[It] . . . is a very painful image to me. It does not contain joy or peace and this does not do justice to Jesus. . . . I hope that our Christian friends will also portray Jesus . . . sitting in the lotus position."[14] The ideal is not to be "disturbed" by anything. When Ram Dass was walking with his guru through Bangladesh, and heart-wrenching human suffering was all around them, the guru's question was "Can you see how perfect it is?"[15] But if the Buddhist ideal is to seek and maintain calm or *apatheia* and "the tranquility of order," the divine presence from the biblical perspective disturbs all "calm" by a divine passion, a divine *perturbatio*. The biblical prophetic tradition intrudes with a justice that disturbs what might have become an "oppressive order" or a "sleepy tranquility."

From a Buddhist perspective, it seems that emptiness is a complete negation of all personality, with no positive understanding of personality at all, whereas the Judeo-Christian tradition finds a supreme and transcendent fulfillment of the individual personality. Thomas Merton, however, makes a distinction between the illusory and exterior ego-self and the authentic human person. What is destroyed in the "death of the old man" is the dissipation of an ego-illusion and not the image of God that we all are.[16]

From a Buddhist point of view, reality is not ontologically linked to history, but rather history is the ground of an endless flux of events. There can be no kingdom of God here on earth, no ultimate in the transitory, because history is not a constitutive category of Reality or of human existence. A human being, at the deepest level, remains untouched by the historical. As Ken Wilber explicates this perspective: "My primordial awareness, and I-I remains untouched by time and space and their *complaints*. Eternity does not mean living forever in time—a rather horrible notion—but living in the timeless moment, prior to time and its *turmoils* altogether" [italics added].[17] Or, as the Buddhist master Bikku put the matter: "We know no history. There is only the passing of worlds."

From the Judeo-Christian point of view, however, there is a ripeness of time when the Spirit of life breaks forth with a whole new possibility for the human community. Certain historical events can carry within them ultimate meaning and make supreme demands on human beings originating from the Mystery of Life. We can begin to grasp this point of view when we understand what the greatest Celtic medieval thinker, Johannes Scotus Eriugena, taught, "In a wonderful and inexpressible way, God is created in his creatures."[18] What this directly implies is that we are God's communication, God's life. God realizes the Godhead in us as a human community. In a real way God needs the human community and cannot be fully God without us. "Thus God says to

Israel . . . My connection with the world is entirely dependent, as it were, on the direction to which your deeds point."[19] Rather than being a limitation on God, this is the realization of the full splendor of God's self communicating Being and Becoming. It is this vision of a non-dual unity between God and the world that is the basis of believing in God's involvement in the world through the specific deeds of human beings and works of human communities.

Our good works of liberation and social responsibility are correspondingly the work of God and are therefore necessary for realizing and constructing the kingdom. "The real truth is . . . that the World to come is actually identical with man's own deeds; it is that portion which he expanded, added and prepared by his own efforts."[20] As the liberation theologian Gustavo Gutiérrez explains: "Biblical faith is, above all, faith in a God who gives self-expression through historical events."[21] History, therefore, is not simply a random flux of events passing over Reality like evanescent clouds but rather an essential constituent of Reality itself. If creation and history can reveal an actual manifestation of the divine Mystery, then human history is a fundamental location for our encounter and realization of God. History is a locus for the ongoing Being and Becoming of the Real and can give essential clues as to the primordial intention of the Divine. In making history we participate in the ongoing shaping of creation. History is, therefore, not only constitutive of reality but also of the substantiality of being human. Emmanuel Levinas once wrote: "Historicity is not a secondary property of man as if man existed first and then became temporal and historical. Historicity and temporality form the very substantiality of man's substance."[22] The historical aspect of the Judeo-Christian tradition we will see later as one of the fundamentally unique contributions of this tradition to the human community.

In trying to honor both these traditions, we could conclude that we discover God by both realizing the kingdom within and engaging in the kingdom without. Both the practice of meditation and that of embracing the sufferings of others introduce us to the divine Mystery. What we attempt in this study is to unite going within and going without, so that they reinforce and interpenetrate one another in a unitive path that at once alternates between and integrates the two divinely infused dynamics.

3

What to Do?

So how do I construct and conduct my life? Where is the fullness of life to be found? Where does my being lead me? Is my highest spiritual call to develop a spirituality that is dominated by interior experiences (psychological analysis, a personal relationship with my Savior, alone with the Alone, and so on) more or less separate from life in the world? Is my religion basically what I do with my solitude? Or do I hear a different call? Do I see my spirituality as fundamentally a responsibility to the world and my neighbor? Religion in this sense is primarily what I do for the other (solidarity). Am I inclined to agree with Thoreau, who claimed one needed a special genius for charity and therefore "as for Doing-good . . . I have tried it fairly, and . . . am satisfied that it does not agree with my constitution"?[1] Emerson states this position even more pointedly:

> Do not tell me . . . of my obligation to put all poor men in good situations. Are they *my* poor? I tell thee, thou foolish philanthropist, that I grudge the dollar, the dime, the cent I give to such men as do not belong to me and to whom I do not belong.[2]

Or do I heed the Christian Saint Basil, who warned that the life of solitude violates the divine law of charity and is injurious to the soul of the solitary in nursing a sense of self-sufficiency and spiritual pride?[3]

If we decide to go exclusively in one direction or the other, then we perhaps have at best a limited and at worst a terrible distortion of the fullness of human existence. When solitude or solidarity are overemphasized or even totalized, then a reductionism has taken place with no awareness of a necessary dialectic where both solitude and solidarity meet and strengthen each other. The end result is that reality becomes mutilated, resulting in all kinds of human distortions.

If our spirituality becomes too interior, there is the danger of becoming awash in what has been called the disease of the infinite. We can become actually addicted to transcendence, where we are inwardly dazzled by what Pablo Neruda calls the "fetish of the incomprehensible." The Buddhist, for example, can talk of excessive Zen devotees as those who "stink of Zen." This kind of spiritual addiction can actually become, in the words of Andrew Harvey, a form of "spiritual masturbation." Because of this form of addiction, Emmanuel Levinas warns of the danger, in a loaded phrase, of "idolizing God." Martin Buber characterizes such spiritual addicts as "theomaniacs" because they so emphasize God and the soul that there is no faithful and responsible solidarity with the world or their neighbor. This can lead us "straight into the hell of the most terrible demonism all the while celebrating it as if it were a path to the divine."[4]

On the other hand, if our spirituality is all exteriority where we remain totally or solely on the horizontal plane of existence, Joseph Campbell has a caution: "Hell is the state of soul that is absolutely committed to its earthly experiences without recognizing the radiance of the divine dimension. It is being stuck simply in the time/space aspect of experience."[5] Dag Hammarskjöld once wrote: "God does not die on the day we cease to believe in a personal deity, but we die on the day when our lives cease to be illumined by the steady radiance, renewed daily, of a wonder, the source of which is beyond reason."[6] Or as Andrew Harvey warns: "We have been brought to a historical moment in which we can't possibly live or survive if we go on pretending that the mind and reason and technological progress are enough. Clearly, they are not enough, and we are going to destroy everything if we continue to believe that they are."[7]

We need to avoid a *spiritual reductionism*, by which the human person is reduced to "states" or "levels of consciousness,"or a *material reductionism*, by which human persons are totally circumscribed by their social, historical, and political reality. Dietrich Bonhoeffer, the great German Lutheran pastor, gives us an example of being able to see the dangers of both dynamics. Jürgen Moltmann describes Bonhoeffer as a person who

> fought passionately against the withdrawn piety of those who put up with every injustice on earth because they have long since resigned themselves to it and only live life here in a half-hearted way. But he opposed with equal passion the flat and trivial this-worldliness of those who consider themselves enlightened. . . . God without the world and the world without God . . . are merely a mutual corroboration of one another.[8]

From a psychological perspective, we find that total extroversion can lead people to lose a sense of their own identity in their vulnerability to and preoccupation with the dominant social agenda. They can become so "horizontalized" and absorbed in their dealings with the world that they forget about or abandon their spiritual roots, identity, and destiny. Extreme introversion, on the other hand, can lead people to become so inwardly preoccupied that they lose contact with external reality altogether. There is also the danger that introverts will equate their ego with their self, and thus their consciousness is so subjectivized that it becomes narcissistic and alienated from the world. The result is that, according to the Dutch painter Piet Mondrian, "concentrating solely on the 'culture of the inward' amounts to nothing more than a half-lived life." Great thinkers, for example, can be brilliant expositors and nourishers of the inner life like Jung, Heidegger, and Joseph Campbell, but become amazingly blind to social injustice or actually caught up in social perversions such as Nazism. The great task that we are attempting to envision is to incorporate these two tendencies toward the interior world of the person and the external world of society not as antithetical but complementary. The goal is to see solitude and solidarity as equiprimordial, coextensive, and codetermining elements of human existence, through which the authentic meaning of a human being is both disclosed and actualized.

4

On Entering Solitude

In order to construct an integral humanity that fuses the polarities of solitude and solidarity into a nutritive inter-communion, we need to look at each particular polarity. Solitude and solidarity do not refer to two different worlds but rather are two dimensions, or fundamental existentials, of one reality. Nevertheless, they are distinct and can only be more easily and more properly understood if we examine them separately. Yin is not Yang.

We will first examine the dynamics of solitude. This does not imply that we must first enter into solitude before we can fruitfully participate in the human community, but simply that withdrawal into solitude is a necessary dynamic for any fully human life. Chapters 5 to 9 seek to explore what can fruitfully happen in solitude, what inner work is necessary, the discovery of our unique identity, and then to see our deepest self in all its fullness.

When we enter into solitude we deliberately pull out of the human anthill, the asphalt jungle, the daily chase. A space is provided where no one is giving us any orders, seducing us with hyped images and rewards, trying in one way or another to manipulate us. The inner pressure circle created by the crowd leaves us, and in this silence we begin to experience gradually, first of all, a whole new sense of time, for example, a-historical/trans-historical, or contemplative time. As a traditionalist, Huston Smith comments that he does not dispute the fact that we are historical beings, or even radically such. But "the question is whether we are totally such, which is to say historical without remainder."[1] Those who consider human beings as historical beings "without remainder" have a great deal of difficulty valuing solitude because they judge it as nothing but a historical distraction from humanity's march toward social development. We are told that we discover our humanity through our deeds, and by studying what we have done historically we discover what we are as human beings. We become who we are through social praxis, and are called, therefore, to take hold of the reins of our own destiny and participate in transforming society. It is through this historical work or praxis that we discover a real awareness of our own being. Confronted with such claims, Mircea Eliade complains:

> I am told you must be at one with your historical moment. Today we are dominated by the social problem—more precisely, by the social problems

posed by the Marxists. You *must*, therefore, respond through your work, in one way or another, to the historical moment in which you live.[2]

Even if solitude is viewed more favorably, we might be told that it must exist in the context of what is valid historically. A dialogue between a Catholic theologian, Rosemary Ruether, and a Catholic monk, Thomas Merton, illustrates this. Ruether told Merton that his life as a hermit in the woods of Kentucky was simply agrarian romanticism, a way of escaping history because, as she put it, "[for] those who wish to be at the kingdom's frontier of history, it is the streaming ghetto of the big city, not the countryside that is the place of the radical overcoming of this world, the place where one renews creation, disposes of oneself and does hand to hand combat with the demons."[3] From this point of view, the countryside, where time is cyclical and follows nature more than historical events, has been bypassed and surpassed by humanity's evolution. The center of gravity is no longer in nature but in human beings, making culture the only creator of humanity.

Our task is a human one: eradicate poverty, disease, injustices, lethal ideologies, and bondages of every sort. But in order to do this we must participate in what is really going on. And nothing much of historical significance is going on in the countryside except what has always gone on (and on). History happens in what is new in our evolutionary process and therefore in fields such as technology, economics, politics, social events. Historical people are plugged into their computers, cable TVs, and newspapers in order to stay abreast of this ongoing historical reality. They stay plugged into what's going on, but the point we will attempt to communicate is the observation made by Raimon Panikkar. Those who are experts at what is going *on* often give short shrift to what is going *in*, that is, "with what happens in the internal universe, those profound recesses of reality to which the human psyche has access."[4]

Although humans are obviously historical beings, we are not only that. We are not circumscribed by the historical. History does not exhaust the clues to what it means to live a full, authentic, and happy life. From Panikkar's perspective, "the fulfillment of human life is no longer seen exclusively, or even mainly, in the historical unfolding (individual or collective) but also, or rather in transtemporal experiences."[5] What Panikkar means by *transhistorical* or *transtemporal* is not in the sense of *transcendence* or "going beyond," but rather as in *transparency*, or "going through" to the core. Or as Chogyam Trungpa says from a Buddhist perspective: "The idea is not getting out of *samsara* or transcending it but getting to the source of it, the background of it . . . a way in not a way out..not so much liberation from but into that ground."[6]

If the historical emphasizes the future and therefore the virtue of hope, the a-historical emphasizes the present and therefore the state of awareness or presence. The emphasis here is not so much the final or ultimate goal of time *(telos)* but the fullness of time *(teleios)*. If history emphasizes what a person does, the a-historical emphasizes who the person is. Who is doing the what (ever)? If the historical emphasizes cultural time, the a-historical emphasizes natural time.

The seasons of the earth measure this sense of time, not the exploits of humanity. The meaning of life is not found primarily in building the Great Society or the "kingdom without," but rather in enjoying life in the here and now. If historical consciousness emphasizes the will and work and getting things done and creating a better future, contemplative time emphasizes joy and bliss and relishing the present moment as fully as possible. If reality in its essence is "a kind of total spontaneity," then "Be here now!" is its anthem. Let the day take care of the day and do not worry about tomorrow.

The ideal life, mystical in nature, is lived in what Elie Wiesel calls a succession of "eternal moments,"[7] metaphysical and ecstatic a-temporal "instants" where linear time is left behind. My fulfillment does not depend on any future development or evolutionary process, but in my realization as a unique human person. Leisure is more important than work; love is more important than hope; the present is more important than the future. The great danger of being swept up into the historical alone is that we can so easily become simply cogs in a social mega-machine. We can become homogenized into a flatland of social definition alone and therefore not be able to see or experience life apart from an unthinking, unconscious herd existence.

Once we become acclimated and accustomed to the silence of contemplative time, one of the first things that we discover is that all is not well with us. We perceive that there is more to our lives than the narrow confines of our present ego experience. We are confronted with the reality that our masked persona is not our true selves. We are not connected to our own integrity. Merton describes one of the first difficulties of interior solitude as the disconcerting task of facing and accepting one's own absurdity. The anguish of realizing that underneath the apparently logical pattern of a more or less 'well organized' and rational life, there lies an abyss of irrationality, confusion, pointlessness and indeed apparent chaos."[8]

So we may well feel anguished because we have lost our way; we have failed to fulfill our true nature. George Gurdjieff characterizes this realization: "I am shocked at what I am and I feel the measure of what I am meant to be."[9] Somehow we realize that we have missed our vocation. We have betrayed the best that was in us. Our accomplishments do not seem to correspond to or resonate with our individual essence. We have been trying to content ourselves with all the wrong answers. We discover that we are standing in our own way. We might even feel shipwrecked as a total failure in the deepest part of our soul. We realize that we are without a center, without a fruitful discipline. We are, in biblical terms, lost. We also discover that over the months and years our human qualities such as goodness, generosity, discipline, patience, diligence, concentration, wisdom, tolerance, and being at peace with ourselves and others have been declining instead of growing. We're in a kind of neutral or reverse gear. So there grows within us an urgent search for real life. P. D. Ouspensky, a disciple of Gurdjief, sums up this self-confrontation: "So long as a man is not horrified at himself, he knows nothing of himself."[10]

As we immerse ourselves in this contemplative atmosphere, we will very likely begin to feel gripped by some wholly other power. We will begin to sense another dimension, an unknown fullness and depth that casts doubt on the whole direction in which we were previously heading. Suddenly a new possibility arises, a promise of life emerges within us that demands an inner change. Our past is not our only potential. It is possible to leave the prison of our conditioning and turn homeward. Whatever we may think of ourselves and no matter how long we have thought it, we can still wake up to Reality. Joseph Campbell counsels us when he says:

> You are more than you think you are. There are dimensions of your being and a potential for realization and consciousness that are not included in your concept of yourself. Your life is broader and deeper than you conceive it to be. What you are living is but a fractional inkling of what is really within you, what gives you life, breadth and depth. But you can live in terms of that depth.[11]

In sensing this split between what we appear to be to others and what we still feel obscurely to be within, we may decide that we no longer want to float along in the general noise. We refuse to any longer impersonate a fake, but rather we choose to begin to uncover our own face, our own skin, our own mind, our own way, our own faith. We feel the need to piece together our own truth.

The modern age promised us a culture of unintimidated, curious, rational, self-reliant individuals, but what it has produced by and large is, to use a Nietzschean phrase, a herd society, full of anxious, timid, conformist, sheeplike clones. The United States is a nation that prides itself on the heritage of rugged individualism, but as a people, by and large, we find anything but rugged individualists. Walter Brueggemann makes this comment: "For all our treasured talk of 'individual freedom,' the force of homogeneity is immense—partly reductive, partly coercive, partly the irresistible effect of affluence, in any case, not hospitable to 'difference.'"[12] Chogyam Trungpa has a similar analysis:

> Everyone in Paris, Berlin, New York, San Francisco, and Tokyo tends to be dressed the same way, eat the same fast food, and drink the same beverages. It is one of the strangest paradoxes about our society. Never has individuality been talked about so much, yet it is uniformity that clearly dominates.[13]

It seems in our modern society people have been socialized into doing anything to belong. Children are raised in clumps, groups, auditoriums, buses, locker rooms, scout dens, malls, and gangs. The great emphasis is placed on how sociable one is, how well one "fits in," how popular one is. One dare not be out of the mainstream. "To be sociable," laments Dag Hammarskjöld, "to talk merely because convention forbids silence, to rub against one another in order to create the illusion of intimacy and contact: what an example of *la condition humaine*."[14] If a person is quiet and contemplative or is psychologically introverted, such a person is deemed to be almost pathological, whereas a highly extroverted person is seen to be perfectly normal, since the emphasis on human maturity is linked to social conformity with a disdain for the solitude necessary to nurture more individual and unique creative capacities.

When we were born, we entered the world with endless possibilities. As we grew up, however, we began to discover those possibilities that were acceptable to our parents and society and those that were not. Whatever our parents or society did not approve of, we learned to hide. We found out that just as only particular parts of our body are allowed to be exposed, so too with our true selves. Society chooses us in parts. Many of our possible choices will find disfavor in some quarter. Our totality is never approved of or accepted. When our natural responses—sadness, enthusiasm, sensuality, spontaneity, inquisitiveness, quirkiness, assertiveness, tenderness—were tempered or criticized, we learned to hide them so we would avoid the sting of disapproval.

If we hungered for the approval and acceptance of others and wanted to avoid the shame or ridicule that we dreaded, we would have to disguise parts of ourselves. We had to become an acceptable persona. The only way we could survive was to create an image, a mask that we hoped would be all right, and that would meet and live up to collective expectations. It became more important for us to *belong* to society than to simply *be*. "Seeming" became more important than "being." The impression we wished to make on others was more important than our true identity. So we ended up in bondage to semblance. But this yielding to the temptation to "seem" in what we say and do in order to be confirmed or approved by the other is what Buber calls "our essential cowardice," and our resisting it, "our essential courage."[15]

If we handle the masking of ourselves with some measure of finesse, we are seen as "good people," or "normal folk," or "nice." (A person may be a serial killer all the while seeming nice to the neighbors.) Our transcendent human realization has been whittled down to "seeming nice." This goodness or niceness can be translated as follows: in order to keep the peace let others write the script of my life. As one frustrated person put it: "I'm just a collection of mirrors, reflecting what everyone expects of me."[16] This comment is reminiscent of the comment made by the main character in Luigi Pirandello's *Naked Masks*, who, seen by everyone in a different light, comments when asked who she is: "I am whoever you believe me to be. . . . And as for myself, I am nobody!"[17] Nice people's whole emotional security and self-esteem is in the hands of others, of the collective. They do not dare seek their own truth but rather a way to appear as good. They might even have become haunted by the possibility that someone might not approve of or be disappointed in their actions. So they might feel compelled to comply with everyone else's wishes, to do good deeds constantly and favors for others to keep in their good graces. They end up, in the words of Carlos Castaneda's Don Juan, "pimping for others,"[18] that is, living a life in compliance with and for the gratification of others. They literally inhibit and imprison the truth of their whole lives because they cannot bear the pain of disapproval or rejection. Thomas Merton once quipped to Daniel Berrigan: "We are our own concentration camp. Too damn docile if you ask me."[19]

This "goodness" can often sour, and the good people can become disillusioned, embittered, and cynical. Good people are potentially noble people who have sacrificed their high hopes long ago. The desert fathers of the early church discovered in their solitude seven deadly sins. One of them is *acedia* (sloth). Sloth is not the sin of youth but of middle age. Its opposite is not hard work but high-mindedness. The humanistic psychologist Abraham Maslow calls this "the Jonah Complex," which is characterized by "fear of one's own greatness," "evasion of one's destiny," or the "repression of the sublime."[20] It occurs when we become disillusioned with life, and so we develop an antipathy toward life and boredom in the face of life's challenges. We become a burnt-out case (like a character in one of Graham Greene's novels),[21] "a closed-in life wherein grows the vice of self-regard."[22] In this self-enclosedness, one becomes tired of life itself, resulting in "a numbness, a way of curling up into oneself . . . the lag of an existent tarrying behind its existing."[23] A repression of passion, a loss of one's vital instincts, an insatiable curiosity of the petty, endless small talk, lack of self-discipline, narrow-mindedness, a strange lack of good will toward others, a cold-hearted mean-spiritedness, contempt for excellence or the good, a constant resentment about everything, a willful autism—all these characterize such a life. It is the paralysis of the soul in flight: the joyless, irritable, and selfish dismissal of life's awesome grandeur.

In order to keep our personal and socialized fiction going without any relapse into our own truth, we are amply provided with what Blaise Pascal called *divertissement* or systematized distraction from what is essential. "The function of diversion," explains Thomas Merton, "is simply to anesthetize the individual as individual, and to plunge him in the warm, apathetic stupor of a collectivity which, like himself, wishes to remain amused."[24] The genius of our culture is to provide all the necessary fillers, new and better ways to escape reality. It convinces us that life would be incredibly dull without distractions and cravings of every kind. We are seduced to live our lives in terms of engrossing and addictive distractions.

Our culture is so chaotically hyped with kinetic information and sensational images that the steady gaze necessary to see life clearly and sanely is next to impossible. So as soon as silence opens up before us, we run away, seek some kind of entertainment, turn on the TV or radio, run to the websites, take some drug, or look for sex. Our life becomes an anxious filling up of vacuums. We always rent the open area of our minds and souls and the rentee is none other than our obsessions, compulsions, and abdications.

There is a law in biology called Romer's Law; it states that life forms advance only when circumstances force them to do so. But given the choice, any life form would prefer to remain the same forever. Inertia is one of the great laws of being. Unfortunately we have become accustomed to our mask and prefer to stay with it rather than try to discover our true face sweating underneath. We resist and fear anything that would rip our mask off or expose the falsity of our ego/persona. We don't want to endure our own reality. Illusion is more comforting.

We conclude that this is the human condition because it makes it easier to live with our own imperfection, easier to ignore our higher or greater or broader possibilities. We prefer the illusion and lies. And this, according to the British theologian Sebastian Moore, is exactly what sin is: the idolization of the ego at its present stage of development.[25] Or as Angela West said: "Sin is about never being able to do a new thing or reach a new place."[26]

We are quite satisfied with letting our masked persona be our whole selves because we fear that if we lose our ego dominance we will lose our identity. We thus destroy all kinds of personal possibilities, remaining only a fragment of our true selves. We cut ourselves off to the point of sterility from the creative powers struggling to flow through us. We have deadened "the nerve of creature hood." We have literally become "cultural ventriloquists." We walk around saturated with disconnected sound bites with which the cultural collective brainwashes us, and then are deluded to think that this is actually our perception of life. And since we come to believe that cultural clichés are in fact our personal conclusions, we can mouth them, at times with great mindless vehemence. Hence, we end up with what Gore Vidal calls "energetic mediocrities."

We end up saying yes to what is not life-giving and no to what is. We have long ago ceased thinking our own thoughts and now we think only those thoughts judiciously manufactured by a culture that ensures the domination of its sterile direction. We look, but we do not see; we act, but we do not think; we plan, but we do not reflect. We learn to consider important what is not and unimportant what is. We know the price of everything but the value of nothing. We consider the superfluous necessary, and essentials arbitrary. We make social progress without any respect for priorities. We end up having no idea why we do what we do; acquire things we have no need of; say things we really do not mean or believe. And the irony is that it seems that those who have the least to say are always saying something; the mindless with a megaphone! The empty cans rattle on! The principle seems to be this: the dumber we get the glibber we become. W. B. Yeats wrote in his famous poem "The Second Coming": "The best lack all conviction, while *the worst are full of passionate intensity*" [italics added]. Or, as Heraclitus observed, "The eyes and ears are bad witnesses for men with barbarian souls."

When there was a great celebration in Boston on the occasion of constructing a magnetic telegraph from Maine to Texas, Henry David Thoreau commented: "Nobody asks the real question: do the people of Maine have anything to say to the people of Texas?"[27] We have endless talk shows that host people who have absolutely nothing of any enduring value to say and totally ignore or marginalize those few and far between wise people in our culture. Those who really do have something to say are deemed unmarketable since they do not fit into the mainstream, that is, socially engineered thought.

With our mask in hand, we find ourselves in a much harried social situation. Just think of what many of our nervous systems undergo every day: noise and more noise from 6:00 a.m. to midnight: muzak, news, talk, gossip, machinery, appliances, phones, traffic, TV, beepers, speed, go, go, go bumper to bumper at breakneck speed, on ramps, off ramps, horns, boom boxes, cellphones, deadlines, appointments, bosses over our shoulders with stop watches. We are under constant pressure to justify ourselves, and the criteria are how much progress we are making, how successful we are, how marketable we are. We do not stand under the judgment of God any more but under social pressure.

It is only through the evidence of social achievement that we can have any sense of self-esteem. So we submit to the social pressure and get lost in the social roles provided for us. Some of us play the part brilliantly and don't even notice that we have lost our very soul. With a shrug we say: whatever! We are like water skiers. We skim over life, trying desperately not to fall in. Very few of us are underwater explorers. Nietzsche had it right when he said: "You could wear no better masks, you men of today than your own faces. Who could possibly find you out?"[28]

In order to achieve we have to "motorize" our whole being in the "zoo of secular hurry." As Max Picard analyzes it:

> The primary factor is movement for its own sake, movement that hits a definite target only by accident, movement that happens before it has been decided why it is happening, and movement that is always ahead of man himself—so far ahead that he has to jump to catch up.[29]

We live in what has become a vast automatic-functioning social machine. Society has so enlarged its demands on us that it has arrogated to itself almost total control of the individual. Our time has been socially disciplined as never before, constantly surveyed by time studies. So we have become split-second dutiful servants. We have no time because we are always trying to save time. We are always on the go. We are always pressed for time. We are in a race against time. There are goals to be set, deadlines to be met, and once met, another is set, and so everyone is revved up on a treadmill, the end of which never, ever, arrives.

Time has become precious because time has become money. Our psyche is on constant red alert for the monetary opportunity. So we are 99 percent ahead of ourselves, tripping over ourselves to make the advantage. Our whole inner psyche is revved up to a very high idle, which leaves us with high anxiety. We go from explosion to exhaustion believing that our hyperactivity of mind and body are signs that we are really alive. There are so many possibilities out there, but our lives are so short. Since we can't prolong our lives to any appreciable degree, we have to make sure we get as much out of life as possible. So we have to step up the pace of our lives in an almost panic that we might miss out on something.

As we move more and more rapidly from place to place, our goal is to collect as many experiences as we can. We are under the illusion that, if we have more and can do more and experience more, we will be more. But simply to participate in events, to collect them sometimes greedily and impulsively, does nothing to deepen our souls or the quality of our lives. After all, there have been many great souls who have flourished in monk cells, in prison cells, in one form of isolation or another. We can have plenty of experiences, but if we never take the time to assimilate them, then we never really experience our experiences. As Aldous Huxley says: "Experience is not what happens to a man; it is what a man does with what happens to him."[30] Or to say it in a different way: we may search for infinite experience without realizing that our inability to access that experience is not the insufficiency of any particular experience but the insufficiency of the one doing the experiencing. Thus it is not a quantitative but a qualitative problem. But this response to an experience is not just a reflective assimilation or a mere *understanding* of that experience. More important, there is a necessary *undergoing* of the experience. That is why Emmanuel Levinas prefers

> the word "ordeal" (epreuve) over "experience" (experience), because the word "experience" expresses always a knowledge of which the I is master. In the word "ordeal" there is at the same time the idea of . . . of a critical "testing" which exceeds the I.[31]

Being afraid of missing out on life, we might very well end up missing out on any meaningful or transformative life. If we are all "yes," wide-eyed, open-mouthed, salivating tongue like a hungry puppy, without any discrimination or proper vessel to contain and nurture these experiences, then we have no way of holding and keeping them within so we can relish them. We need a psychic container that allows us not simply to leak out all over the place, but rather allows us to keep back and stop short in our eagerness for simply "more." As fifteenth-century philosopher Marsilio Ficino, who was considered by his contemporaries as a man who "did" the least of all men, taught: "When the external act decreases, the internal act is increased."

We almost inevitably buy into the foremost technology for shattering human consciousness and restructuring our psyches for motorized living: television. Television draws us into a perceptual universe much faster than ordinary life, setting its own visual pace at its own electronic speed. Since TV images move much faster than a person can react, you have to chase after them with your mind in an attempt to absorb this glut of images. Since we cannot stop this accelerated barrage of images, we have to clear all our other channels of perception and reception to accommodate our psyche to this incessant flow. Attempts to reflect on them, or spend time contemplatively with them, or apply our critical analysis to them, are totally impossible. The result is that the TV is creating a new kind of human person whose nervous system has been accelerated into a form that accommodates the technology before it.

At the same time, we are losing our capacity to be attuned to the natural world. We are literally on speed. We are becoming speed junkies. This revved-up psyche produces anything but an alert, aware, reflective, incisive mind. Just the opposite! It gives birth to a passive, disconnected, unable-to-deal-with-nuance, superficial, uncreative dolt. As Jerry Mander summarizes: "Our whole culture and the physical shape of the environment, no more or less than our minds and feelings, have been computerized, linearized, suburbanized, freewayized, and packaged for sale."[32] Or, as James Baldwin once said to Andrew Harvey: "The bomb has already gone off . . . the psychic bomb. The master bomb! It goes off and nobody notices. It destroys hearts, souls, and minds, while leaving the bodies and the refrigerator intact."[33]

5

A Second Education from Within

If solitude opens us up to a "space of liberty, of silence, in which possibilities are allowed to surface and new choices beyond routine choices become manifest,"[1] then what possibilities and choices emerge? One of the most fundamental choices confronting us is choosing between acquiescing to the social engineering of our very soul and beginning a very painful process of rediscovering our true identity. In order to come home to ourselves, we should realize that what we really need is a radical reeducation from head to toe.

We usually identify education as that which we have received from our culture through its traditions, teachers, and social agenda. But this is only partially correct. There is a far more profound education, yet one which most people never receive. Our social education might provide us something in our lives with which to identify, but if left there our lives remain nothing more than the construction of others as we adopt their viewpoints as our own. By becoming well-adjusted members of the collective, individuals are released from their heroic mission of seeking their inner authority. We find ourselves in a kind of consensus trance. We are brainwashed into believing, for example, that life is meaningless unless we reach respectable levels of consumption. By misrepresenting real needs and by manipulating false needs, we are socialized into society's vested interests. The collective, seeking to mobilize us for the social project, demands that we become functional operatives for its own purposes.

If the truth be told, our culture, while proclaiming high ideals, is essentially indifferent to such values as beauty, art, and education. The reason why most politicians say we need to raise the level of education is not so that students receive the broadest form of education and become well-rounded individuals, but so that the United States can remain competitive in the global market. As a result, students no longer go to college to discover the manifold ways of being human, but rather simply to get a good-paying job. The universities where the humanities and the sciences had traditionally been custodians of the human spirit have now become custodians of the market. The pursuit of excellence has been replaced by the vision of climbing up the corporate ladder. Our idea of vocation has degenerated into a mere function. As David Fideler observes, "The realization of an individual's intrinsic humanity through art, creativity, and learning is replaced by yet another end: acquiring the trappings of social status."[2]

More and more of our colleges and universities have demoted the importance of the humanities and are being transformed into trade and business schools. Instead of opening students' eyes to vaster worlds they hadn't known existed, students are deluged with facts and figures that result in the killing of the spirit.[3] Universities have become, in the words of Clark Kerr, factories "for the production of knowledge and technicians to service society's many bureaucracies."[4] And what we end up with is people who are unfit for "anything except to take part in an elaborate and completely artificial charade which they and their contemporaries have conspired to call 'life.'"[5] Or, as the former president of Johns Hopkins University, Steven Miller, concluded in an interview: "The University is rooted in the scientific method and the scientific method cannot provide a sense of values. As a result, we're turning out skilled barbarians."[6]

The French philosopher Michel Foucault masterfully reminds us that what society holds up to be normal, good, and noble is not determined so much by an objective pursuit of the truth as by the power structures and power groups within that society. Virtue is that which helps bring about the social system's interest. These strategic social interests are valued over principles, ends are valued over means, efficiency over depth, and quantity over quality. Objects become subjects, and subjects become objects. The supremacy of the peripheral and banal "virtues" such as utility (being marketable), performance, adaptability, being competitive, being number one in effect smother the essential mystery of the person. In Pascal's terms, the *esprit de geometric*, or the spirit of calculation, is valued over the *esprit de finesse*, or the spirit of intuition and empathy with others.[7]

We are induced to be uniform in our thinking and disciplined in our initiatives, and in order to achieve social coherence, we are oftentimes pressured to make a sacrilegious renunciation of our selves. We are convinced to perform "spiritual self-castration" as we renounce our truth in favor of the social agenda. As the Marxist philosopher Herbert Marcuse pointed out, the one-dimensional human being has become the prototype of first-world citizens. Our multifaceted personal reality is now reduced to manageable and marketable personas. Collectivization can ultimately so atomize and indeed rape the souls of individuals that we are reduced merely to the utilitarian aspects of our human possibilities. But if we are to survive as our authentic selves, we need to retreat from our "cultural hypnotism" and deconstruct what we have so often blindly assimilated.

We need to undergo a second education, one which will take us beyond the common social denominator. Although we would be wise to assimilate as many positive, useful, and transformative influences as we can from our culture, in the end our ultimate true task is to move in the direction of a fully personal vision. "Man's being is not only given to him," Paul Tillich reminds us, "but is also demanded of him. He is responsible for it, literally; he is required to answer, if he is asked, what he has made of himself. He who asks him is his judge, namely, he himself."[8] This second education will be far more personal and revelatory because it comes from us; through a process where truth is not introduced into the mind from without but is "led out" from within. Meister Eckhart maintained: "Whatever I want to express in its truest meaning must emerge from within me and pass through an inner form. It cannot come from outside to the inside but must emerge from within."[9] We will find ourselves inevitably drawn into totally new and unexplored realms, which will call us forth into an all-encompassing lifestyle demanding completely original initiatives.

When Chogyam Trungpa was abbot of a Buddhist monastery in Tibet, the Chinese communists invaded their land. The monks decided to flee for safety. When they were all about to leave, one of the monks rushed up to Chogyam Trungpa and anxiously asked: "What are we going to do now?" And Trungpa's reply was: "There is no longer any 'we.' From now on, brother, everybody has to learn how to stand on his own two feet."[10] There comes that point in our lives where we have to decide whether to stand on our own two feet or not. To go fruitfully into solitude is to pass from doing what others do to doing what we do; from saying what others say to saying what we say; from thinking what others think to thinking what we think; from desiring what others desire to desiring what we desire. We have to dare to let our lives take their intended form and defy any pattern that is not our own. "For this I came into the world!" (Jn 18:37). We have to be able to say with Dostoyevsky: "This is what I must do. If others don't like it they can go to hell." When Martin Luther nailed his ninety-nine theses on the door of the Cathedral of Wittenberg, he said: "Here I stand, I can do no other."[11] Or as Saint Francis of Assisi told his followers on his deathbed: "I pray that you will discover your way as I discovered mine."

We are not here to live someone else's life. We can live only one life, and that is ours. Sin for Abraham Heschel was the refusal of humans to become who they are,[12] and for Sebastian Moore it was seeing our life through someone else's eyes. So we have to find out for ourselves that we have to decide for ourselves what we are to make of ourselves. We have to learn to recognize our own depths. Imitation can be deadly, even if it is the imitation of Christ. As Carl Jung once commented: "It is no easy matter to live a life that is modeled on Christ. But it is unspeakably harder to live one's own life as truly as Christ lived his."[13]

When we begin to get a sense of our self through this self-introduction, Nietzsche believed that in the "second-metamorphosis," where we begin to believe in ourselves and our own entrails, our spirit must become a "lion who would conquer his freedom and be master in his desert."[14] We must transform ourselves from a helpless puppet controlled by unconscious and collective forces into a self-aware, free person determining our own destiny. Emerson believed: "That is always best which gives me to myself. The sublime is excited in me by the great stoical doctrine, obey thyself. That which shows God in me fortifies me. That which shows God out of me, makes me a wart and a wen."[15]

We must, therefore, no longer have a common conscience with the herd but rather free ourselves from this yoke, from the happiness of slaves, and become creators of new laws, our own laws. We must then hang our will over ourselves as our judge and avenger of our own ten commandments, which emerge from the essence of who we are. We begin to measure ourselves against our own reality. In this way we become, in the words of Nietzsche, a new beginning, a self-propelled wheel, a first movement, a sacred yes. We become a source of light, which is at the same time our strength. This is my way; where is yours? "For this is what I am," claimed Nietzsche, "through and through: reeling, reeling in, raising up, raising, a raiser, cultivator, and disciplinarian, who once counseled himself, not for nothing: Become what you are!"[16]

We have to face the stark fact, however, that this process of self-education and self-recovery is no easy task. Solitude is not only a place where we can relax and become refreshed, but it is also, and more importantly, a reality that requires intensive inner work, a disciplined choice demanding blood, sweat, and tears. "Treading the spiritual path is painful. It is a constant unmasking, peeling off of layer after layer of masks. It involves insult after insult."[17]

Perhaps one of the first disciplines required in solitude is *learning how to slow down*. We have to begin to deal with our speed, our restlessness, our constant busyness. We have been so motorized by our society that we are just whizzing past life rather than relishing it. How much of our lives do we dash through? We have become multi-taskers, a euphemism for trying to do two or more things at the same time: answering the phone, sweeping the floor, watching TV, and printing out reports on the computer all at the same time. We have become like the man in his car who was pulled over by the cops because he had one cell phone in one ear, another in the other, conducting a conference call while steering the wheel with his elbows! Health professionals are facing new epidemics of "hurry sickness," which is producing frantic people in the midst of a frantic society.

Nothing gets our full attention. We ignore what is before us in anxious anticipation of what we expect to soon be before us. In our rushing around for what is next, we need to deliberately stop, catch our breath, and bring ourselves back to a consciousness of what we are about at this moment. Rushing through a task indicates that we do not care about what we are doing because we are trying to get it over with. And to the extent that we want anything simply over and done with, we are merely passing time, spending time, wasting time: *on* time perhaps, but not *in* time. Marcel Legault describes the modern individual pointedly:

> They cling to events . . .
> are haunted by necessities . . .
> devoured by activities . . .
> carried away by circumstances . . .
> not yet been truly born to their humanity . . .
> never succeed in finding their own breath.[18]

That is why Chogyam Trungpa counsels:

> You must not make an impulsive move in any situation. . . . Whenever there is an impulse to do something, you should not just do it; you should work with the impulse. If you are working with it, then you will not act frivolously; you want really to see it and taste it properly, devoid of frivolousness.[19]

Another very fruitful discipline for our inner work is what we could call the discipline of weeding our inner garden. Not only have our lives been motorized, but they have also been cluttered up with useless thoughts, useless activities, and useless possessions. Our garden has not been weeded. So part of a solitude praxis is simplification. "Simplicity, simplicity, simplicity!" cried Thoreau. "Let your affairs be of two or three, and not a hundred or a thousand."[20] Clutter indicates that we fail to distinguish between what is superfluous and what is essential. Brother David Steindl-Rast often teaches that "there is a close relation between the struggle to put things in order within yourself, within your life, and the ordering of the space around you. . . . It takes a long time to see that orderliness and cleanliness is not just cleaning the room, but it is getting your life in order."[21] Clutter indicates that we are failing to discern and appreciate what in reality is real and contributes to the fulfillment of our authentic destiny from that which is merely the result of greedy, distracted, impulsive, fleeting desires leading nowhere.

Grabbing indiscriminately for everything, we end up cherishing nothing, at least nothing worthwhile. That is why Buddhist talk about developing a "lofty dryness,"[22] which is not calling for an absence of the sensuous or the cessation of vitality as in a dried-up well, but rather demands the absence of the superficial, the unnecessary. It recognizes when enough is enough of anything. Nothing is ever lost when we suppress the superfluous. Everything extraneous is stripped from our lives so that only the essentials are left. In the same vein Heraclitus recommended that we live in an atmosphere of what he called "dry luster," which he saw as the "best and wisest condition of the spirit."

But it is important to note here that simplification is not a process in which we scorn material values or develop contempt for temporal goods, eliminating every human pleasure until our focus is reduced to the One True Reality. "If you are over-concerned with looking for the real always beyond everything, you may very well leave reality behind,"[23] warns Raimon Panikkar. Rather simplification of the clutter, of the extraneous, gives room in our human space so that we can gradually embrace all things of value. Nor does simplification imply ugliness or even homeliness. Simplification can add to the beauty of our lives when it becomes, in the words of the architect Paolo Soleri, an "elegant frugality."

A further fruitful solitude praxis is what Chogyam Trungpa calls the "appreciation of the cool boredom of the natural world." Compared to media existence, which has so maniacally over-stimulated the American culture, nature can seem rather boring. Trees never tire of being trees, mountains are always mountains, the ocean is always the ocean, and birds are always about being birds. But when we turn off all our gadgets of distraction and attempt to retune ourselves to nature, what might seem at first boring can become a "cool boredom, like a mountain river which flows and flows and flows methodically and repetitiously but is very cooling and refreshing."[24] One learns to become attentive to the radiance of the most simple, everyday things. Thoreau maintained: "Every man is tasked to make his life, even in its details, worthy of the contemplation of his most elevated and critical hour."[25] And it is in this seemingly, dry, boring atmosphere that great human creativity can emerge. It has been suggested that the great intellectual flowering of New England in the nineteenth century (Hawthorne, Emerson, Melville, Thoreau, Longfellow, and others) resulted in part from the very thinness of the New England atmosphere, an understimulation that made introspection a sort of cultural resource.

Our distracted, hyped, motorized, cluttered lives point to perhaps the most essential inner praxis of all: *working with our consciousness.* We need to slow down not only our anxious activity but also our hyped-up minds. It is not as though once all the outside conditionings and distractions are removed, our true selves emerge ready made and at our immediate disposal. Far from it! We still have to deal with our inner demons and the state of our mind. We will also come to the unsettling realization that most of our thoughts and emotions have become as involuntary as our heart rate and blood pressure.

When we are confronted with our inner world, we will be astonished at our restlessness, at the variety of conflicting emotions, at the stream of unconscious thoughts and images that seize control of our minds. "The epitome of the human realm," according to Chogyam Trungpa, "is to be stuck in a huge traffic jam of discursive thought."[26] That is why Thomas Merton believed that the root of all our problems is that our consciousness is so fouled up that we can not apprehend reality as it fully and really is. We are not only unaware of our true nature, but also of the true nature of everyone and everything in our world. "The greatest need of our time," maintained Merton, "is to clean out the enormous rubbish that clutters our minds. . . . Without this housecleaning we cannot begin to see. Unless we see, we cannot think."[27] We, therefore, need to develop an "ecology of the mind," so that we can begin to approach reality as we most truly are and see what's before us clearly and precisely so we can approach life with care and mindfulness.

The Hindus refer to the everyday mind that we usually approach the world with and which we in turn bring into solitude as the "monkey mind." Psychologists tell us that the average mind is only capable of thinking about one thing for about three and one-half seconds before it bounces all around like a ping pong ball chasing a trail of senseless irrelevancies. And if action follows mind, then we see what Gurdjieff saw: most people cannot follow any course of action for any reasonable length of time.

We discover very quickly in any form of meditation that the motions of our everyday mind, as the Hindus describe it, are about as orderly as that of a crazed monkey cavorting in a cage. Worse than this, it is more like the prancing of a drunken, crazed monkey. Even this does not do it justice. It is more like a drunken, crazed monkey who has St. Vitas dance. No, our minds are even more restless than this. They are like a drunken, crazed monkey who has St. Vitas dance, and who has just been stung by a wasp. This is the kind of monkey mind or our habitual disease of uncontrolled thoughts that we have to learn to simplify and clarify so that we can live more directly and fully. Without mastering our thoughts, we cannot master our actions, since our mind determines our actions (and vice versa).

One of the ways our vision is radically impaired and our actions are misguided is through a profusion of negative thoughts. Unless our negative thoughts are liberated, we can too easily give in to a chain reaction. We discover that the mind can have incredible momentum and can very easily drag us along like a wild raging river. A tiny thought can blossom into a full-blown storm cloud very quickly. The thought of dislike, for example, can transform into one of animosity and then hatred and then take over the mind with such gusto that we might very easily express it in words or actions. The Dalai Lama warns us that "when we indulge our negative thoughts and feelings inevitably we become accustomed to them. As a result, gradually we become more prone to them and more controlled by them. And we become habituated to exploding in the face of displeasing circumstances."[28] This is true for all negative thoughts such as greed, fear, hatred, jealousy, anger, and so on. If these negative thoughts are given free reign they can possess, dominate, and even destroy not only our peace of mind, but our lives as well. We can either devolve into toxic individuals or evolve into equanimous ones. "Purify, purify," Andrew Harvey insists, "not to 'get out' of here, but to come more completely and totally in, to arrive here completely present. Neti-neti acts as a constant, acidic washing away of anything that prevents you from meeting the moment in ecstasy."[29]

Whatever type of thoughts preoccupies us, whether they are negative or merely distractions, one of the initial techniques in attempting to calm and slow down the mind is to train the mind in one-pointed concentration, by which we learn to concentrate and focus on one thing alone. William James once made the point that "the faculty of voluntarily bringing back a wandering attention, over and over again, is the very root of judgment, character and will. . . . An education which should improve this faculty would be *the* education *par excellence*."[30] This one-pointed concentration can focus on, for example breath, as in Zazen, or on a word such as a mantra, or on a visual pattern (Yantra/Icon). It is only when we know how to pay attention to something or someone that we come to know the other and be present to the other. And when we say "pay attention," it is a very telling phrase, because we have to struggle through our own inner incoherence, self-absorption, and socialized mindset. We need to go from a distracted and diffused consciousness to a focused one. This rigorous training of attention, we discover, is an essential element of the required training in virtually all wisdom traditions.

This practice can begin by adopting a form of sitting meditation, where we directly work with our mental processes, or by pursuing a form of active meditation, where we work on our actions and mind together. When Thomas Merton asked Thich Nhat Hahn how he was taught to meditate in a Buddhist monastery, Nhat Hahn responded that, when one first enters the monastery, one is not even allowed to meditate for three or four years. Before you can meditate you have to learn to close doors. What is the point of going around slamming doors, kicking everything around mindlessly, uncontrolled physical energy popping off in all directions, and then for half an hour trying to be mindful? Or, from another angle, as a young martial artist explained the need for an active form of meditation: "After three years of meditation I felt real good mentally, but I couldn't accomplish much in the physical world. I was spaced out. I was what you call a cosmic oatmeal cookie. . . . I needed a mental/physical/spiritual balance." The whole point of these meditational practices and techniques is not to have certain kinds of special inner experiences or merely to develop an attentive mind for an hour or so but to be able to live attentively all the time.

Sitting or active meditation aims not simply at learning how to concentrate, but further, how to realize the spaciousness of consciousness, or how to go from a focused consciousness to a more flexible, broader, fully attentive consciousness. A concentrative mind is not necessarily an attentive mind, but a mind that is in a state of full attention can concentrate at will. The mental practice that facilitates this state of attention has been sometimes called bare attention. Unlike concentration, bare attention does not try to cut off all sense stimuli except the one in focus. Rather, it seeks to be open yet undistracted by or unattached to all stimuli. It is the difference between a spotlight and a floodlight. The mind is trained to see everything yet clutch nothing. It is like the roving eye of the mariner, "who never attaches himself to what he sees, whose very glance is roving, floating, sailing on, who looks at every person and object with a sense of the enormousness of the world and of the tides and currents that carry us onward."[31]

Although it is crucial to be able to concentrate, there is a caution. We can become so tunnel-visioned in our concentration of whatever orientation that in effect we bracket out the rest of life. The ability to concentrate needs to be expanded into total attention. In terms of Western spirituality, prayer can become so concentrative and cocoon-like that one can get "lost in prayer," where the outside world is totally shut out. Psychologists such as Erich Neumann might characterize such a state as merely plunging into the maternal "uroboros."[32] But on a higher plane, there is a form of prayer where one's awareness of the world becomes increasingly sharp and crystal clear. This distinction is exemplified in a rabbinic story of two highly esteemed rabbis, a father and his son. One day the father was visiting his son when he heard a baby crying. He found his son beside his baby boy in a crib, "lost in prayer." He shook his son and said: "My son, I never knew you had such a little mind, because when I am in the deepest meditation I can hear a fly buzzing about."[33]

6

Self-discovery

Once we have slowed down sufficiently, uncluttered our minds and our life space, and begun to be attuned to vertical (contemplative) time as well as horizontal time; once our consciousness has been cleared of the rubble and can be attentive to reality; once we being to realize the spaciousness of consciousness, we can begin to be reintroduced to our selves on many different levels. We begin to be more sensitive to that which is most genuine in us and to that which betrays us. We can begin to trust our own perspective and, in the words of Howard Thurman, learn to "cherish the grain of our own wood."[1]

We can begin to have confidence in our own intelligence and trust the invisible gauges that we carry within us. Our creative imagination begins to be liberated. We are freed from the boundaries of the established patterns of the past. We may very well experience some "trans-rational, almost visionary images of our deepest reality that arise from the inner shaping tendencies we carry with us."[2] We begin to see a whole range of possibilities that we had never imagined before. Our ego is no longer our dictator. We discover, as Merton pointed out, that much of what we thought was real now seems fictitious. What seemed truth now seems shallow or even false. What we previously called our personality we find can overshadow our potential personality and can deprive us of our true identity. What we have been calling our self is really in many ways that which has been veiling our self. And that which has been our *I* can be a barrier to our becoming.

We discover that we are not like anyone else, because each human being is gifted with something unique and extraordinary. We experience what the Native Americans have taught us—that our particular personality, our particular way, our particular set of life circumstances have never been tried before. It is as though life were experimenting with us in its ceaseless attempt at bringing about new and more unique life forms. Martin Buber always rejected people's attempts to peg him as a philosopher or a theologian or in some other traditional category. He declared himself to be "an atypical man." Thomas Merton insisted:

> I am accused of living in the woods like Thoreau instead of living in the desert like John the Baptist. All I can answer is that I am not living "like

anybody." . . . It is a compelling necessity for me to be free to embrace the necessity of my own nature.[3]

With the inspiration of so many before us, we have to begin to see ourselves, as Chogyam Trungpa suggests, as the first settlers in a no-man's land where we have nothing at all and have to do and make everything with our bare hands. We have to start fresh, start from scratch, as if we were Adam and Eve. Each step on our own is worth more than all the knowledge and insight of others. In the words of Walt Whitman:

Sail forth—steer for the deep water only
Reckless O Soul, exploring, I with thee and thou with me
For we are bound where mariner has not yet dared to go
And we will risk the ship, ourselves and all.[4]

As we allow ourselves to be more and more exposed to our depths, we will discover, as the Sufis teach, that there are twenty-two thousand veils that we have to peal away to expose our deepest nature. "Man discovers and senses," intuits Raimon Panikkar, "an inbuilt *more* in his own being which at once belongs to and transcends his own private being."[5] We discover in ourselves, beyond the reach of our ego, reason, and psyche, beyond or below the unconscious, that we possess at the deepest level of our being a faculty called the organ of knowledge or what Plato called the "eye of the soul." The Buddhists call this faculty Bodhi, whereas the medieval theologians referred to it as the Intellect. Through this faculty we experience an altogether different dimension of Reality. It is of a more ontological, transcendent, mystical nature. It is not reason, nor is it feeling, sensitivity, intelligence, or instinct alone. It is all of them and more. It is the most profound manifestation of our intrinsic being.

Through the eye of the soul we come to an intuitive, passionate apprehension, a kind of rapturous recognition that we have roots in the infinite depths of existence. According to the Catholic theologian Karl Rahner, a fundamental act of transcendence constitutes our very essence. It constitutes the inner structure of our being. We discover that our personhood emerges out of a divine, sacred spring. We are created from the beginning to be vehicles of the self-manifestation of the unmanifest. We are "theomorphic" beings because "God is the transcendent mystery immanent in us. . . . We realize that we 'remain' in something, that being within us, is greater than we are, transcends us."[6] Therefore, we have the capacity to understand not only our true nature, but also the nature of ultimate Reality, at least inchoately (through a glass darkly), since only like can know like.

Through the eye of the soul we can come to manifest the non-manifest in our being. We can manifest something that is at once real and yet waiting to be realized. This yet-to-be manifest reality is what the great Sufi mystic and metaphysician Ibn al Arabi called our "divine Name," which becomes visible in a particularized and individual form, our self. This divine Name becomes at once our Lord and our self. The revelation that the divine Mystery makes in every creature is in a unique and personalized mode, a different, hitherto unrevealed name of God different than every other divine Name. Every creature has it own Name, its own Lord, and therefore, its own logos, its own entelechy, and its secret coincidence with its "interior word."

There is no one expression of Reality. As the Russian personalists (such as Berdyaev, Soloviev, and Shestov) believed, the ground of existence is not a single entity of any kind but rather a myriad of souls in ecstatic play, in a primordial unity. God is many, albeit a unified many. If Hindus, for example, point to an undifferentiated unity, this approach is rather the belief in a differentiated union. The divine Name or my Lord, which is my essence, will be necessarily different from anyone else's. There is no one, direct, permanent path to realization of the divine Mystery. Each individual destiny has a unique gateway to Reality and must find its own spiritual belonging and direction. As Beatrice Bruteau explains: "The single large life in which I participate is a community of whole selves. . . . Far from being absorbed or dissolved . . . my interior sense of self-possession, or self-being, is more intense and clearer, in the sense of being more luminous and more truly 'I.'"[7]

Spiritualities that attempt to lead us directly to the All, or Emptiness (Buddhist) bypass the very mode and manifestation that could lead us there: our own identity. We would be in effect ignoring and disregarding the very manifestation we were created for; we would be counting as nothing the very raison d'etre of our creation. Who am I? would be a meaningless question since the illusory I dissolves into the All. From a Judeo-Christian perspective, the self always retains its own ontological status since it is not identical with God or totally absorbed into the All. As Raimon Panikkar explains:

> I am not a spare part which can be exchanged. If I do not enact what I am, no one else will. Here no one else can help me out, no one can replace me, since it is not a matter of doing a certain job, of having a certain function. It is a matter of being, not having. The point is that something within me is ultimate and cannot be reversed.[8]

In Jewish mysticism, for example, never "does the identity and individuality of the mystic become blurred even at the height of ecstatic passion."[9] In one of Carl Jung's *Sermons* found in his last great work, *Mysterium Coniunctionis*, he articulated the danger of dissolving in the All:

> What is the harm, ye ask, in not distinguishing oneself? If we do not distinguish, we get beyond our own nature, away from creature. We fall into indistinctiveness. . . . We fall into the pleroma itself and cease to be creatures. We are given over to dissolution in the nothingness. This is the death of the creature.[10]

It is this understanding of one's special Name or Lord, this sacred psychology, this metaphysical anthropology that secures the very foundation for our radical autonomy as an individual, not as a floating ion in a meaningless flux but as a unique theophany of the very essence of Reality. It is the radical substantiation of the dignity of the human person. To live a life totally unacquainted with our personal Lord is to live a life alienated from whom we most truly are and the reality we are called to manifest in this world. The heart and soul of this approach to Reality is, therefore, the long unremitting quest for a decisive encounter and identification with our Lord, our "divine DNA." As the Jungian psychologist Jean Houston expresses it, we are being asked before all else:

> Who is your double in the extended realm of your soul? For whom are you here as the asymmetrical partner, the ecotype of your archetype? Who is it who is yearning for you, calling to you, who is the beloved you are always trying to remember?[11]

Paradoxically, we experience this Lord, or divine Name, as "other" than ourselves yet at the core of ourselves. This quintessence of otherness is yet the quintessence of our essential being. Our identity is grounded in an awareness at once within me and yet beyond me. This "Thou," which is "that-which-is-not-I," is at once wholly other and yet is oneself as self. We "behold" the self, whereas we "have" an ego, which is a person's "my": my way, my style, my work, my possessions, my spouse. Sogyal Rinpoche, in *The Tibetan Book of Living and Dying*, puts it like this: "Two people have been living in you all your life. One is your ego, garrulous, demanding, hysterical, calculating; the other is the hidden spiritual being, whose still voice of wisdom you have only rarely heard or attended to."[12]

We as free human beings encounter our Lord as a counter-image to our freedom, not as a limit but rather as a completion. It is not as if we are talking about two separate essences that could exist on their own without each other, but a bi-unity, forming at once a dialogical polarity as well as a unity. "The seeing through which I know him," explains Ibn al Arabi, "is the same seeing through which he knows me."[13] Martin Buber describes this encounter of the self with one's Lord precisely:

> He must sacrifice his little will which is unfree and ruled by things and drives, to his great will that moves away from being determined to find destiny. Now he no longer interferes, nor does he merely allow things to happen. He listens to that which grows, to the way of being in the world, not in order to be carried along by it but rather in order to actualize it in the manner in which it, needing him, wants to be actualized by him—with human spirit and human deed, with human life and human death.[14]

This intuition about the divine Names and hence one's Lord is by no means unique to Ibn al Arabi, for it is found in one form or another in most of the spiritual, religious, philosophical, and psychological traditions of the world. Joseph Campbell called this intuition "the most sophisticated notion of the deity anywhere I know of, this notion of a chosen deity that is going to be your guide."[15] For the ancient Greeks, the basic injunction was to "accept your destiny," and your destiny was determined neither by social consensus nor from one's psychic level of instinct, but from what the Greeks called your *daimon.* At birth, each person is given a certain *daimon,* concerning which Socrates said, "I am subject to a divine or supernatural experience . . . a sort of voice which comes to me."[16]

This *daimon* is our true secret self, our personal destiny, a guiding principle that moves within us allowing us to live life out of our own strength and not relying on outside forces. The *daimon* is our ideal possibility, not the way we now find ourselves. We are born as a potentiality not as a fully actualized human being. Reaching our destiny demands we respond to Pindar's admonition: "Become what you are!"[17]

For Socrates, this *daimon* would indicate at crucial moments what course he should take. When he was about to make a decision in life, he would listen to this deepest voice inside and make his decisions based on those indicators and not rely simply on some rational analysis or socially agreed upon moral maxims. And it was generally not an easy path, but rather a task and a challenge. It is very difficult being your being. "The most difficult discipline is to be what you are."[18] As in a poem by e e cummings: "to be nobody but yourself . . . / means to fight the hardest battle which any human being can fight." William Butler Yeats explains:

> When I think of life as a struggle with the Daimon, who would ever set us to the hardest work among those not impossible, I understand why there is a deep enmity between a man and his destiny, and why a man loves nothing but his destiny.[19]

The *daimon* never urged Socrates toward any particular course of future action, but rather made itself known to Socrates primarily as a "naysayer," an intuitive warning system, a moral barometer, a divine obstruction, arresting him at the edge of any misstep, cautioning and inhibiting him against anything that would try to pull him out of his unique "shape." It was often a "counter voice" or another will contrary to his conscious point of view. There was something within him all the time that was aware of another and greater reality, in the presence of which his life might be lived. So there is this inner struggle between Socrates' conscious goals and the indicators of his deep daimonic presence since the *daimon* could move him in directions that he would rather not go. ("Not my will but thine be done" [Mt 26:39].) And if one does not listen to one's *daimon*, Schopenhauer offers a warning in his journals: "Thus

I was advised for my own good by a certain inner voice, which I have been all my life ready to follow, as on rare occasions when I acted against it I invariably found cause to regret it bitterly."[20]

This inner *daimon*, therefore, works to limit our lives to only those possibilities that are truly ours. Often this naysaying manifests itself as physical symptoms or inner psychic disturbances, which are seeking to hold us back from some enterprise or relationship that for us would be false or destructive. What might superficially seem as a catastrophe or a great disappointment might be the only way our inner guide has of keeping us true to our life-giving path. As Michael Ventura suggests: "It's like having a much older man inside who talks to you, quietly, usually kindly, tolerantly, and sometimes sternly when you're really fucking up, always with humor . . . the best part of you."[21]

7

Working with Our Inner Alchemy

Our gradual exposure to our deepest self necessarily leads us to a form of self-acquaintance where we discover aspects of ourselves that do not necessarily jive with what we might judge as "morally positive," at least according to society's dominant ethical values or our corresponding ego ideal. We find ourselves drawn, attracted, and pulled toward our realization by the energies that constitute our essence. Inner work consists of recognizing those energies, working with them, corralling them, channeling them, allowing them to be transformed into their deepest and highest realization.

There is a Tantric dictum that states: "One must rise by that which one falls."[1] The inner quest is not an attempt to destroy, repress, suppress, or ignore those energies within us that might appear dangerous or even potentially destructive and then take a "flight into the light," in search of a type of "pure energy" or "pure consciousness." This Tantric wisdom, according to Andrew Harvey,

> does not aim for an unnatural perfection or a flight into some life of body-denying absolute, does not over privilege the "pure" and the "transcendent," but works patiently, all-embracing, with alchemical subtlety, towards a wholeness in which the transcendent and mystical are not separate from the immanent and practical, but are joined with them in indivisible sacred union.[2]

The goal of inner work, therefore, is not perfection but completeness. Perfection, Otto Rank insisted, is a disease, an ego quest pure and simple. Interestingly, the Greek word used in the New Testament for perfection is *Teleioi*, which means "to be full grown, adult, complete, and whole." The true saint is not some super-angelic person, but one who lives his or her unique truth. The "whole" person is never blameless or guiltless or pure but is one in whom all sides of the self have been combined inexplicably into a total person. Such persons live the whole range of their capacities.

Of course, we are afraid to take an unflinching look at our true self in all its aspects because our ego will be obliged to step down from its moral pedestal. But the energies we experience within are the only ones that we have and can work with. The danger, the spiritual delusion, is to attempt to leap over our real energies, the very "stuff" of our realization, and seek some higher, purer experience or consciousness. We can become so alien, distant, or separate from our true energies that we literally have nothing left to work with except our constructed angelic fiction. "Whoever uproots his instincts uproots his strength," warns Nikos Kazanzakis, " . . . for with time, satiety and discipline this dark matter may turn to spirit."

In the Buddhist tradition, seeking an ecology of the mind involves a process known as clarifying muddy waters. Water is essentially pure and clear, but when it is turbulent it often stirs up the mud. Our consciousness is also essentially clear and open but muddied by the turbulence of conflicting thoughts and emotions. If we want the muddy waters to become clear, the best thing to do is to let the water sit, and that is exactly what sitting meditation is all about. The point, however, is not to try to get rid of the mud, because all these conflicting thoughts and emotions are telling us something about ourselves. These thoughts and emotions spring up for a reason. Inner work, therefore, consists of both quieting the mind but also exploring the mud, because we discover that the mud not only points to inner disturbances but it also contains many essential minerals and nutrients necessary for our growth. The image presented to us by the Buddhists is that of the lotus flower, this most beautiful of flowers blossoming in the midst of mud, whose roots are sunk deep into the muddy water that continues to nourish it. As Parker Palmer says, "Those fearsome forces within us may turn out to be our closest companions and most knowledgeable guides on the spiritual journey."[3] So we have to explore the mud, or the darker seemingly dirtier and messier parts of our consciousness.

One of the most ancient schools of mysticism is alchemy, which in its broadest sense is the transforming of lower energies, metaphorically called baser metals, into higher energies, metaphorically gold. The aim is personal transformation, but the key to this transformation is knowing and dealing with the ingredients of our personal alchemy. If we do not deal with our seemingly baser energies, no metamorphosis is possible. This is a very difficult form of inner work, but if we have the courage to face up to everything we discover within and leave nothing unexplored, if we walk slowly and deliberately through the sometimes terrifying labyrinthine recesses of our inner world, we will discover the whole subterranean part of ourselves that we consider dangerous and unacceptable, for example, the whole world of uncivilized desires and feelings.

We need to access what the East calls *kufu* or the ability to remove all our emotional and intellectual inhibitions so that we can bring forth whatever is stored in this labyrinth without any ego interference. As Aldo Carotenuto insists:

> One must be audacious enough to continually live one's shadow side, otherwise one really and truly sins against oneself. The basic question we must ask ourselves in drawing up the balance sheet of our lives is this: "Did I live as I really was?" If I cannot answer yes, I have not truly lived.[4]

Or, as Jesus says in the Gospel of Thomas: "If you bring forth what is within you, what is within you will save you; if you don't bring forth what is within you, what is within you will destroy you."[5]

For Jung, this "shadow" is 90 percent gold. At first, it might seem that we are mired in a kind of inner chaos, but there is a great deal of potency in this chaos. Every energy in the chaos has the potential of being upgraded. Behind every impulse we discover a higher possibility. There is nothing in us—no urge, no desire that does not contain many valuable clues to our true identity. Many of the most frightening energies are messengers of our creative potential. So the task is not to drop the lower but to seek to attain the higher possibilities. The lower will merge with the higher on its own accord. We must never consider our instincts as too impure or our sensuousness too peripheral or our feelings too fleeting. Rather, "everything must be included and integrated. What is wanted is not the abstracted self but the whole, undiminished man."[6]

Saint Paul, for example, was one of the most violent of men. There was this rage, this fierceness, and this enormous aggressiveness. At first he had it turned against the followers of Jesus. He was a major persecutor. But when he had undergone his conversion experience he did not all of a sudden become gentle as a lamb, a milquetoast messenger. He was able to transform this aggressive, fierce, raging energy into becoming one of Christianity's most potent defenders.

When we discover, for example, anger within us, and we are willing to work with it, then it can gradually be channeled into a positive, powerful force. Individuals with a highly critical nature can develop the gift of discernment, by which they are able to size up a situation very accurately and sometimes with deadly insight. Chogyam Trungpa expresses it this way:

> Each person . . . has his or her own particular quality. It may be a great kind of violence or great laziness, but one has just to take that particular quality and not regard it necessarily as a fault or a blockage, for this *is* the bodhi [awakened mind and heart] which is in oneself; it is the seed, or rather the full potentiality for giving birth [to his awakened mind and heart]. . . . He may be habitually drunk or habitually violent, but that character is his potentiality. And in order to give birth to bodhi . . . that . . . energetic, dynamic aspect of violence can be made to serve the energy aspect of the spiritual life.[7]

Albert Camus once made a similar point: "It seemed better to accept my pride and try to make use of it, rather than give myself . . . principles stronger than my character."[8]

One of the great obstacles to self-realization is getting stuck at our present level of ego development or "plateau-ing" on our interior growth, refusing or being afraid of responding to life's call. All authentic paths demand the ultimate effort. That is why so many spiritual paths are compared to the athletic quest—because of the incredible effort that must be made. Therefore, this effort means being willing to pay an enormous price. It even means, in the words of Blake, sometimes having to "go beyond your boundaries to discover where your boundaries are." Those who insist on restricting their lives to tranquil, safe havens where they never have to confront and deal with shocks and crises consign themselves to live in an unaware, flat, gray, anonymous, lowest-common-denominator existence. Rainer Maria Rilke says of an artist that which could be said of any spiritual path: "Works of art always spring from those who have faced the danger, gone to the very end of an experience, to the point beyond which no human being can go. The further one dares to go, the more decent, the more personal, the more unique a life becomes."[9]

But there is a corresponding danger to be aware of. As Rilke counseled, we should never remain behind our heart yet never be in advance of it either. We have to do our inner work from where we are, fully where we are, not where we would like to imagine ourselves to be, or where others would have us. There is an old proverb that states: No bird soars too high, if it soars with its own wings. There is a real danger of a spiritual ambitiousness, which only produces the most bogus of spiritualities. "It is difficult," observes the potter M. C. Richards, "to stand forth in one's growing, if one is not permitted to live through one's unripeness, clumsiness, unreadyness, as well as one's grace and aptitude."[10] The Bhagavad Gita teaches: "Better is one's own dharma imperfectly performed, than the dharma of another performed to perfection."[11] Or as Raimon Panikkar warns: "To want to achieve an ideal that is too high or inappropriate leads to total deception and fiasco."[12]

Although it is true that you can judge a tree by its fruits, it is also true that we should not judge a tree until it has time to produce its fruits. There is a date tree, for example, that takes seventy years to bear fruit. Choa-Yi, a well-known scholar during the Ch'ing Dynasty, said that a person is not to be judged until the lid of the coffin is closed. When we live out of where we genuinely are, we have to be willing to face the reality that we might be at a very immature stage of realization. Raimon Panikkar states: "Humility, to me, means the courage to be imperfect, not finished."[13] Joseph Campbell makes a very similar point when he maintains that "as long as you're re-incarnating, you are imperfect. So you have to be loyal to your imperfection. . . . Decide to be imperfect, reconcile yourself to that and go ahead."[14] The great spiritual figure Thomas Merton, toward the end of his life, could confess:

In order to be honest with myself . . . I find it necessary to take the facts of my own life as they are, and admit . . . that nothing in my life is ideal, and nothing fits the accepted formulas. I am the first one to declare that I am not what I ought to be. . . . As I grow older I find it more and more necessary to respect the mystery of one's personal life, everyone's.[15]

8

The Further Journey

Through the eye of the *soul* we discover our own unique divine Name. But the journey is not now over. Although the soul always retains its intrinsic ontological, theological, and mystical constitution, it never stands in radical isolation. Rather, we discover in our ontological depths that we are relational beings. Through the eye of the *heart*, we discover that we are called deeper into the holy Mystery, where there is revealed to us an infinite compassion that embraces all life. It is out of this endless flow of compassion that we are immediately and intrinsically linked to the other, to all others, to the whole of creation. There exists not only our unique identity but also the absolute identity of everyone else and that interrelationship of identities is held together in love.

What we finally come to experience is that the deeper we go in, the more radically we are directed outward. As Thomas Merton teaches:

> One of the paradoxes of the mystical life is this: that a man cannot enter into the deepest center of himself and pass through that center into God, unless he is able to pass entirely out of himself and give himself to other people in the purity of a selfless love. . . . The more I become identified with God, the more will I be identified with all the others who are identified with Him. . . . We shall love one another and God with the same Love with which He loves us and Himself. This love is God Himself.[1]

Or, we could also say that when we love, we are "in God," for as Saint Augustine provocatively stated, "Love is God."[2] Where there is love, there is God. Love is the very presence of the Divine.

Buddhism also shares this fundamental insight into Reality. For Buddhism, *Dharmakaya* is the source of all things. Buddhist scholar D. T. Suzuki explains that the essential characteristics of *Dharmakaya*,[3] or the cosmic God Manifest, are *prayna* (wisdom) and *karuna* (compassion), which Suzuki translates as love. Wisdom and love are at the very heart of reality. Wisdom *(prayna)* is the ability to see reality as it is. Wisdom dispels the clouds of *Maya*, or illusion, demolishes our false beliefs, and introduces us to a new world of values based on compassion *(karuna)*.

We experience wisdom and compassion in a dynamic twofold movement, not unlike Plato's insight. The upward movement is the ascent from the world of *maya* to the experience of enlightenment. This path requires a series of negations of our ordinary way of thinking and acting in order to lead us to a new way of being. The downward movement is the return from the experience of enlightenment to a renewed affirmation of human existence in the world. The downward path of the return proceeds in the opposite manner from the ascent, through a series of affirmations, since everything in the world is interconnected and interdependent.

These two directions correspond to the fundamental Buddhist virtues. The upward path or a path of withdrawal is the path of wisdom. The downward path or the path of engagement is the path of compassion. Wisdom and compassion are inseparable. To see things as they are is to have compassion on all sentient beings. One comes to realize that ultimately wisdom and compassion are two aspects of one experience. These two directions, the ascent and descent, moving away and moving toward, are simultaneously identical and not identical. Although the realization of this unity is attained by different priorities and praxes, both the Judeo-Christian tradition and the Buddhist tradition at a very deep level intuit this union of withdrawal and engagement, wisdom and compassion.

At the heart of the matter is this great irony of how deep interior silence gives birth to infinite compassion. Solitude and solidarity birth each other. Solidarity needs to be constantly fed and finds its firmest footing in a profound solitude, and solitude—if it is humanly real and healthy—will necessarily flow into compassion. We discover that the drive to realize our true nature in solitude flows from the same source as the drive to alleviate the suffering of others. In fact we discover that the alleviation of the suffering of others is the flowering of our true nature. The deeper we move into our selves, the more we recognize hitherto unimagined social responsibilities. Allen Ginsberg once wrote: "Why I meditate is to become more peaceful. Why I meditate is to revolutionize the world." The Jewish teacher Hillel, a contemporary of Jesus, sums it up perfectly: "If I am not for myself, who will be? If I am only for myself, what am I?"[4]

PART II

COMPASSIONATE SOLIDARITY

9

Solidarity Mysticism

If solitude emphasizes interiority, solidarity exposes us to a radical exteriority. In solitude, we are called to withdraw from our regular round of social life, to go within and discover such human treasures as wisdom, contemplation, thought, creativity, imagination, memory, leisure, and so forth. Solidarity, on the other hand, calls us forth into the community. If the vocation of solitude is one of "sensitizing the world, 'conscientizing' man to his transcendent, vertical reality,"[1] the vocation of solidarity is to sensitize and conscienticize human persons to the horizontal reality of the suffering in the human community. Solidarity mysticism bids us to open our eyes and see the situation in the world: to read the signs of the times, to behold the beauty of creation, and to appreciate the worth of the other. If solitude exposes us to our solitary daimonic identity—our transpersonal ground—then solidarity reveals the corporate nature of our selfhood. We discover that in the mystery of our being there is the mystery of the other. If solitude draws us into a vertical mysticism that emphasizes a transformation through contemplation, solidarity draws us into a horizontal mysticism, a horizontal transcendence, where transformation is attained through gnosis-as-action, an "engaged love," an active, moral, public mysticism; a mysticism of responsibility; a mysticism of immersion and participation.

A holistic spirituality that incorporates both solitude and solidarity is rooted in the divine Mystery. The masters of suspicion (Freud, Marx, and Nietzsche) have dismissed, even ridiculed, any belief in God because in one way or another they consider such belief to rob humanity of its dignity and independence. If we can grant that much of their negative characterizations of traditional belief in God contain some truth to them, then perhaps this situation calls for a reinterpretation of our understanding of God.

The first chapter articulated a vision of the divine Mystery that spoke of God unmanifest, which corresponds to the Christian Father. Out of God unmanifest emerged God manifest corresponding to the Christian God the Son. And finally, there is the Love between the Father and the Son, which Christians call Spirit. But perhaps at this point we need to push this vision further and speak more precisely. Karl Rahner puts forward an understanding and vision of the divine Mystery that is decidedly not the God that the masters of suspicion critiqued. His vision may provide the deepest primordial reality out of which solidarity mysticism can be awakened and nurtured. This is what Rahner says: "The absolute One [God unmanifest] in the pure freedom of his infinite unrelatedness, which he always preserves, possesses the possibility of himself becoming the other [God manifest]." Then Rahner makes a crucial point:

> He possesses the possibility of establishing the other as his own reality by dispossessing himself, he himself, he as the self-giving fullness. Because he can do this, because this is his free and primary possibility, for this reason he is defined in scripture as love.[2]

In other words, at the heart of Reality is a dispossessing of self through self-giving fullness in love. And it is from this dispossessing, self-giving fullness that solidarity mysticism flows.

If the divine Mystery is self-giving love, it manifests itself not only as being, but also as gift, becoming, doing. Solitary, traditional mysticism not only emphasizes wisdom/gnosis over love, but it also favors being over action or doing. This is because, from this tradition's viewpoint, being is seen to have priority over becoming. It points to the delight of being, the radiance of being. As the East would say, at the heart of being are *Sat Chit Ananda* or suchness, wisdom, and bliss. If being is more important than doing, then a receptive mode toward life is favored over a responsive one. Or we could say that this spirituality is decidedly more feminine than masculine. It is as if it views spirituality to be, by its very nature, feminine. Therefore, this solitary mysticism delights in existence as such and is not driven toward any particular tasks or obligations. This form of mysticism tends to have sympathy for the Greek doctrine of *apatheia* or what the East would refer to as serenity or tranquility. The ideal person from this perspective would be *homo apatheticos* (tranquil man) where the ontological notion of serenity and stability is often accompanied by the psychological view of emotions as disturbances of the soul. If the heart of all Reality is total bliss and serenity, then the more we realize this serenity or *apatheia* in our being, the closer we are to God/Reality.

With solidarity mysticism a whole new turn is taken. Not that it totally denies or abrogates the solitary approach, but it perceives a polarity. There is another whole dimension that has been left out or has not yet been revealed. Solidarity mysticism points to a dynamic concept of being in which being cannot be separated from becoming or doing. "To think," declares Levinas, "is no longer to contemplate, but to be engaged, merged with what we think, launched!—the dramatic event of being-in-the-world."[3] The essence of being/becoming calls forth not only receptivity but also responsibility. The fathomless shores of compassion flow outward to the world and humanity in the decisive mode of justice. Therefore, if *Sat Chit Ananda* (suchness, wisdom, and bliss) is the divine revelation of the East, love/justice are the two great divine Names for the Judeo-Christian tradition.

Being, therefore, is not the totality of reality, because there is becoming, and becoming involves action, movement, and doing. In the Judeo-Christian tradition being and becoming are characterized not only by serenity but also, as Abraham Heschel points out, by a "sense of challenge, a commitment, a state of tension, consternation and dismay." Or, as Heschel says in another way, God is encountered "not as universal, general pure Being, but always . . . in a specific pathos that comes with a demand in a concrete situation."[4] The God/Reality is not only *apatheia* but also a *pathos* that leads the human community not only to an experience, but also to a task. If the Eastern sage is tranquil, the Western prophet is intensely present and fervently involved.

Solitary mysticism has traditionally been concerned with what we do with our solitude, as the philosopher Alfred North Whitehead states.[5] Most of what we have understood as spirituality has had to do with silent prayer, an intense one-on-one love affair with God, mystical ecstasy, contemplation, *samadhi*, *nirvana*, and so on. This spiritual approach is so abundantly explored in spiritual literature that we need not reexamine it here, except to offer a caution:

> There is in any [solitary] mysticism something disquieting and even objectively dangerous. Mysticism turns into the cloak that renders the mystic invisible. His soul is open to God, but because it is open *only* to God, it is invisible for the rest of the world and cut off from it.[6]

Beyond this caution, unfortunately in our time this profound inward experience has been so trivialized and psychologized that many present-day spiritualities have become little more than therapeutic devises where our relationship with God is simply a way of making us feel better, of "massaging our feelings. We pray for comfort but do not expect to be challenged."[7] This inward-gazing spirituality fixates on such questions as: I am anxious; how can I cope? But a holistic spirituality is not only concerned with what we do in solitude but also with what we do in community. The question solidarity spirituality would ask is: My neighbor is oppressed. What is my responsibility?

Dorothee Soelle points to the broad implications of this spirituality when she insists that a solidarity mysticism

> seeks to erase the distinction between a mystical internal and a political external. Everything that is within needs to be externalized so it doesn't spoil, like the manna from the desert that was hoarded for future consumption. There is no experience of God that can be so privatized that it becomes and remains the property of one owner, the privilege of a person of leisure, the esoteric domain of the initiated.[8]

Solidarity mysticism is born and nurtured in an experience of reality not available to those who choose the path of solitude alone. The mysticism of solidarity does not approach the transcendent by fleeing the immanent but discovers the transcendent as the very mystery and sacredness of the immanent.

As Buber would say: It is "a realistic and active mysticism, i.e., a mysticism for which the world is not an illusion from which man must turn away in order to reach true being."[9]

The mysticism of love and solidarity does not put aside the concern for others for the sake of finding ourselves. Rather, it is in the giving of ourselves for the other that we fully discover our whole identity. It is only by ceasing to identify our life's quest with our own good alone that we can begin to realize that our good is totally bound up with the good of all others. As Sarvepalli Radhakrishnan would see it from a Hindu perspective: "The resurrection is not the rise of the dead from their tombs but the passage from the death of self-absorption to the life of unselfish love."[10] Instead of seeking all kinds of sophisticated ways out of dealing with our neighbor and the world, solidarity brings us down from transcendence into immanence,

> down from the safety of detachment into the misery and glory of love. Down from mystical illumination into heart-illumined action that is prepared to risk defeat, derision, and all kinds of desolation. . . . Instead of trying to escape time at any cost, it takes time and kisses it on the lips and accepts all its conditions and sufferings, all its ordeals just as they are. . . . No escape, no escape.[11]

The ontological basis of experiencing the divine Mystery primarily as wisdom is rooted in the soul's capacity called the eye of the soul, which radically exposes the person to divine wisdom or gnosis. But there is also within us an affective power of the soul on the same ontological level as the eye of the soul that is called by the Buddhists *bodhicitta* or "the awakened mind-heart." It is called by the Sufis the eye of the heart, and *synderesis*[12] by the medieval Scholastics. We are born with a primordial capacity of basic goodness or a natural inclination toward doing the good. Or as some would have it, we are "hard wired" to do the good. Beatrice Bruteau explains: "One discovers at the center of one's own being an enormous flux and 'through-flux' of agape-energy."[13] In Deuteronomy we find: "This commandment which I command you this day is not too difficult for you, neither is it far off. . . . It is very near to you; it is . . . in your heart, so that you can do it" (Dt 30:11–14). Therefore, there is within us all an innate predilection toward both wisdom and the good. If the praxis of contemplation allows divine Wisdom to flow through us, the praxis of service to our neighbor allows divine Love to flow in our lives. Both eye of the soul and eye of the heart are loci of and fundamental entries into the divine dimension.

Mysticism in the broadest sense is an intense presence before or union with the divine Mystery. This experience or presence traditionally has been called, at least in the West, prayer. Although there is a form of prayer that is communal (for example, the liturgy), what we have traditionally understood as prayer has been largely a private experience. But although the spiritual reality is experienced within, it does not come about by merely turning within. A unitive relationship with God or the Real, which is designated as prayer in spiritual literature, occurs not just in the splendid intimacy of the soul alone with the Alone (Plotinus), but also in the turning toward the other in love and responsibility. As Martin Buber says: "The encounter with God does not come to man in order that he may henceforth attend to God but in order that he may prove its meaning in action in the world."[14] Leon Brunschvicg makes a similar point when he states that

> preoccupation with our salvation is a remnant of self-love, a trace of natural egocentrism from which we must be torn by the religious life. As long as you only think salvation, you turn your back on God. God is God, only for the person who overcomes the temptation to degrade him and use him for his own ends.[15]

In prayer, we are not only invited to "come" but also to "go," not only to "be" but to "do." Prayer is not only *Ora pro me* (pray for *me*) or *Ora pro nobis* (pray for *us*) but *Ora pro aliis* (pray for the *others*), *Ora pro omnibus* (pray for *all people*), *Ora pro pauperiis* (pray for the *poor*). Rather than only a passive act or a withdrawal from the world, prayer can also be a way of waking and summoning us to do good in the world. Otherwise, prayer can become what Emerson called "a disease of the will." As the Dalai Lama observes: "It is easier to meditate than to actually do something for others. I feel that merely to meditate . . . is to take the passive option. Our meditation should form the basis of action, for seizing the opportunity to do something."[16]

There is always the real danger that an isolationistic prayer can produce in us a conscience that never becomes bothersome but rather becomes part of a religion that has been diminished into "the churches and sermons of an institutionalized degradation."[17] There is that type of prayer that can so separate us from the condition of our brothers and sisters that we can end up with the horrible spectacle of a Roman Catholic church adjoining the extermination camp in Auschwitz, daily offering communion to the officers of the camp who daily drove thousands of people to be killed in the gas chambers. That is why Abraham Heschel insists that "prayer is meaningless unless it is subversive, unless it seeks to overthrow and to ruin the pyramids of callousness, hatred, opportunism, falsehoods."[18] Or as Johann Baptist Metz would pointedly say: "Prayer is the oldest form of the struggle of human beings to keep their own self and their identity before the highest danger."[19] To paraphrase Emmanuel Levinas, tell me the dangers you are risking, and I will tell you if you are praying. Cesar Chavez, the great leader of the American farm workers, prepared himself for every struggle for the rights of poor migrants by prayer and fasting. He once fasted and prayed for twenty-four days before a large and dangerous strike. Every time he prepared himself, his enemies would say, "Watch out! Cesar Chavez is up to something. He's praying!"

Thus, this divine love flowing through us flourishes not only by being experienced in ecstatic passivity, but by being enacted. It is in the doing of love that the divine dimension becomes most profoundly present. The first of the ten *paramitas* or transformative practices of Buddhism is generosity. Once a student monk asked his teacher: "Why do the practices begin with generosity and not meditation?" And the master answered: "Practice it and then we'll talk." In *The Brothers Karamazov*, Father Zossima assures a histrionic woman, who is desperate to know whether or not God exists, that although the existence of God cannot be proved, you can become convinced of it by practicing "love in action." As he counseled:

> Strive to love your neighbor actively and indefatigably. In so far as you advance in love you will grow surer of the reality of God. . . . If you attain to perfect self-forgetfulness in the love of your neighbor, then you will believe without doubt, and no doubt can possibly enter your soul. This has been tried. This is certain. . . . I am sorry I can say nothing more consoling to you, for love in action is a harsh and dreadful thing.[20]

Love, therefore, is not only experienced but also enacted. It is above all else a doing. In the Judeo-Christian tradition, however, we are brought further along and with more precision. In looking away from self-preoccupation toward the other, we take a first step in the journey of solidarity mysticism. But we have only just begun. There is still much more. From the Judeo-Christian perspective the divine reality is intrinsically not only love and compassion but also justice. The God of love is also the God of justice. God is not only compassionate but is also passionate for justice. The implication for humanity is that in our lives love and justice are intrinsically related, for justice is the social or systematic form of love. Thus even more is demanded of us than aiding the neighbor: one must aid all humankind. To be is not only to be for the *singular* other but for the many others. As Richard A. Cohen points out, "Humanism . . . is not merely the affirmation of the dignity of one person, of each individual alone; it is also an affirmation of the dignity of all humanity, the affirmation of an interhuman morality, community, and social justice."[21] Cohen further points out that "aiding all mankind demands a different sort of aid than the infinite solicitude that one desires to give the other. It requires, in a word, justice."[22] We move then from an "I-I" to an "I-Thou" to an "I-We," toward a universal "we," the "we" of a completely redeemed world, a world of complete love and justice, or the kingdom of God. Cohen concludes:

> If the ethical dimension of the face-to-face relation is the authentic entry or dimension of the divine . . . then the wider impact of this dimension, meaning the spread of morality, up to its social and political institutionalization (in other words, the spread and establishment of justice), means at the same time the spread of G-d's presence on earth . . . the infinite ethical responsibilities and obligations of the face-to-face turn out to be insufficiently moral. There arises a further demand, for

justice, justice for all. Ethics satisfying its own demand for justice would be G-d's "supreme and ultimate presence."[23]

If we have any knowledge of traditional mysticism, which involves the purgative, illuminative, and finally the unitive life with the divine Mystery, we might conclude that solidarity mysticism is not as profound an experience and, therefore, while valuable, it is inferior to the traditional approach. But as Edward Schillebeeckx says, solidarity mysticism or what he calls "political love," from a whole new area of experience, "knows the same conversion and metanoia, the same ascesis and detachment of self, the same suffering and dark nights, the same losing of oneself in the other,"[24] as we find in traditional mysticism.

This process of self-purification is not inferior to classical mysticism but rather complements it and situates it in the social reality of the world. This purification process lies in the disinterested partisanship for the poor, the oppressed, the exploited, and in the social consequences of such realities as exile, torture, execution, martyrdom. And as we will see, it is this solidarity mysticism that reflects more precisely the mysticism of Jesus and the prophets.

We have to face the fact, however, that whether we are talking about religious traditions from the East or the West, spirituality/mysticism has been mainly seen as the domain of the inward, as if spirituality is only found in one's private experience of or relationship to God (Reality/Emptiness). Either we find some form of private mystical union with God in the Western traditions (especially in the Christian tradition), or a purifying of awareness and a raising of consciousness to a non-dual reality in the Eastern traditions. But we rarely discover any ontological spiritual or mystical dimension to the human praxis of human solidarity or justice. At best, solidarity and justice are seen as "the result of" the essential Reality that is discovered within the privacy of the solitary soul. (It should be noted here that there is no evidence at all to suggest that meditation or reaching higher stages of consciousness leads to any necessary flowing out into compassion or social justice.) Huston Smith raises the question: "Are compassion and justice rooted in ultimate reality, or are they only admirable human virtues?" And he answers: "It argues nothing against justice and compassion to say that those virtues are less important than God."[25] God, from this perspective, is not intrinsically Love, whereas from the Judeo-Christian perspective, the very essence of God is love and justice.

But where are those religious traditions and voices that call us not only to turn within but to turn toward the other in solidarity? And further, where are those religious traditions that call us to seek social justice for all peoples as a fundamental praxis of our faith? Must we wait for all to reach enlightenment before we can address social realities? And in this pursuit of social justice, where are those traditions that understand that the poor do not simply happen to be poor, but they are poor because of the way society is organized in economic structures? This is the question posed by Marx. And further, what traditions see that evil or sin assumes political and economic form, as structures and systems? Hence, which traditions not only seek to liberate individuals from their personal sins, but also seek to liberate social systems from their structural sins? Can we be in solidarity with those who are suffering on a personal basis while absenting ourselves from their social liberation? Can we say that we are with you but cannot do anything for you except perhaps through episodic acts of the works of mercy? Must such structural questions and solutions be left to the rich and powerful minority and their technical elites or to the "grace of God" in God's good time?

These are the burning questions for all of those who live below poverty in destitution (over one billion people). If poverty means subsistence living on the bare essentials, destitution means not having even the bare essentials. Destitution entails conditions of malnutrition; high infant mortality; endemic diseases; less than subsistence wages; unemployment; absence of education; and lack of modern medical care, housing, clean water, sanitation, security, and so on. Do not religious traditions that are turned totally inward and try to remain historically indifferent or innocent, and refuse to take responsibility for these brutal facts, in fact become collusive with those historical human systems that are the agents of this suffering? Are they not only "opium" for the people but don't they serve to bless people's irresponsibility toward their neighbors, at least in any systematic sense? By their silence, are they in a kind of connivance with the prevailing world economic and political systems? Can this kind of naive or sometimes not so naive spirituality actually function as part of the ideological apparatus of these systems, since they may serve as a hollowed force not only for legitimating the suffering of the subjugated, but also for achieving their domestication?

"Man does not live by bread alone" an aristocratic spirituality reminds the hungry; "slaves be obedient to your masters or bosses" has been their counsel to the subjugated. "No system is perfect" and "the poor you will always have with you" is their convenient political philosophy of inevitability. "Identify with Christ on the cross" is their mysticism offered to suffering humanity. Pius IX sums up this approach with the paternal advisory:

> Let Our poor recall the teachings of Christ Himself that they should not be sad at their condition, since their poverty makes lighter their journey to salvation, provided that they bear their need with patience and are poor not only in possessions, but in spirit too.[26]

Robert McAfee Brown characterizes this passive approach:

> People were told, "See the Son of God there on the cross? Is he crying out? Is he trying to rock the boat? Is he trying to organize a labor union? No, he's accepting God's will for him. Who are you to think you have a right to complain? Your situation might be difficult, but how much more difficult was Jesus'"?[27]

By remaining either a-historical and/or apolitical; or by adopting a theology of the inevitable that accepts the prevailing world order as given; or by being so convinced of a human being's innate sinfulness that one abandons any hope of political progress and hands it all over to the mercy of God—is not this type of religion a legitimate subject for the masters of suspicion to ruthlessly expose, as did the prophets of old? A Marxist might rightly ask: "What sort of solidarity, if any, do you religionists maintain with the world's oppressed? What are you doing to promote the creation of social structures likely to generate more social justice for the greatest possible number of people?"[28]

Has not the ecclesiastical church in fact functioned as a respected member of those closed dominant groups that the economic machine and social system have benefited? How can a church that has contributed so much historically to the injustice and oppression in the world claim to be the leading light of solidarity with humanity and its liberation? What does it say when we also have to face the fact that the whole emancipatory process of modern revolutions that has promoted the widening of the sphere of human liberation has been accomplished behind the Christian church's back, beside it, or against it; that the contribution of not only the Christian churches but also of Eastern religions was minimal if not downright antagonistic?

Karl Marx called religion "the opiate of the people"; Freud called it a "collective neurosis"; while Friedrich Nietzsche dismissed Christianity as mere "Platonism for the people." Although much truth can be found in the critiques of these masters of suspicion, we do not have to accept their reductionistic solutions that fall short of a complete anthropology and satisfactory vision of Reality. All religious traditions in some way see a human being as fundamentally *homo religiosus*. Therefore, they would reject reducing human nature to merely a result of social influences, or a blank slate on which to create whatever one chooses. Rather, at the deepest level of human subjectivity and experience, there is already a pre-apprehension of holy Mystery. In the deepest core of the soul there is an altogether other dimension that Paul Tillich calls the "mystical a-priori," or Karl Rahner calls the "supernatural existential," where the full human identity opens up to the divine horizon. Therefore, regardless of the social, cultural, economic, and political situation, there are "transcendental longings" in the human heart.

It is out of this primordial human/divine realm that all the great religious traditions flow. For all their faults and historical failings, we can still find within the traditional religions revelations worthy of our profound attention. While intellectual honesty necessitates that we "interrogate" the scriptures, we should also be correspondingly willing to be interrogated *by* them, since these scriptures represent the most profound spiritualities of the human community. These traditions do not represent mediocre achievements but the contributions of spiritual geniuses who have handed down to us treasures that we could not have acquired by ourselves. Chogyam Trungpa critiques those who too quickly dismiss the religious traditions:

> Throwing away tradition and wisdom that have been developed through many centuries is like tossing the extraordinary exertion and sacrifice that human beings have made out the window, like dirty socks. This is certainly not the best way to maintain the best human society.[29]

These traditions would never have made such a deep impression on the human community if they did not find resonance within the deepest center of the human experience. William Penn once said: "There is something nearer to us than scriptures, to wit, the word in the heart from which all scriptures come." It is not as if the religious traditions and texts have value and authority because they are sacred, but rather they have become sacred to the human community because they lay bare universal truths. Or, as Raimon Panikkar posits, if these traditions have made an indelible impression on the human community it is because "already in ourselves we made a connection with that which we saw as true. That is to say, we wouldn't have accepted their revelations or teachings if we did not see it as a part of our reality."[30]

The masters of suspicion have perhaps rightly pointed in the direction of what has been called a hermeneutics of suspicion, or indeed, a deconstruction. But this is not done for the purpose of razing or leveling these traditions but rather to shake them loose from their sedimented forms in order to return to their life-giving sources. Thus the hermeneutics of suspicion gives rise to the hermeneutics of retrieval. Like an archeologist, we have to dig beyond the dirt of decay, overlay, and routinization to uncover the original vision and dynamism of the traditions. We seek to discover what is living and stirring deep within them and to release it, set it free, give it new life, a new future. And for the purposes of this study, we search to discover if we can unfold the sociopolitical potentiality of these faiths. With the increase of globalization, an encounter with the liberating potential of Eastern religions will reveal to the West that a worldwide liberation movement needs a worldwide interreligious dialogue by which we can tap into the liberative potential of such non-Western religions as Buddhism.

10

Engaged Buddhism

If we first turn to an Eastern tradition such as Buddhism, what do we find concerning social solidarity? One of the basic laws of early Buddhism known as Theravada or Hinayana Buddhism is the belief in karma, which regards all states and conditions of a person's life as the direct result of one's previous actions in former lives. Therefore, people are responsible for their present individual and social condition. The earliest vision of Buddhism was primarily an individually oriented life in which persons sought "nirvanic freedom" from the coils of their individual karma. If they banded together in the *sangha* (monastic community), it was for the purpose of achieving this goal. They saw society as only a collection of individual karmic characteristics. This not only produced a kind of fatalism for their personal life and their social situation, but for society as a whole. Any attempt to improve society in a collective way was totally futile. It was only by means of a one-by-one improvement of individuals that society could be changed.

There is, in addition, a pronounced tendency in Eastern religions, and Buddhism is no exception, to denigrate action in the higher stages of spiritual enlightenment. One of the signs of an unenlightened mind is an excessive concern about transforming the world. Reality is already whole—perfect and complete—so an enlightened person has no desire whatsoever to do anything other than nothing in particular. Only when we are fully detached from any desire for world transformation does true compassion for the world emerge.

The greatest blessing a person can bestow on the world and all life is to sit silently, infusing the world with this compassion even though its effects may not be immediately experienced or recognized. This may create what Rupert Sheldrake calls a "morphic field," which affects all reality in a so far incomprehensible but recognizable way. Mattieu Ricard, an articulate Buddhist scholar, takes a step closer to historical engagement, but there is still no idea that a person can wake up to Reality through the historical. As he states, indicating Buddhist priorities:

> You could say that action on the world is *desirable* [notice not imperative] while inner transformation is indispensable. . . . [Or further, even though the nature of the world is illusory] it's perfectly *legitimate* [as if it needed

> legitimation] to remedy suffering by all available means and to do whatever can be done to increase the well-being of all.[1]

Interestingly, we could interject here that Saint Augustine, who has so greatly influenced Christian spirituality, also maintained that the active way of helping others is a "necessary good, but still sorrowful; the other [the life of contemplation] is better and perfectly blessed."[2]

Although at first glance there is much in early Buddhism that would appear to negate the value of active participation in world transformation, we can find fundamental Buddhist viewpoints, especially from the later Mahayana tradition, which point to the solidarity side of this basic human dialectic. From this Buddhist perspective, all Reality is seen as interconnected and interdependent, flowing from the principle of "dependent co-arising," where every reality arises from every other reality. Because this is, that is. Everything implies everything else. It is a process that is without beginning or end, and thus the interconnectedness of all things is indestructible. This radical sense of interdependence and interpenetration is one of the essential messages of Buddhism.

All things are not only interdependent but also impermanent, because nothing has a separate, independent self. The impermanence of all beings is important because it points not only to the interconnectedness of everything, but also to the selfless nature of all that exists. Nothing can exist by itself. To be real is to "inter-depend." Or, as Thich Nhat Hahn says: "To be is to inter-be. Everything co-exists. You cannot be by yourself alone. You have to inter-be with everything."[3] There is no aspect of a person that can exist as an entity unto itself. To be real is to be interdependent. Every person is included in every part and in the whole of the universe. True wisdom is identification with the reality before us. If we do not penetrate reality, we do not understand it. This means that there is a universal brotherhood and sisterhood among all beings.

This perspective of inter-being influenced the Bodhisattva ideal, which appeared in the later phase of Buddhism, Mahayana Buddhism. The original belief that one who is sick cannot cure others before one is cured oneself came to be radically transformed by the Bodhisattva tradition. This Mahayana tradition came about because, as Chogyam Trungpa pointed out,

> the path of individual salvation was not completely fulfilling. Something was missing: we had not yet worked with other people. . . . Our whole approach seemed to become an ingrown toe-nail: we were eating ourselves up rather than expanding and working with others.[4]

The newly envisioned Buddhist saint was no longer the solitary sage (Arhat) but the Bodhisattva, who is no longer just himself or herself but is in complete identification with all beings and things. "Taking the bodhisattva vow," Chogyam Trungpa explains, "implies that instead of holding onto our individual territory . . . we are willing to take on great responsibility, immense responsibility."[5] The crucial point here is that a Bodhisattva cures oneself, not simply or even primarily through solitary monastic *(sangha)* praxis, but by curing others. On the one hand, "if you leap into Mahayana without having ever fully addressed Hinayana, you can open yourself up to all kinds of delusions and as a result, have nothing to offer others. One's aloneness must first be fully established."[6] But this is only the initial stage.

Taking the Bodhisattva vow is a radical leap whereby a commitment is made to put others before oneself. The life of a Bodhisattva is "one of seeing everyone as one's guest, constantly."[7] It is only by fully embracing the experience of others, which naturally entails experiencing their sickness and suffering, that one can further and fully realize oneself as identical to the others. By taking the Bodhisattva vow,

> we actually present ourselves as the property of sentient beings: depending on the situation, we are willing to be a highway, a boat, a floor, or a house. We allow other sentient beings to use us in what ever way they choose. As the earth sustains the atmosphere and outer space accommodates the stars, galaxies, and all the rest, we are willing to carry the burdens of the world.[8]

As one Tibetan Buddhist monk said:

> Ah, you know, when you really love, it's like feeling everyone is your body. When you have a burn on your body, your hand instinctively goes to that place. And that is what you see when you come to the state of bodhisattva-hood. Wherever there is pain, you instinctively move towards it, because everyone is your body and every pain is your pain.[9]

Out of this Mahayana tradition a political theory can develop that proposes systems of social organization that best facilitate the attainment of enlightenment or nirvana. For this tradition the key to deciding which governments are best is to discover those that enlarge everyone's opportunity for the attainment of wisdom. Life, liberty, and the pursuit of wisdom, and not the pursuit of happiness, are the standards. An oligarchy or even a benign dictatorship would be preferable to a democratic form of government that is dependent upon and therefore champions consumerism rather than the pursuit of wisdom.

With this as a starting point, we are witnessing today a new form of Buddhism called engaged Buddhism, where a fresh synthesis is attempted between Buddhism's traditional spirituality and Western political thought. Transcendental insight and social justice can inform and reinforce one another. Any inner peace that does not generate some kind of active response to the pain of the world would be seen as suspect or perhaps even a false inner peace. Compassion is naturally put into action. "When a village is being bombed and children and adults are suffering from wounds and death," asks Thich Nhat

Hahn, "can a Buddhist sit still in his un-bombed temple? Truly if he has wisdom and compassion, he will be able to practice Buddhism while [notice not "by"] helping other people."[10]

Although there are many strains in the Eastern traditions that point to a fundamental solidarity with the other, undoubtedly it is the Judeo-Christian biblical tradition that reveals a prioritization of solidarity as a foundational element of its religious faith. As Andrew Harvey puts it: "The Eastern traditions have wonderful things to offer us, astonishing revelations, vast depths of mystical understanding, but they largely lack what Christ brings to the table of the world: a burning sense of present action, of present life, an absolute insistence on justice."[11]

11

The Hebrew Tradition

In retrieving the core of the Judeo-Christian tradition, we need to first uncover the Hebrew God. This does not imply any necessary disconnect from the Christian God, but merely points to a formative process by which there is a certain evolution of understanding about the nature of the divine Mystery. If we can say that one's experience of God or the ultimate Mystery reveals one's fundamental outlook on life, then, who or what is the Hebrew God and what way of life is elicited? If God-talk is in actuality the ultimate model, insight, symbol of Reality, then the Israelite portrait of God reveals the Hebrew soul and exemplified way of life.

The purpose of this retrieval, however, is not an overview as such, but exploring the tradition to discover those strands that are helpful and perhaps normative in trying to grasp the essential nature of the divine Mystery. In doing this, it is important to recognize that our spiritual ancestors passed on to us through their scriptures and traditions insights and outlooks on life that were sometimes revelatory and sometimes distortions about the nature of Reality. The Hebrew understanding of God can vary widely. But the fundamental core contribution of Hebrew insight that I believe will have eternal significance for the ongoing world community is how history and justice reveal the divine dimension of Reality. So there is every reason to turn to Judaism with "certitude of its value, its dignity, and its mission,"[1] not so much in the sense that it represents a particularistic, time-bound ethos but rather a universalistic ideal for Jews and non-Jews alike.

This will be a constructive approach, since there is a purposeful decision to jettison those strands of the Hebrew tradition that are at the very least difficult to see as useful in a pursuit of a fundamental, normative understanding of the divine Mystery. One such negative strand of the Hebrew tradition is what Jack Nelson-Pallmeyer[2] refers to as the violence of the Hebrew God. Judaism, as with all major religions, is deeply ambivalent when it comes to God and violence. As Vanessa Baird points out, "All the major religions have their compassionate and peace-loving messages, but they also possess deeply violent roots and traditions."[3] Elise Boulding, who has examined peace in the major religions, finds that "sacred texts are flooded with images of a vengeful and violent god. The warrior-god has dominated the stories of our faith communities so that the other story of human caring and compassion and reconciliation is often difficult to hear."[4]

However one decides to explain the emergence of this violence in the Hebrew tradition, there is no doubt that this is one way in which the Hebrew God is understood in this tradition. Jack Nelson-Pallmeyer points out: "How much horrific violence was attributed to God in the Bible . . . that . . . had 'sacred' or 'holy' texts in which God's dominant character was said to be compassionate but equally steeped in violence?"[5] Therefore, it is imperative to acknowledge and confront this aspect of the Hebrew tradition. God directed his people to use bloody conquest under the banner of the divine Will to conquer a territory occupied by others. God used empires to punish his people when they sinned. If you obey God you will prosper, but if you disobey God you will suffer. God helps the chosen people to crush any enemy who stands in the way of fulfilling the divine plan. Defeat of an enemy was total, including the slaughter of innocent women and children. As Nelson-Pallmeyer says: "God becomes an instrument of human revenge. Compassion and salvation are militarized, that is, understood as the crushing defeat of enemies within or at the end of history."[6]

No matter how reasonable this critique of the Hebrew tradition is, we could ask, what modern texts are superior? What have modern texts in the Western tradition offered that have proven so superior that they negate or render obsolete the whole Hebrew corpus? Freud? Nietzsche? Marx? Hegel? Heidegger? Jung? Derrida? Whose work has so transcended the wisdom of the Hebrews that we can dismiss the Hebrew scriptures once and for all? Have these modern texts been able to save the twentieth century from terrible violence? As Peter replied to Jesus when asked if he was about to abandon Jesus: "To whom shall we go?" (Jn 6:68).

As we, therefore, with confidence study the Jewish tradition, an important point needs to be first observed. There is in the Hebrew tradition a tension between what Richard Horsley refers to as the "great tradition" and the "little tradition." The Hebrew scriptures, or the Torah, present the fundamental revelations, events, stories, and beliefs that form the Jewish tradition. On the one hand, the very core of their sacred tradition consisted in how their God had decisively and repeatedly delivered the Hebrew people from both foreign and domestic domination. The Hebrew tradition, therefore, contains a fundamental liberative element. But there also emerged the temple tradition, which arose concomitantly with the rise of the monarchy.

In the beginning, Israel was a federation of tribes with no ruling class over their heads and no established temple cult. Their vision was a free and egalitarian peasant society under the direct kingship of their God, unmediated by anyone or any institution, that is, a radical theocracy. The Israelites lived securely this way for nearly two hundred years. But with the advent of the Iron Age, new military technologies developed that enabled their neighboring Philistine warlords, who up till now they were able to contain, to become an increasing threat to Israelite security. It was at this time the Israelites turned to centralized religio-political structures (monarchy/temple) to resist this new threat. The monarchy that was established began to stand in a mediating role between the Israelites and their God. And the divine legitimation of this new monarchic order became centered in the temple built by Solomon on the sacred Mt. Zion. This became the substance of the "great tradition," which had as its role the legitimation of the centrality of the temple in Judea and the support of the temple and priests by tithes and offerings.

Since the Hebrew scriptures were written in a largely agrarian society, and since the only people who could write were the elite, this meant that those who wrote the Torah were probably in the employ of the monarchy/temple establishment. Although both the liberative and temple traditions are found in the Torah, the establishment emphasized the temple tradition to the extent that it became the "great tradition." Since the liberative tradition favored the peasant society, the vast majority of the people favored this tradition. But since it took second place in the dominant temple religion, it became the "little tradition." The prophetic tradition became a strong and enduring defender of this "little tradition" and held it up as a fundamental standard in its confrontation with the increasingly predatory nature of temple religion. Without going into it now, although Christianity today has become mainly a temple religion with its fixation on buildings and liturgy, we will discover that Jesus sided with the "little tradition" over the temple advocates. And that will be the approach of this study. We have come to the point that what is worth saving and perhaps normative of the divine Mystery from this Judaic tradition is the liberative element of equality and justice minus the often violent ways in which this vision was secured and realized.

Ancient peoples, primal peoples as well as the cultures of Asia, Europe, and the Americas, believed in, as an absolute given of reality, the great wheel of Being or what Mircea Eliade termed "the myth of the eternal return." This created a consciousness where everything moved in a great circle, where all reality of nature was saturated with Divinity, where all reality continually and eternally repeated itself. All reality, therefore, was determined. This eternal-return consciousness experienced time as sacred, and what this sacred time pointed to was the primordial time of creation. It revealed what the gods did at the beginning of time, and this became archetypal time for all human life. This sacred time was timeless, for both the past and the future were contained within it. Real time, therefore, has no beginning or end but passes through a perpetual cycle of birth, death, and rebirth.

All the actions of human life acquire their reality only to the extent that they participate in this sacred, cyclical, archetypal time. All human industry receives its meaning and value solely to the extent to which it repeats and communes with the primordial acts of the gods. Every act that lacks an exemplary model is meaningless. Therefore, the only history that concerned primordial people was the sacred history of the gods. The upshot of this is that this visionary view of life was essentially anti-historical. Profane history for the ancients was the remembrance of those events that were divergences from sacred time because they had no archetypal model. Therefore, these events were considered "unmeaning," even sin, because they were a fall into profanity.

The Jews were the first of the ancient peoples who refused to be circumscribed by these sacred cycles. Although the Jewish liturgical life sometimes reflected nature's cycles, because these cycles reflected the creation of their creator God, the Jews also broke loose of these cycles. For the first time, the notion of linear time appears; the universe was seen as the cosmic plan of God with definite goals and a future vision for humanity as well. Their new way of thinking about and experiencing life was unique, so there is some justification in asserting that "this is the only new idea that human beings have ever had."[7] The real world is not simply unchanging, forever repeatable, but it has a beginning, a history, and a fullness of time. Thus Judaism starts in Genesis, continues in history, and ends in eschatology. The world is understood as a creation with a culmination. And this Hebrew God invites the people to be God's partner in the work of creation. What we have in essence is "a community of shared vision on the march, with memory of an inauguration, awareness of presence crisis, and a voice that spoke into the future."[8] Thomas Cahill sums it up: "No people have ever insisted more firmly than the Jews that history has a purpose and humanity is destiny."[9]

The great and overwhelming adventures exemplified in the stories of Abraham and Moses make history real to human consciousness. The Jewish people experienced YHWH, we are told, through their conscience, in a "still, small voice." This mysterious voice spoke to Abraham at the beginning of the second millennium BCE by disclosing to Abraham that he was to have a whole new destiny. And when Abraham put faith and trust in this voice, his whole life was uprooted. In contrast to the eternal divine stasis, the first great escape from the determinism of cyclical existence was made by the first Hebrew, Abraham. He was called to leave the highly developed and comfortable city of Ur and journey into uncertainty. He was led to separate himself from the spacial gods of his father's house and to follow the God of time and the future.

Abraham's escape made him the first Hebrew, for the very word *Hebrew (Ivri)* means "one who crossed over." Abraham introduces to the whole ancient world the radical new notion of journey, that you can leave where you are, break free from your bonds and boundaries, and go to a new place. Thus the idea of linear history first appears in the ancient world. The idea of plot, suspense, and ultimate resolution that was introduced by the Hebrews and that has become so ingrained in us today was virtually unknown to the circle consciousness of their neighbors. Abraham was not only called forth to a new destiny and a new identity but also, in time, he became the father of a new nation, Israel. This new destiny, therefore, was not only for Abraham alone, but it was also "familial, national and even (in a mysterious sense yet to be defined) global."[10]

This vocation of Abraham would find its full flowering in Moses, who also heard the mysterious Voice, which called him to lead his tribal people out of their Egyptian bondage and into a new life of freedom. One commentator noted, "Until the Exodus no slave had ever succeeded in leaving Egypt." In the social consciousness of Egypt, no one could ever leave his or her place. Individuals were born into their cyclical-determined existence and destined to go round and round with it. This exodus from Egypt would become the fundamental event, the center of history, for Israel. And it would be the Hebrews' traumatic experience in Egypt that would constitute the very humanity of the Jews, since it necessarily allies the Hebrew people to the wretched persecuted peoples of the world. These two profound religious experiences and journeys of Abraham and Moses, the listening and the responding of both men, exemplified what Judaism was and who its God was. And it pointed to something unique among the peoples of the world.

For the first time, these stories show humanity what it is like to journey from the old to the new, from stasis to dynamism, from fate to free will, from slavery to freedom. They announce the possibility of constructing a society that can be built on justice, compassion, and freedom. The future of the world is not fated but is in covenant with Yahweh and dependent on human choice, on what humans do in the present. To be a Jew, therefore, is to accept responsibility for the world, and to be alert to poverty, suffering, and the loneliness of others. It is to be convicted that one must contribute something to the human heritage, leaving the world better than it would have been if one had not existed. And in order to do the will of YHWH, each person must continually listen to the "still, small voice" speaking in her or his consciousness, the great law inscribed in our hearts.

The Israelites looked at the liberating events in their history as the revelation of YHWH. Certain historical events had a way of awakening in the Hebrew soul what were really the heart and depth realities of the human adventure. Hence, the Israelite's eye was trained to take human events seriously, because in some very crucial events, it was to be learned clearly what YHWH willed and what YHWH was about.

If God could be encountered through certain historical events, then the God of the Jews was relational. This sharply contrasted with the god of the Greek philosophers, who was an isolated and self-enclosed Being, unconcerned about human affairs. But the Hebrew God was a relational and interrelational Reality. The mysterious revelation of YHWH's name in the theophany of Moses while expressing YHWH's transcendence also revealed that this transcendence is not absent but a promised involvement in Israel's misery and enslavement. Jack Miles makes an important observation concerning the name YHWH:

> The three words in question are extremely familiar Hebrew words: *ehyeh* ("I am") *aser* ("who" or "that which") *ehyeh* ("I am"). The word *ehyeh* can mean "I shall be" as well as "I am." . . . Thus, rather than saying that

> [God's] name is "I Am Who I Am," God could be saying: "I am what I shall be," in effect, "You'll find out who I am."[11]

Therefore, YHWH is what Abraham Heschel refers to as a "covenantal transcendence," a transcendent relatedness in history. If the ancient Greek philosophers saw God as impassible and immutable, YHWH is revealed as passion and pathos, one who has the power to care, the capacity to weep, the sympathy to grieve, and the energy to rejoice. YHWH has an aching concern for an unredeemed earth full of unnecessary pain: "I saw the oppression of my people. . . . I heard their complaints against the oppressors, I stopped to see their sufferings and I descended to liberate them" (Ex 3:7–8).

The Hebrews also parted from the dominant view of the neighborhood gods, which were tied into the royal courts with their priesthoods, armies, and tribute systems. Rather, their God was associated with a group of slaves who later lived as a federation of tribes. If the neighborhood gods demanded elaborate rituals, their God demanded justice. If the neighborhood gods favored the rich and the powerful, YHWH showed a decided preference for the needs of the poor and the weak. As Karl Barth explains:

> In the relations and events in the life of God's people, God always takes a stand unconditionally and passionately on this side and this side alone: against the lofty and on behalf of the lowly; against those who already enjoy right and privilege, and on behalf of those who are denied and deprived of it.[12]

John Dominic Crossan made the comment that if he were to sum up both the Hebrew and Christian scriptures, he would choose Psalm 82, which points to YHWH's unique identity among the gods:

> YHWH arises in the divine assembly; he judges in the midst of the gods. "How long will you judge unjustly and favor the cause of the wicked? Defend the lowly and the fatherless; render justice to the afflicted and the destitute. Rescue the lowly and the poor; from the land of the wicked deliver them." (Ps 82:1–3)

The whole aim of YHWH's Torah is "that there will never be any poor among you" (Dt 15:4). Unique to the Hebrew tradition, the ethical is at the very heart of God/Reality. We discover a moral ontology of God. The Hebrew God is intrinsically concerned with the human condition.

And it is not just any morality. More difficult virtues are demanded by solidarity than by private morality. If our society conveniently identifies morality primarily with private sins of the flesh such as sexual misconduct, the God of the Hebrews identifies it fundamentally with social justice. In our society, for example, the sin of sodomy immediately conjures up sexual misconduct of a sexual minority and is juridically defined as such, but not for the Hebrew prophets. As Isaiah cried out:

> Hear the word of the Lord.
> You chieftains of Sodom;
> give ear to our God's instruction,
> you folk of Gomorrah!
>
> Assemblies with iniquity, I cannot abide. . . .
> Cease to do evil;
> learn to do good.
> Devote yourself to justice;
> aid the wronged;
> uphold the rights of the orphan;
> defend the widow's cause. (Is 1:10, 16–17)

And the prophet Ezekiel: "Only this was the sin of your sister Sodom: arrogance! She and her daughters had plenty of bread and untroubled tranquility; yet she did not support the poor and the needy. In their haughtiness, they committed abominations before me; and so I removed them, as you saw" (Ez 16:49–50). The real sodomites are not homosexuals, but those who ignore justice with "untroubled tranquility."

Thus Jeremiah tells us: "This is the name they gave him, the Lord of Justice" (Jer 23:6). It is only by justice that "the holy God shows himself as Holy" (Is 5:12). Justice is the foundation of God's throne and the grounding of divine Majesty (Ps 97:3).

> Thus says the Lord: Let not the wise man glory in his wisdom, nor the strong man glory in his strength, nor the rich man glory in his riches; but rather let him who glories, glory in this, that in his providence he knows me, knows that I the Lord bring about kindness and justice and uprightness on the earth. (Jer 9:22–24)

Justice is identified with the will and even with the being of YHWH. Accordingly, we should speak of justice *(Sedaqhah)* as the very essence of YHWH. YHWH is described not in ontological, but in ethical terms. Or rather, the ethical is raised to the ontological level, an ontological ethics. We are at the most primordial level when we are dealing with a moral ontology of God.

If holiness is the goal of all Jewish morality, then this holiness is seen as closeness to a God who is justice; by doing justice one comes close to God. To be filled with a passion for justice and to grieve with all who grieve was to be "theomorphous." As Abraham Heschel pointed out, the fundamental experience of the prophets was a fellowship with the feelings of God so that they would awaken to God's passion for the welfare of the people.

Holiness is also expressed as knowledge of God. The Hebrews, however, do not come to know their God primarily through speculative thought or by solitary mystical absorption, but rather by enacting merciful justice for the poor. "To know God is to do justice" (Jer 22:13–17). God is not only contemplated but also "done" or practiced. And the God who is contemplated is essentially a "doer." As N. H. Snaith remarks, "The Hebrews do not say that Jehovah is, or that Jehovah exists, but that He does."[13] Doing a "doing God" is doing justice with a compassionate heart, and this God-doing was the biblical form of mystagogy. Not to execute justice is not to worship YHWH.

Isaiah's exhortation to achieve justice in human relations is not fulfilled by some adjunct social-action group at the local synagogue but is the very definition of worship. Without care for the poor, linkage to God is ruptured. We know we are at the center of Hebrew faith because when Job was confronted with his faithfulness to YHWH, in his defense he pointed to what he saw as the heart of that faithfulness: doing justice. He proclaimed that he had been "eyes to the blind, feet to the lame, a father to the needy"; he saved the orphan, the widow, and "the poor man when he called for help." He took up the "cause of persons he didn't even know"(Job 29:12–20).

Once the core of a religious tradition is retrieved, we need to confront the present times and evaluate what is going on and how one is to live authentically in this our time under the light of this tradition. If we are seeking an integral humanity, where reality has both an inward and outward dimension, then we need to challenge any attempt to reduce human existence to either pole. If the Hebrew tradition has a great strength, surely it is its insistence on solidarity and justice. In our time we see a marked tendency to reduce spirituality to the inward or to temple religion, where the focus is on church buildings and what occurs in the private souls of the worshipers. All that has contributed to this tendency will be challenged by the Hebrew tradition.

Destruction of solidarity can be accomplished by either a false inwardness or a degraded outwardness. Selfishness can abound either in self-absorption or through self-aggrandizement; materialism can be either spiritual (Chogyam Trungpa, for example, talks of "spiritual materialism")[14] or socioeconomic. Drawing from the Hebrew tradition, such eminent voices as Martin Buber and Emmanuel Levinas have confronted especially those forms of inward-fixated spiritualities or inward-turning psychologies of modern times that seek to trivialize, ignore, disparage, or even dismiss the historical, social, ethical, and political dimensions of human life.

Martin Buber criticized both Carl Jung and Søren Kierkegaard for reducing human existence to the inward, subjective side of the dialectic. He saw both Jung and Kierkegaard as attempting to evade the concrete situations of human beings in the world. He opposed those who wanted to psychologize the world by drawing it into the sphere of one's feelings, one's thoughts, or one's analyses; those who tried to subsume all reality under psychological categories; those who attempted to detach the soul completely from its basic character of relationship by the bending back of the spirit onto itself; those who referred all events and meaning back to the psyche.

He saw Jung's psychology as a kind of psychologism wherein Jung reduced religion to a living relationship with psychical events alone. Psychology is raised to the status of metaphysics since truth is reduced to the psychic where one's touchstone with reality is the collective psyche, or self. Jung, according to Buber, "proclaims the new religion, the only one which can still be true, the religion of pure psychic immanence."[15] It is only in the psyche that humans can harbor the Divine. There is no divine core in a person beyond the psyche where divine revelation may occur. God is no longer seen as an autonomous essence, but it is the unconscious that creates the idea of the Divine. God thus becomes merely a function of the unconscious as an "autonomous psychic content."

For Buber, however, insofar as the soul is comprehended exclusively as *I*, it is comprehended in amputation, in abstraction, not in its whole existence. In opposition to Jung, the true human way leads a soul that places reality within itself to a soul that enters into the whole of reality. Authentic religion for Buber was the willingness to meet what comes to us in our life in the world and to go forth from that meeting as one summoned and sent. The *I* that exists through the "shoreless becoming of the deed" is no isolated self. On the contrary, the self comes into being in its mutual contact with the unique reality that it meets outside itself in the world.

Buber also challenged the subjectivization of religion where one's relationship with God was seen exclusively as a one-on-one, alone relationship with the Alone. If "demythologizing" of the Christian faith was all the rage with the Existentialists, Buber rather focused on the "deprivitization" of religion. "Meeting with God," Buber insisted, "does not come to man in order that he may concern himself with God, but in order that he may confirm that there is meaning in the world."[16]

Perhaps no one subjectivized the Christian faith more than Søren Kierkegaard. Kierkegaard rejected the importance of society and culture because he believed that God could not be found in creation. Therefore, individuals should back away from society, which he saw as basically the crowd, and go within. For him, the "crowd is untruth!" Knowledge of other people constitutes a danger and a distraction from interest in one's own existence. The really significant other is not the human other, but the divine Other—God. He saw relationships with other people as secondary, superficial, inessential, and even as obstacles to the "single one's" relationship to the absolute. People literally got in Kierkegaard's way, because it is only the internal, the private, the inward that counts. As Kierkegaard said in an essay entitled "That Individual": "Every man should be chary about having to do with 'the others' . . . and essentially should talk only with God and with himself—for only one attains the goal." One's inner essence, therefore, had nothing to do with one's social self. The social self should be depreciated and devalued, since it was for him a "temptation to finitude." As a result, Kierkegaard found it necessary to cut off his relationship to Regine Olsen, to whom he was engaged, since it was seemingly an obstacle to his solitary relationship with God.

In contrast to Kierkegaard, Buber believed that there is no such thing as an I-Thou relationship with God that comes when one turns away from one's brothers and sisters in the world. As Buber said, in light of Kierkegaard's rejection of Regine Olsen, "God wants to come to him by means of the Regines he has created and not by renunciation of them."[17] Buber's religion was a "religion of Reality." Religion must touch individuals in the challenge of their existence. Outside the world there is no salvation. He wanted nothing to do with a religion that fetched forth things for the use of human subjectivity alone; that was in the spiritual hunt for precious moments of the soul; that saw authentic religion as happening within the person, in the encapsulated sphere of the soul. For him, what was important was not religious *experiences* but rather religious *life*.

He turned away from this interiorization of religious life toward the irreducible and far less agreeable concreteness of being in the world. Religious life comes about not from the exclusion of otherness, but rather from the meeting with otherness in the world and not apart from it. What was crucial was not some kind of expansion of consciousness to the All, but awareness of otherness in the "lived concrete." Buber rejected any kind of mysticism that lifted one out of the world and saw the world of everyday life as an obstacle or at best a means toward one's moments of illumination and ecstasy. Presence of God must be actualized in deeds for the other, not in interior experiences. Authentic religion moves away from any ecstasy above or outside the world toward a unity of existence that finds its center in one's relationships in the world.

Another great Jewish voice that thunders out against any inward fixation is Emmanuel Levinas, who is "without doubt the philosopher who has given Judaism its most exacting expression."[18] Like Martin Buber, Levinas expounded a philosophy of intersubjectivity. But whereas Buber described interpersonal relationships in terms of mutuality, communion, and reciprocity, Levinas described the relation between oneself and the other in terms of command, duty, and responsibility. The relationship that Buber described between the I *and* the Thou is reversible and mutual, expressed by the conjunction *and*. Whereas, the relationship of the "I *for* the Thou" is expressed by Levinas in the dative form: *for*. "With the appearance of the human—and this is my entire philosophy," states Levinas, "there is something more important than my life, and this is the life of the other."[19] Levinas complements Buber, whose *I-Thou* was primarily a personal relationship but not primarily or exclusively an ethical one. Levinas insists that I-thou relationships primordially involve not only meeting the other in a personal way but also taking responsibility for the other. He identifies with Dostoyevsky, who said through his character Alyosha in *The Brothers Karamazov*: "We are all responsible for everyone else—but I am more responsible than all the others."[20]

For Levinas, the biblical God does not arise in our solitary, serene soul that is shut up in itself, but rather only amid the suffering and sighs of those who are oppressed. "Before the oppression of the humble, the sighing of the poor, *at that time I arise*, says the lord" (Ps 12:6). In light of this, Levinas critiques Kierkegaard as Buber did, but with a vengeance. He saw Kierkegaard as transforming all spiritual seeking into an inner drama alone. Life's secret was the secret of the *I* which was infinitely needy and distressed over itself; a subjectivity tensed on itself; a kind of torment over oneself. Levinas referred to this inner absorption as narcissistic and melodramatic. Kierkegaardian faith was "the going forth from self, the only possible going forth for subjectivity . . . the solitary tete-a-tete with what Kierkegaard admits of nothing but the tete-tete with God."[21] Kierkegaard described the encounter with God as a religious subjectivity that was higher than the ethical; what Kierkegaard called the "teleological suspension of the ethical," since the ethical had only to do with human beings. The result was that his discourse directed to the outer world was one of anger and invective. Suffering the truth does not open a person to other people but to God alone in solitude. For Levinas, this approach carries within it an immense irresponsibility. As he said sarcastically: "Egoism is not an ugly vice of the subjects, but its ontology." His philosophy or spirituality, to employ Husserl's term, was an "egology." Hence, Kierkegaard "bequeathed to the history of philosophy an exhibitionistic immodest subjectivity."[22]

For Levinas, the presence or absence of God is not determined by mystical gifts of the soul, whereby access to God is gained by a mystical encounter in which a person is removed from the social world and caught up in a singular rapture with the Divine. It is not a quest for the Divine that "retreats into the immanence and interiority of subjectivity where one mystically engages in a 'private meeting with a consoling God.'"[23] Levinas insists that the Hebrew scriptures "lead us not towards the mystery of God, but towards the human tasks of man. [Judaism] . . . is a humanism. Only simpletons make it into a theological arithmetic."[24] Rather, one is called to "the responsibility that rids the I of its imperialism and egotism *(even the egotism of salvation)*" (italics added).[25] The God of Abraham, of Isaac, and of Jacob had no private meetings. Moral dignity is "no longer played out in a *tete-a-tete* with God, but . . . sorted out between men. The Jewish God has never tolerated these *tete-a-tetes*. He was always the God of the multitudes."[26]

For Judaism, "to know God means to know what has to be done."[27] And in response to an abstractive theology, Levinas insists that the first question is not What must I believe? but What must I do? "The way in which Man possesses the truth," claims Levinas, "does not consist in contemplating it in God, but in verifying it through his life. *Human truth, both Christian and Jewish, is verification. . . . Human truth is a testimony offered by a life.*"[28] It is the other who is first, and there the question of my sovereign consciousness is no longer the first question. The way to seek union with and to follow this God is by approaching our neighbor with that same divine concern which is attentive to the fate of the "widow and orphan, the stranger and the poor man." Man, therefore, is the site of transcendence. "Holiness is the *ascension* to the *human* in being [a *transascendence*, in Jean Wahl's words] . . . in the passage from one to the other."[29] It is the "denuclearization" of the self where moral exigencies overload and uplift the self above and beyond the self to greater responsibilities than it has for itself. This is a transcendence that does not get lost in vertical transcendence. There is no recourse to religious experiences. We are talking here about a transcendence that transcends ethically. Levinas does not deny the holy, but he interprets it ethically. This is how Levinas describes this spiritual process:

> The dimension of the divine opens forth from the human face. A relation with the Transcendent . . . is a social relation. It is here that the Transcendent, infinitely other, solicits us and appeals to us. The proximity of the Other, the proximity of the neighbor, is . . . an ineluctable moment of the revelation of an absolute presence. . . . His very epiphany consists in soliciting us by his destitution in the face of the stranger, the widow, and the orphan. . . . Our relation with the Metaphysical is an ethical behavior and not theology. . . . God rises his supreme and ultimate presence as correlative to the justice rendered unto men.[30]

Holiness is precisely and concretely the love of neighbor. There is no religion without responsibility. When I am in the act of loving and serving the other, God is present. God belongs to the order of ethics. God is best thought of as a holy "ought," where God's name can only be uttered in the context of ethical praxis. This human praxis is the "dimension of the divine."

God does not create the *I* to have the *I* acknowledge

> an infinite debt, praising and adoring the creator God in gratitude, honoring its parent. . . . In being loved man is called upon to live up to G-d's love, to complete G-d's creation, to emulate G-d by loving otherness in turn. This means, concretely, that I must love the neighbor ("thou") and redeem the world. . . . The proper way for man to return G-d's love is not simply or solely by loving G-d directly and exclusively in return, but to love *as* G-d loves and what G-d loves, i.e., man's fellow creatures.[31]

Richard A. Cohen makes the comment that "the entirety of Levinas's thought can be correctly characterized as a long and profound meditation on the significance of the face."[32] In the face of the other I hear the word of God. This is not just a metaphor; it is literally true. The word of God is inscribed in the face of the other, in the encounter with the other. It is important to note that Levinas is not pointing to an "incarnation" of God in the other in which the other and God would be equivalent. Levinas would see this as idolatry. He talks in terms of what he calls God's "trace," where God is not the other but becomes present to us in the other. It is in this encounter that God is revealed. The real individual awakening is the "awakening of me by the other, of me by the stranger, of me by the stateless person . . . an awakening that signifies responsibility for the other who must be fed and clothed."[33]

The first word of the other's "face" is obligation, which no "interiority" permits avoiding. Subjectivity is not for itself; it is essentially for the other. My ego is called to do something it doesn't want to do. But it is only in the laying down of the ego's sovereignty that we find the very spirituality of the soul. The *I* is called to free itself from its attempt to return to self, from its auto-affirmation, from its egotism, and answer for the other. The word *I* here means, "Here I am, answering for everything and every one." I have responsibility for the other as "having-the-other-in-my-skin."[34] The other is in me and in the midst of my very identification. Responsibility is the essential, primary, and fundamental structure of my subjectivity. It is a primary principle of my individuation. If the fundamental sin for Jung was being unconscious, the fundamental sin for Levinas was being irresponsible. We become truly human when we find the resources to respond to the call.

Hence, from the first I am in an ethical situation. *I-Thou* is therefore not only psychological, but also primarily ontological. Pre-existing the plane of ontology is the ethical plane, or better, the ethical is the ontological. Here we have an ethical interpretation of transcendence, an ethical ontology. "Ethics is not the corollary of the vision of God, it is that very vision."[35] Thus, as John D. Caputo sums up Levinas's approach:

> To stay related to God, to maintain a link with God, I should bid adieu to God, *Adieu a Dieu*, and welcome the stranger. For it is only by loving and welcoming the stranger, by responding *in the name of* the God who loves the stranger, that God can be God. I pray to God to rid me of God. God can be God only if my relationship to God is oblique while my relationship to my neighbor is direct. . . . That means that the name of God must be *translated into hospitality*.[36]

12

Jesus and His Radical Gospel

Surely we will see that the Judeo-Christian tradition has as its foundation an immersion in the divine Mystery through a solidarity with creation and all humankind. It has been acknowledged, to give an immediate example, that Christianity introduced a new humanism into the mainstream of Indian history, affirming equality of persons as a religious value. As one Hindu scholar concedes: "Hinduism has learned one great thing from Christianity . . . that the way of God lies through the service of man. . . . The emphasis on 'seva,' the service of man as a method of realizing God came through our contact with Christianity."[1] It must be noted, however, that this biblical priority has hardly been the mainstay of traditional Christianity. "Christianity cast off its conformity to Christ a long time ago,"[2] concludes Johann Baptist Metz. The church as an ecclesiastical establishment gradually began to cover up the biblical priority of justice and Jesus' option for the poor in much the same way that the temple establishment of Judaism covered up the God of justice in Jesus' time. As Sebastian Kappen points out, "The alienation of Christian faith and practice from the historical Jesus took place along three principle lines—cultic, dogmatic and institutional."[3]

First of all, the Gospels repeatedly show that the historical Jesus subordinated cultic worship to justice, mercy, and love. Jesus does not relate the observance of the Sabbath to the glory and honor of God, but as he said: "The Sabbath was made for the sake of man and not man for the Sabbath" (Mk 2:27). Any cult not born of love of neighbor is an aberration and a futile gesture: "If, when you are bringing your gift to the altar, you suddenly remember your brother has a grievance against you, leave your gift where it is before the altar. First, go and make peace with your brother and only then come back and offer your gift" (Mt 5:23–24). Emmanuel Levinas points to a similar tendency in Hebrew spirituality where religion for many means, most fundamentally, a liturgical relation with God. Levinas complained about how Israel's destiny was being "reduced to the interiority of a house of prayer. Charitable works were an extension of this piety. The rabbis became ecclesiastics. . . . Judaism transformed its spiritual life into a *privatissime* business."[4]

According to Hebrew law, Jesus was a layman, not a priest, because he was born of a tribe "no member of which has ever officiated at the altar" (Heb

7:13). Rather, Jesus saw himself in the line of the prophets, and so did his disciples and the common folk. We never find Jesus around an altar offering sacrifices or organizing public worship. With the exception of the last supper, we almost never find Jesus gathered with his disciples for anything that would even remotely resemble what we today call liturgy. For Jesus, neither the temple nor the synagogue was central to worship, because it was not the altar but the world that was the center of his life. "It was in the heart of the world . . . in and through the myriad facets of the life of his people that he communed with the God of his fathers."[5] Jesus taught in Mark (12:33) that love of God and neighbor was worth more than any "burnt offerings or sacrifices." E. Lohmeyer, commenting on this passage from Mark concludes:

> Within the holy temple area, even within sight of the reeking altars themselves, the complete overthrow of sacrifice and Temple is proclaimed. . . . Man does not require any particular holy sacrifice or mediation of priests. . . . His relationship to God is determined not by what he gives to God at a holy place but by whether or not he loves God in his neighbor.[6]

Cult then is radically disempowered. With this prophetic insistence of Jesus, "a silent step, tremendous in its silence, is taken from cultic constraint into the freedom of moral action."[7]

Jesus taught people to worship in the desert, on mountaintops, in communal gatherings in homes, in "spirit and truth," in secret, with one or two. In the Synoptic Gospels, Jesus did not offer himself as an object of worship: "Why do you call me good? Only your father in heaven is good" (Mk 10:18). No sooner did Jesus pass from the scene, however, than a cult developed around not the Jesus of history, but almost exclusively the trans-historical Christ of glory. The result was that Jesus was removed from our daily life and ensconced in a tabernacle, "a separate home for him furnished with flowers, candles, holy water and incense."[8] Gradually Jesus was not only divorced from his historical existence but was also fragmented into a plethora of devotions: Sacred Heart, Crown of Thorns, Precious Blood, Five Wounds,[9] and so forth. Kappen concludes: "By the Middle Ages Christianity had become a cult centered religion. Mercy, justice and love became secondary to the Eucharistic cult and devotions. . . . A non-cultic prophetic movement had ended up as a cultic religion."[10]

Second, the history of dogma and catechesis shows a parallel process of alienation. "They do me empty reverence, making dogmas out of human precepts" (Mt 15:9). As Hans Küng has pointed out, doctrine and tradition soon began to be more central to the church than discipleship to Jesus. Christians began to be instructed that what they believed about Jesus was more important than following him. It became more important to understand Christianity correctly than for the Christian reality actually to take place.[11] The upshot was that the Gospels were reduced to dogmas, creeds, and catechisms.

Christianity went from dharma to dogmas; from radicalism to rigorism. From the dynamism of Jesus' life and way, the Christian community ended up with fossilized forms of belief, what Emerson called "diseases of the intellect," congealments of the Spirit, "sapless abstracts," depositing themselves in the consciousness of Christians "like some inert matter . . . handed down in these ossified forms from one generation to another."[12] Jesus in the Synoptics was a member of the human community who grew in wisdom, who had limitations, who was a subject of anger, tension, grief, and fear. But as Jesus was transmuted through the Greco-Roman mode of conceptualization, he emerged fragmented into a host of abstractions: person, nature, hypostasis, body, soul, substance. Kappen observes: "What cult did at the level of action [from discipleship to devotions], theology did at the level of thought. Jesus was reduced to a mere sum of formal concepts."[13] The result has been in our time what W. D. Davies indicts in his study *The Sermon on the Mount:*

> With a few exceptions, interpreters of the New Testament have been largely absorbed in kerygmatic or strictly theological questions. The moral teaching of Jesus, although acknowledged, has been sharply distinguished from the kerygma of the Church and then treated as a Cinderella. Scholars have sometimes been even self-consciously anxious to relegate his teaching to a markedly subordinate place in the exposition of the faith of the New Testament.[14]

Finally, we have to face the institutional obscuration of the historical Jesus. Jesus clearly rejected power—whether religious, economic, or political—as a means to usher in the kingdom of God. But when the Emperor Constantine established Christianity as the state religion, Christian clerical officials began to enjoy prestige and power. As Kappen notes:

> The temptation Jesus overcame in the desert his disciples succumbed to all too easily. . . . The tragic consequence of all this is that Jesus of Nazareth is the most forgotten person among the very people who claim to be his disciples. He lies buried under the weight of accumulated layers of rituals, rubrics, laws, concepts, legends, myths, superstitions, and institutions. . . . His voice smothered and his spirit stifled. If he still acts and makes his presence felt in history, it is less through the official church than through honest dissenters among Christians.[15]

"The whole history of Anno Domino, after Christ, may be interpreted as a maneuver to evade the dangerous Christ."[16] All we have to do is look at the unedifying legacy of the atrocities of the Inquisition, the witch burnings, the Crusades, the justification of imperialism, the perpetuation of sexism, racism, anti-Semitism, homophobia, and so on as ample examples of this Gospel waywardness. The church, for example, only began to address the situation of the poor and weak as a social class when they had become a powerful social force.

Awakening from a "dogmatic slumber,"[17] the first papal social encyclical, *Rerum Novarum*, came forty years after the *Communist Manifesto*.

For a century, all that the entire world saw were documents anathematizing every political and social liberation movement. As Johann Baptist Metz sums it up: "There is, so to speak, no single great social criticism made in our history—revolution, enlightenment, reason, or even love and freedom—which has not been disavowed at one time or another by historical Christianity and its institutions."[18] And even further we could conclude that "there is no exaggeration in saying that the Church has sometimes been more in the service of established (dis)order than in the service of establishing a new [just] order. . . . It has even gone so far as to take positive steps to reinforce an unjust order."[19] In spite of this historical record, we nevertheless can find abundant sources of solidarity in the Christian scriptures and tradition. We can in fact be overwhelmed at their life-giving insights into humanity, the world, society, and the divine Mystery.

As we investigate the New Testament witness, what vision of the divine Mystery do we encounter? It is the Christian conviction that we know God through Jesus. (This is not to imply that there is some kind of disjuncture between the Hebrew and Christian scriptures, or that Jesus was not very much a Jew.) Jesus reveals in his person and way of life the very nature of God. We come to know the Father through the Son. So if we want to know who the God of the New Testament is, we look to Jesus. Jesus brought to humanity a radical understanding of God. It was so profound that from then on his followers were determined not to talk of God without reference to Jesus or to talk of Jesus without reference to God. And if the essence of the way of Jesus was the gift of his life unto death, then it is this total self-gifting that is of the essence of Divinity. This Jesus, who identifies his very self with the poor, the oppressed, and the executed innocent, is manifesting the very identity of God.

Jesus' way was informed by his intimate experience of God, the *Mysterium Tremendum* as the infinitely embracing compassionate One. His fundamental spiritual vision of the universe was that it is pervaded with compassion and goodness. The universe is not morally neutral but is imbued by a force that inclines it toward compassion, generosity, and the alleviation of unnecessary suffering. This is why Kazoh Kitamori calls for concentrating not so much on the "theology of the *word* of God," but further and more precisely on the "theology of the *pain* of God."[20]

The depth of Jesus's mystic/ontic experience was of such a radical nature that it led him to challenge provocatively the central paradigm of the Jewish community of his time in interpreting the Torah, namely, holiness or purity. "You shall be holy [pure] because I am holy [pure]" (Lv 11:45) becomes "be compassion as God is compassionate" (Lk 6:36). Grounded in his radical intimacy with his Abba, compassion was the core value in Jesus' interpretation of the Torah, and it was in conformity to this paradigm that Jesus insisted that the people of God were to structure their collective life. Jesus referred to his vision of a transformed Israel, in union with the compassionate Father, as the kingdom of God.

Jesus compared this kingdom to fire with which Jesus came to ignite the world, and with which he himself was burning. Jesus seized upon this rare phrase, *the kingdom of God*, as the "heuristic scheme" under which he synthesized the whole salvific activity of YHWH in Hebrew theology. It was a vision of God, the world, humankind, and creation as a whole, as well as of each individual human person. It was the central theme and reference point of most of his parables, the subject of a large number of his sayings, and the content of his symbolic actions. So central was the theme of the kingdom of God to Jesus that Karl Rahner concluded: "Jesus preached the Kingdom of God, not himself."[21] Jesus was not the absolute for himself. He did not present himself as the core of faith; he did not preach himself. Rather, Jesus preached, on the one hand, what his being revealed and manifested in Jesus' "way" (immanence of the kingdom) and something coming soon, brought about by God (transcendence of the kingdom).

The kingdom is the consummation of history, the final fulfillment of humankind's spiritual and social destiny, and the accomplishment of God's own intention for the whole of creation. The spirit of Christ labors in history to build up the bonds of solidarity among all peoples until their union is brought to fulfillment in the kingdom of God. Leonardo Boff articulates: "It is a total, global and structural transfiguration and revolution of the reality of human beings; it is the cosmos purified of all evils and full of the reality of God."[22] John Fuellenbach describes the kingdom of God as "social, political, personal (respectful of individual freedom), universal in intent, transcendent in origin, earthly in realization, present in sign, and future in fullness."[23]

Israel, led by God's revelation, was a nation of people who discovered their God active in history, and it was the Jews who discovered this historical dimension of religious faith. Jesus was very much a Jew, and he experienced reality and his God as a Jew. Therefore, a Jesus abstracted from a historical dimension is unthinkable. God, for Jesus, was not a metaphysical being who could be thought of or related to in the God-Self, set aside from creation, human beings, and their history. Although Jesus shared a profound and intense personal intimacy with his Father, the Father was constitutively bound up with human history. God's relationship to history, for the Jew and therefore for Jesus, was essential to God. For it was that divine Mystery which at certain crucial times manifested divine compassion in given human, historical events. Therefore, it is in human history, not some parallel supernatural history, that the kingdom comes. This is not to say that the being of God is circumscribed by history but to insist that God cannot be thought of as totally abstracted from it either.

It is in the person of Jesus that we first and foremost discover this kingdom. If the mystery of a person is only accessible to us (and then only obliquely) in his or her passions and actions, then the inner core, the mystical identity of Jesus (therefore kingdom), is where his profound inner experience of his

Father led him and what it led him to do. Jesus' inaugural sermon made this direction abundantly clear:

> The spirit of the Lord is upon me, for He has consecrated me to preach the good news to the poor; He has sent me to announce to the prisoners their release and to the blind the recovery of their sight; to set the down-trodden at liberty, to proclaim the year of the Lord's favor. (Lk 4:18–19/ Is 61:1–2, 5–6)

Of all the texts that Jesus could have chosen, he chose a text from Isaiah that did not in any way seek to legitimize the priority of any kind of ritual/juridical/temple holiness but rather the tradition of liberation and justice, a text that placed him squarely in the prophetic tradition. In quoting the passage from Isaiah, it is important to note that Jesus leaves out a phrase: "And the day of our God's vengeance" (Is 61:2b). This indicates Jesus' experience of God as compassion in whom vengeance plays no part.

In Jesus' inaugural address ("I have come to bring good news to the poor"); in his response to John's query about his identity ("Go and tell John what you hear and see: the blind receive their sight, the lame walk, the lepers are cleansed, the deaf hear, the dead are raised, and the poor have good news brought to them" [Mt 11:4–5]); and at the beginning of the Sermon on the Mount, both in Matthew and Luke ("Blessed are you who are poor [in spirit]"), we are introduced to one of Jesus' essential priorities. Jesus centers his whole ministry among the poor, making *poor* and *gospel* correlative terms. Poverty is by far the most comprehensive term to describe the ethos of the Jesus event. In Matthew's Gospel the poor are the only necessary sacrament of salvation (Mt 25). Jesus never appears apart from the poor. "The backdrop of Jesus' activity is always the suffering of the masses, the poor, the weak, those deprived of their dignity. Jesus' entrails wrench in its presence, and it is these wrenched entrails that shape all that Jesus is: his knowing, his hoping, his actions, and his celebration."[24] It is, in turn, the adoption of evangelical poverty that defines a follower of Jesus. Only those who are radically poor are eminently qualified to be witnesses of the kingdom.

Whereas for Jesus celibacy was an evangelical counsel, a charism given to a few, poverty was to be the basic spirituality of all his disciples (obligatory poverty and optional celibacy). God's main competitor was not sex or marriage, but mammon. Hence, it is poverty, not celibacy, that can guarantee one's undivided devotion to God's reign. Therefore, solidarity with the poor is not merely one demand among many, but is indeed the primary, fundamental Christian demand, without which one's moral concerns are not only compromised but evacuated of any moral power or persuasiveness. In light of this Aloysius Pieris asserts that there is "no salvation outside God's covenant with the poor."[25] Poverty was not an evangelical counsel for a few but rather the primary praxis and spirituality of all Christian disciples. What has occurred in the Catholic Church regarding her priests and religious, however, is the "policy of 'obligatory celibacy and optional poverty' . . . the exact converse of what Jesus had intended."[26]

Jesus, in line with all the prophets, made it clear that social responsibility for the poor and oppressed was essential to the covenant with YHWH and thus took priority over worship (Mt 5:23–25/Is 1:11–17). Kinship with the poor itself becomes mystagogy, bestowing upon disciples of Jesus kinship with the reality of God, initiating them into the very mystery of God, for solidarity with the poor is constitutive of the divine Mystery. There is a transcendental correlation between God and the oppressed. That is why Aloysius Pieris sees the incarnation as "the scandalous agreement (covenant) between God and slaves, embodied in Jesus who sided with the non-persons as a sign and proof of the Divine nature."[27] By sharing his life with the despised and forgotten, Jesus revealed that God ignored all those who are high and mighty and wealthy in the world in favor of the weak, meek, and lowly. God is, therefore, to be found in the below, and the mystery of reality is revealed only from the below, thereby challenging all other hierarchies of values. Reality is not perceived from the perspective of the priest and Levite, who on their way to a worship service—and who with good theological reasons—walk right past the man who lies half-dead in the ditch, but from the perspective of that man who has been robbed and is now lying there on the side of the road.

Jesus shares the common perspective in the Bible that poverty is not simply a natural phenomenon but the result of the avoidable and undesirable consequences of injustice and exploitation. Therefore, the rich gained their riches by and large at the expense of the poor. The kingdom of God that Jesus' teachings announced was the kingdom of the poor—and the rich, as long as they held onto their wealth, could have no part in it. When Jesus said that it would take a miracle for the rich to enter this kingdom, the miracle was not that they would somehow enter holding onto their wealth. The miracle would be that their hearts would be so radically changed that they would share their wealth with the poor. The only way to enter the kingdom is by way of a redistribution of wealth.

Wealth is an evil only when accumulated and not shared. Bread too is a "sin against the body of the Lord" (1 Cor 11:21, 27) if consumed by a few while others starve. But when broken and shared, it is his body that we consume and become. If wealth is distributed "according to need" (Acts 4:35) so "that there be no needy person" (Acts 4:34), it ceases to be mammon. It becomes sacramental. Perhaps one of the greatest midrashes on Jesus' teaching about wealth comes from one of the fathers of the church, Saint Basil (in accord with *all* the church fathers):

> If each kept only what is required for his current needs, and left the surplus for the needy, wealth and poverty would be abolished. . . . The bread you keep belongs to another who is starving, the coat that lies in your chest is stolen from the naked, the shoes that rot in your house are stolen from the man who goes unshod, the money you have laid aside is

> stolen from the poverty stricken. In this way you are the oppressors of as many people as you could help. No, it is not your rapaciousness that is here condemned, but your refusal to share.[28]

This compassion was not only a personal quality of Jesus reflecting the essence of his Father, but it also became a theo/socio/political paradigm expressing his alternative vision of life embodied in the movement that came into existence around him. The implication for a disciple is clear: I live out my encounter with the Father not only in solitude and contemplation, but also in my encounter with my brothers and sisters. And as long as there remain terrible injustices in the world or as long as there is the human condition, it is compassion with an unapologetic preference: those who are the object of that injustice. In short, the mysticism of Jesus is the immersion of the person into the compassionate love of the Father that sets ablaze our hearts to lay down our lives out of love for one another.

In Jesus' Lord's Prayer, Jesus wed personal and social concerns. The first part of the prayer, with its cry to Abba, showed Jesus' great intimacy with his Father, in which he invited his disciples to participate. But this intimacy did not cause Jesus to lose his focus or concern for the people's needs; hence the prayer speaks of the provision of bread and the forgiveness of debts. If contemplative language expresses the gratuity of God's love, prophetic language expresses the demands that love makes. With Jesus, these two realities unite and become one. As Leonardo Boff writes:

> The God who calls upon us is the same God who drives us on in a commitment to liberation. He commands us to unite the passion of God with the passion of the oppressed. More precisely, he demands that the passion of God in Jesus Christ be lived out in the passion of our suffering and needy brothers and sisters.[29]

Jesus had much in common with John the Baptist, and with all the prophets. After all, when John called for the people's repentance and they asked, "Well, what are we to do?" John replied: "If you have two coats, give to those who have none. Whosoever has food to eat must do likewise" (Lk 3:10–11). Jesus was in total agreement with this biblical priority, but Jesus chose a different way to realize the gospel of the poor. It is helpful to contrast the approach of Jesus and John the Baptist as found in the Gospels to clarify further the revelation of Jesus.

Whereas John lived at a distance and in separation from "sinners," Jesus lived in public, out in the open for all to see and have intimate access to. He was within the reach of everyone's request. The poor, and those deemed sinners by the religious authorities, did not need to go in search of him as with John the Baptist because Jesus sought them out. If the approach of John the Baptist was to confront the sins of the people, Jesus' main thrust was to address the suffering of the people. Johann Baptist Metz concludes: "This sensitivity for the wronged-other rather than the sinful-other marked Jesus' way as a 'new kind of life.'"[30] Indeed, the whole tenor of his ministry was not one of severity but of joy because the kingdom is here in our midst.

Whereas John's call to conversion was essentially bound up with ascetic, penitential practices, Jesus' praxis involved compassion, being non-judgmental, healing, and forgiveness. Whereas John's preaching was characterized by an apodictic, imperative moral "ought," Jesus' preaching was more invitational: "Come and see!" Jesus revealed not so much a divine demand as a divine seduction, a drawing—not a hammer but a magnet. And thus Jesus' preaching created an overwhelmingly joyous atmosphere. The people, says Schillebeeckx, "simply adored him because they knew: in him we are aware of receiving a gift, a present from God to us."[31] Or as Schillebeeckx summarizes: "If John came across to the people as a grim ascetic, in complete harmony with his message of God's approaching and inexorable judgment, as a sort of dirge . . . Jesus came across as a song."[32]

Jesus realized that the only way to reveal God's compassion and solidarity with the poor was for him to cast his lot with those whose lives were so often marked by injustice. As Albert Nolan writes: "A sympathy with the poor that is unwilling to share their suffering would be a useless emotion. One cannot share the blessings of the poor unless one is willing to share their sufferings."[33] The very root meaning of compassion, *com passion*, means "to suffer with," "to suffer along side the other." As Robert McAfee Brown teaches, compassion "is rooted in closeness (a suffering with) rather than in some abstract kind of concern that is manifested at a distance. In compassion, both geographic and psychic distance is overcome."[34] This is why Edward Schillebeeckx suggests that perhaps the only meaningful vow Christians should take today is the "vow of solidarity with the poor," committing themselves solemnly to organize their lives and to make choices in such a way that they will remain as close as possible to the poor and socially deprived. "It is not enough," Aloysius Pieris insists, "to consider the poor passively as the sacramental recipients of our ministry, as if their function in life were merely to help us, the rich, to save our souls by retaining them as perpetual objects of our compassion."[35]

Jesus left the security of his own family group and assumed the total condition of the poor, mixing often with those considered the lowest of the low by his social/religious contemporaries ("making himself poor though he was rich" [2 Cor 8:9]). The call to discipleship is not just an assent of our minds and hearts but a total re-ordering of our socioeconomic relationships. Jesus puts the matter clearly: "Every one of you who does not renounce all his possessions cannot be my disciple" (Lk 14:33). The praxis of Jesus involves an exodus from one's social placement ("they left everything and followed him" [Lk 5:11]), leaving behind one's ties and interests, security and comfort, good name and prestige; putting at risk one's peace of mind, one's health, even one's life. It was a kenosis, a decentering of one's involution and a turning to and centering on the other, a going down into the world of the poor, adopting the social position of the poor, and accepting it as one's own. Jesus did not just "do things" for the poor; he did not simply show them "charity," but his identity was bound up with them. It was not simply a practice of service to the poor but also a practice in the midst of the poor. The poor became the locus—the place—of his praxis.

He learned the sufferings of the people through experiential knowledge. He made their sufferings his own. He became one with them, and he was very comfortable in their company. He freely mixed with everyone in total disregard of social status and religious or political consequences. As Edward Schillebeeckx says in summary: "Christianity is completely convicted—a conviction found in no other religion—that the only way to God is via the poor."[36]

The poor are seen as a revelation of Divinity. When Jesus instructed his followers about future discipleship, when he would no longer be with them, he insisted that the way his inspirited presence would continue in history would not be primarily in worship of his person or in some trans-historical ritual or rigid moral laws or giving assent to precise dogmatic formulas, but rather in the person of the poor. As Metz says so precisely: "Christianity itself is not in the first instance a doctrine to be preserved in maximum 'purity' but a praxis to be lived more radically."[37] Today Jesus continues to be visibly and palpably available in the flesh and blood of those whom he himself has designated as his vicars on earth: the little ones, the least of the brothers and sisters. The church's claim to be Christ's vicar on earth is challenged by Jesus' claim to have chosen the poor as his vicar on earth.[38] Thus, in contrast to a temple theology that emphasizes the liturgy as the summit of the Christian life, the life of Jesus pointed to the transformation of life through the crucifying praxis of solidarity with the poor, which led to the *via cruces* as the *fons et lumen* of following him.

Jesus, therefore, was not led by the Spirit to withdraw from the world and live in the desert, as John did. He did not opt for that form of monasticism where a group of people seek their own peace and purity by separation from the world, live a ritually pure life of ascetic abandonment and withdrawal, and set up an alternative idealistic community, as the Essenes chose to do. Still less did he seek to establish placid retreat centers where the affluent leisure class could indulge in short spurts of mental tranquility, far from the maddening crowd. The story of the transfiguration gives clear indications as to where Jesus was calling his disciples. Here is a contemplative, mystical moment for the disciples on a mountaintop. The disciples want to stay, to extend and nurture their ecstasy, but Jesus insists that they leave and go back down with him to the people, where Jesus immediately cures an epileptic boy. From ecstasy to epilepsy! (Mt 17:14–18). From mountaintop contemplation to immersion in the pain of the world! We have a spirituality of both inner experience and social praxis inseparable from each other, a transcendence that quickly leads to a trans-descendence.

This in no way ignores the reality that Jesus was a man of deep and frequent prayer. All throughout his ministry Jesus often withdrew into solitude (Lk 9:18) so he could nourish his being with the life and love of his Abba. It was this constant return to his deepest center that kept the ministry of Jesus aware, focused, wise, serene, circumspect, clear-headed, tender-hearted, joyful, and passionate without being fanatic. But this contemplative life of Jesus was always closely wedded to his ministry of announcing the kingdom. Jesus did not institutionalize his withdrawal or remain hidden in it. Thus Bishop Pedro Casaldaliga describes Christians as "contemplatives while on the way; decoding reality . . . running up against the God who is present in the processes of people and in the process within each of us. Contemplatives on the march . . . trying to walk with your feet in the challenging reality of history."[39]

Nor did Jesus seek to work within the religious establishment of his day, accommodating himself to it, watching and tempering his every word to suit the authorities, so as to inch his way to some modest reform. He was not interested in simply a religious renewal or revival, but in a total personal conversion and social revolution. Aloysius Pieris characterizes the instincts of Jesus as a "revolutionary urge, a psychosocial impulse, to generate a new humanity."[40] When Jesus preached in the synagogues, his words were often so explosive that he would be immediately ejected. Jesus cut to the quick and made quite clear with whom he was in solidarity. The only people Jesus was interested in "accommodating" were those who were suffering.

The marginalized discovered in their midst this Jesus about whom they sensed something different. He was eminently approachable. One could get near him, and not be dismissed, and one thus came away feeling respected, affirmed, empowered, and healed. As Bhagwan Shree Rajneesh observed:

> There are people, if you meet them you feel an unburdening. . . . You feel light, you feel flowing, you feel more vibrant, more alive—as if they had taken a great burden . . . off your chest. As if they had poured some nectar into your being. You feel a dance left within your heart, you seek their company. You enjoy it because you are nourished by their presence.[41]

If Jesus' ministry to the poor took on an initial priority, it was this unburdening, this transformative healing. In fact, almost all of Jesus' exercise of spiritual power initially revolved around healing brokenness. Jesus was very conscious of the human and psychological fact that brokenness needed to be healed before people could be open to preaching and teaching. So Jesus restored the poor in body and mind and brought them back into life-giving relationships within the community.

Jesus saw in his exorcisms an indication that the divine creative forces were overcoming the rule of the demonic destructive forces. Healing, restoration, and liberation were taking place in and through his ministry, which was the great hope for the "age to come." But the healing that Jesus did was not done to prop himself up as some kind of traveling celebrity or wonderworker. Rather, healing was the outflow of an intimate encounter, an overcoming of all barriers, divisions, and defenses. God was becoming intimate with people. Heart, power, and compassion were in his hands that blessed, his arms that embraced, his lips that kissed. As Ulrich Luz describes the impact of Jesus' ministry thus far:

> All around Jesus, people are being made healthy and are being fed, being freed from demons and coming to themselves, being transformed from outsiders to central figures, becoming important because they are important to God.[42]

One of the signature ways that Jesus demonstrated his solidarity with the poor was through table fellowship. Table fellowship was the central expression of social intercourse in the ancient world, and Jesus' acceptance of anyone and everyone—whether outcasts or public sinners—into table fellowship became one of the central characteristics of his movement. "The Lord raises up the poor from the dust, and the beggar from the ant heap, to make them sit with princes and inherit a seat of honor" (1 Sm 2:8). Jesus never defined the kingdom, but rather presented its meaning in symbolic actions, primarily through healings, exorcism, and table fellowship with sinners. Meals were his favorite way of demonstrating that the kingdom had already arrived. These meals were no ordinary meals for nourishment alone, nor were they simply polite get-togethers. Still less were they routine rituals with passive participants. Rather, they were festive parties where everyone was invited, where everyone was made to feel at home, and where there was no fasting but feasting and enjoying one another's company. And these joyous banquets were such a common feature of Jesus' mission that he was accused of being a glutton and a drunkard (Mt 11:19). The joy of table fellowship was a preview of the joyful kingdom community being formed in their midst. Their meals could not have been anything else but festive, since, as Edward Schillebeeckx says: "It was an existential impossibility of being sad in the company of Jesus. His very presence liberated them."[43]

Because everyone was invited and no one was excluded, these meals had the effect of accepting and celebrating all men and women as friends and equals. The intimate physical and personal contact Jesus had with his guests implied forgiveness to sinners, allowing them to feel clean and acceptable for the first time. The rejected no longer felt humiliated. Jesus let them know that they were beautiful and worthy of respect. His form of table fellowship bestowed dignity on those who had been stripped of all dignity. Non-persons had become persons. As Virgil Elizondo writes: "Through him, and with him, and in him, the prostitutes, the tax collectors, the Samaritans (who stand for the rejected and despised neighbor), the public sinners of society and all the hoi poloi passed from being a faceless and nameless mass of individuals to a community of friends."[44]

The simple act of sharing a meal, however, had tremendous religious and social significance in the social world of Jesus. The major tool of social and religious ostracism was the refusal of table fellowship to all those deemed outside one's group. The Jewish religious establishment had very specific rules and regulations as to who could and could not be invited to table fellowship. There were very strict divisions between those who were pure and impure, those who were holy and unholy, and those who were righteous and wicked. For Jesus to invite those who were officially banned from table fellowship, with no questions asked, no requirements to be met, challenged all the social taboos that kept people apart, and threatened the central ordering principle of the whole Jewish religious structure. The table fellowship of Jesus became a primary vehicle of social protest by which Jesus radically, boldly, and provocatively called into question the holiness code, which was the cornerstone of the cultural dynamics of the official Jewish faith of his day. It understandably became a primary source of the hostility that his ministry generated. We are left not with a pious ritual but a social event and religious praxis of enormous impact.

The import of Jesus' ministry was not lost on his family and relatives, who understood all too well that Jesus was courting disaster. One time when Jesus was enjoying table fellowship with his usual motley crew, his family—including his mother—came to take him home and bring him to his senses. But when Jesus was told that his family was outside demanding he leave and come home with them, Jesus made it abundantly clear that his mission was with these little ones, and his new family members were those who joined him in this unparalleled form of table fellowship. Solidarity with the *marginales* took precedence over every other form of solidarity, whether familial, ethnic, religious, or national. The solidarity that Jesus envisioned and enacted was not exclusive but inclusive, not nationalistic or separatist but universal. This was what Israel was supposed to be in the mind and heart of God: an inclusive community reflecting the inclusive heart of its Father.

Thus, we necessarily come to where the path of Jesus finally leads: Jerusalem. Dietrich Bonhoeffer wrote, "When Jesus calls a person, he bids him come and die."[45] We are now steeped in the most serious of matters. Jesus does not go to Jerusalem as a pilgrim in order to demonstrate his blind faithfulness to the law or his unquestioning allegiance to the temple. For the sake of those he loves, Jesus sets out to confront the very center of the powers that are undermining and destroying the inclusive vision of his Father. We are speaking of powers in the sense of, as Walter Wink writes, "the inner essence of earthly realities in their physical and institutional concretizations." Wink explains:

> For we are contending against the spirituality of institutions, against the ideologies and metaphors and legitimations that prop them up, against the greed and covetousness, against the individual egocentricities that give them life, against the individual egocentrism that the Powers so easily hook into, against the idolatry that puts short term gain against the long term good of the whole.[46]

Jesus understood very well (with the fresh memory of John the Baptist's execution) that this face-to-face denunciation of the religious/political establishment could cost him his life. But he was undaunted. He would not recognize any high priest's authority; telling them that they had been dismissed by God; insulting them in front of all the people by saying that prostitutes and tax-collectors would get into the kingdom before them. He cursed a fig tree that was a figure for the temple, which bore no fruit (Mk 11:12–25).

The consciousness of Jesus did not focus on the architectural grandeur of the temple or its elaborate rituals and ceremonies. The overriding concern of Jesus was that the temple was supposed to embody the inclusivity of his Father's compassion, but it had become a center of operations that exploited and robbed the poor. If the original idea of the temple was as a central storehouse where everyone contributed tithing and then redistributed to those who were without, the temple now had become a place where goods were accumulated for the sake of a few.

So here were moneychangers making money off the poor for the profit of high priests who administered the "House of God." Jesus saw the matter clearly. Ched Myers, at one of his workshops at the Center for Action and Contemplation, said that rather than a holy place where the people were enfranchised, the temple disenfranchised them. Rather than trying to restore the integrity of the community, the temple system was actually stratifying that community. Rather than redistributing the wealth, the temple system accumulated the wealth and concentrated it in the hands of a few. Obviously it was not in Jesus' heart to legitimize what the temple had become but rather to disrupt its unjust operations. Albert Nolan concludes:

> It would have been impossible for the men of Jesus' time to have thought of him as an eminently religious man who steered clear of political revolution. They would have seen him as a blasphemously irreligious man who under the cloak of religion was undermining all the values upon which religion, politics, economics and society were based. He was a dangerous and subtly subversive revolutionary.[47]

"If you are to be my disciple," Jesus says emphatically, "deny yourself, pick up your cross, and follow me" (Lk 9:23). The self-denial Jesus is talking about, however, is not some form of personal asceticism, but the willingness to risk one's comfort and welfare, even one's life for the sake of the gospel and the kingdom. The cross in Jesus' time was a public cross, and it was anything but a religious icon (or jewelry to be worn around the neck or a wall decoration). Even less was it a teaching instrument for passivity and acquiescence. The cross was a metaphor for the capital punishment meted out on the grounds of insurgency or perceived threat to the status quo. Therefore, Johann Baptist Metz concludes that the significance of Jesus' cross

> does not stand in the exclusive privacy of the individual, nor in the sanctuary of a purely religious existence, but outside the threshold of sheltered privacy and the screen of the purely religious. . . . This public aspect cannot be taken back, dissolved or hushed up.[48]

The way of the cross, the final phase of the path of Jesus, demonstrates the utter seriousness of this path. A path is that way of life that is so much a part of who you are that you are willing to die for it. And the path of Jesus was eminently that. There are those powers at work in the world whose dominion is built on the oppression of the poor. The ultimate threat of these powers is punishment by torture or death, and it is the fear of this threat that keeps the dominant order intact and the people under control. But when one defies that threat and is not intimidated by it, then people like Jesus begin the process of shattering the power's reign of death. When Jesus died on the cross, the world dominated by the powers had in a very real sense ended their hegemony. "Not the wisdom of philosophical speculation, not the power of politics of a social Darwinism, not the security syndrome of 'Western democracies,'" declares Thorwald Lorenzen, "but the cross of the Risen Christ becomes the hermeneutical key for interpreting reality."[49] We either look upon the death of Jesus on the cross as the ultimate defeat of Jesus by the powers, or we cast our lot and our life with a new power that has been unleashed in this world that defies the power of oppression, greed, and violence and establishes the undefeatable power of love.

If the historical Jesus initiated and animated the "way" that will forever identify his true disciples, it is the resurrected Jesus (now referred to as Christ[50]) who continues to animate that praxis in history through his disciples. Jesus Christ not only entered history and showed his disciples the way but now trans-historically through the Spirit continues to live his life in them, and it is through this gracious empowerment that they can now "walk even as he walked" (1 Jn 2:6) and "do as he has done" (Jn 13:15), "love as he loved" (Eph 5:2), "forgive as he forgave" (Col 3:13), "have this mind, which was also in Christ Jesus" (Phil 2:5), and therefore are able to "follow the example he has left us" (1 Pt 2:21), and "lay down our lives for the brethren" as he did (1 Jn 3:16).

"God has raised a crucified one, and from this moment forward there is hope for the crucified in history."[51] The same God who raised Jesus from the dead is the ground and telos of history, and reserves the final world in history for God-Self. Therefore the resurrection is a grasping of the future as promise, where the believer leans forward into the future, participating with all creation in a longing for the kingdom to come.

It is the overwhelming experience of trust that the blood spilled by Jesus and his disciples will be vindicated, and through that, the pain of the world will be healed. His disciples do not encounter this resurrected presence of Jesus by standing gazing up into the heavens, which is a metaphor for a spirituality that, either despairing of or capitulating to the world, preaches leaping over the historical reality of the world into the lush fields of heavenly abodes.

Rather, they will encounter the resurrected Jesus by confidently involving themselves in the crucifying path of personal and world transformation and liberation.

Just as grace is not "cheap," as Bonhoeffer noted in *The Cost of Discipleship*, hope does not come cheaply either. But grounding in Jesus' cross and resurrection and anticipating a totally redeemed future of transformation and liberation, faith turned into hope now takes on the constitutive characteristic of having a mobilizing, revolutionizing, and critical effect upon the individual and history. Therefore, the resurrection allows faith to unfold into hope and demands the praxis of discipleship where this hope becomes concrete. It forces us to confront what Romano Guardini once called the "incredible inertia of the actual."[52] It refuses to let us strike a compromise with the factual, not because it relativizes the concrete, but rather because

> it is like a powerful magnet. It mobilizes. It moves human beings time and again to give their best to make the Reign come true. . . . It says no to the present and points toward a future within history. Hope says yes to the absolute future, already present, which comes to meet every human being but is always future in the sense that it is never totally achieved and known. It always keeps its character of being something to come, an unforseeable surprise, wholly new.[53]

13

Toward a Judeo-Christian Future Vision

In attempting to retrieve the biblical foundations of a Judeo-Christian approach to the world by utilizing the witness of the Hebrew prophetic tradition, the way of Jesus, the witness of the early Christian community, the church fathers, Jewish and Christian philosophers and theologians, and the social documents of the Christian churches, what would emerge as a Judeo-Christian response to the present world situation, to the present global market social system and its effect on the world community?

The Dignity of the Human Person

Perhaps the most fundamental principle that emerges out of the whole Judeo-Christian tradition is the dignity of each human being. Every person is a visible image of the invisible Mystery and therefore has an inalienable dignity and absolute significance that is not dependent on nationality, race, sex, or economic status or on any human moral condition, human labor, or accomplishment. The human person is not essentially *homo economicus* or *homo consumptor*, but rather is essentially *theomorphic*. As Psalm 8:5–6 proclaims: "You have made him a little less than the angels, you have crowned him with glory and honor; you have set him over the works of your hands, you have subjected all things under his feet." Or, as Jesus says, "Even the hairs on your head are all numbered" (Lk 2:7; Mt 10:30). Because of this dignity, the biblical God battles for the basic right of each human being for abundant life. Not one person must be dehumanized. This principle of human dignity has become the cornerstone of the Roman Catholic Church's social teaching. As José Comblin observes: "When we consider the development of the doctrine of the Roman Catholic Church over the course of the present century, it becomes clear that the theme of the dignity of the human person, is the core and fulcrum of the 'social teaching of the church.'"[1]

In a time when we see, especially in the First World, the increasing instrumentalization and routinization of the person and a society that privileges and rewards conformity, the conviction of the dignity of each individual must be radically reaffirmed. In this global economy, where so many human beings are becoming dispensable, the Catholic bishops of America have declared that "the dignity of the human person, realized in community with others, is the criterion against which all aspects of economic life must be measured. . . . Every economic decision and institution must be judged in light of whether it protects or undermines the dignity of the human person."[2]

The "Corporateness" of Selfhood

The second fundamental of the Judeo-Christian social vision is the belief in the corporateness of selfhood. The Jesus event acknowledges the other as part of the self, especially the marginal other and even the enemy other. When Jesus says "love your neighbor as yourself," this needs to be understood in at least two ways. It means not only that we are to love others the way we love ourselves, but that we are to love others *because* they are ourselves. As Frederick Herzog says: "The commandment to love the other as oneself is not an invitation to love an alien other, but finally to discover the other as co-constitutive of one's self."[3] Or, as Thomas Merton teaches:

> The inner self sees the other not as a limitation upon itself but as its complement, its "other self," and is even in a certain sense identified with the other, so that the two "are one." This unity in love is one of the most characteristic works of the inner self, so that paradoxically the inner "I" is not only isolated but at the same time united with others in a higher plane. . . . The Christian is not merely "alone with the alone" in the neo-platonic sense, but he is one with all his brothers in Christ.[4]

With Jesus, the Divine-Self joined humanity at the level of non-persons, and through this divine act of solidarity, personhood becomes a communal phenomenon. "If one member suffers, all suffer together with it" (1 Cor 12:26). "Let each of you look not to your own interests, but to the interest of others" (Phil 2:4). We discover that our identity is a corporate selfhood. From the Christian perspective, the neighbor is part of me. My neighbor's poverty is my poverty. The fate of all peoples is also my fate. It is when there is an exclusion of the other from one's selfhood that society becomes corrupted, and we see one group lording it over the other, preying on the other, making the other valueless, invisible, and scorned. This corporate self, however, must be radically distinguished from "mass man," Heidegger's "The They,"[5] or what Dostoyevsky's Grand Inquisitor called the "the unanimous ant heap," where there is no personal identity other than one's social self, which is technologically engineered for collective undertakings or is simply the falling of the self into a collective trance. Whereas the corporate self completes a human being, mass/collective self swallows one up and one simply disappears.

The Prioritization of the Common Good

The third fundamental principle of the Judeo-Christian social vision is the prioritization of the common good. The whole biblical tradition teaches that the earth is the Lord's and the fullness thereof. The gift of creation is meant for all. There is a universal destination of the earth's goods, since whatever belongs to God belongs to all, including those not yet born. Therefore civil society exists for the common good and must necessarily be concerned with the interests of all people; individual interests are given their due but always in proportion to the needs of the community. This common good embraces the sum total of those conditions of social living whereby people can achieve a fully human life. Pope John XXIII stated: "All people have a right to life, food, clothing, shelter, rest, medical care, education and employment."[6] If people must go homeless and hungry, then they are being denied their basic rights.

At a time when we have not reached a global consensus that to eat is a basic right and not just a good (the position of the US government), Pope John Paul II insisted in *Sollicitudo Rei Socialis* that "the goods of creation are meant for all. . . . The strong nations must feel responsible for the other nations, based on the equality of all peoples and with respect for the differences" (no. 37). In article 25 of the UN *Universal Declaration of Human Rights*, this principle is reinforced:

> Everyone has the right to a standard of living adequate for the health and well being of himself and his family including food, clothing, housing, and medical care and necessary social services and the right to security in the event of unemployment, sickness, disability, widowhood, old age, or other lack of livelihood in circumstances beyond his control.

The right to private property is not an absolute or unconditional right. Saint Thomas Aquinas taught that "man should not consider his material possessions as his own, but as common to all. . . . Whatever people have in abundance should sustain the poor." Aquinas, in tune with the biblical view of human social existence, held that people are not justified in keeping for their exclusive use what they do not need, when others lack necessities. Those who are unwilling to share from their surplus with their neighbor violate the tenth commandment, since they are coveting what does not belong to them. Therefore, the more fortunate should share some of their possessions so as to place their goods more generously at the service of others. When we give our possessions to the poor, we are handing over to them what is theirs. Saint Ambrose confronted those who claim their own rights without wishing to be answerable to the common good: "What has been given in common for the use of all, you have arrogated to yourself. The world is given to all, not only to the rich." As Pope John Paul II sums up so precisely in *Sollicitudo Rei Socialis*:

> This [solidarity] then is not a feeling of vague compassion or shallow distress at the misfortune of so many people, both near and far. On the contrary, it is a firm and persevering determination to commit oneself to the common good. That is to say, to the good of all and each individual because we are all really responsible for all. This determination is based on the solid conviction that what is hindering full development is that desire for profit and that thirst for power. . . . These attitudes and "structures of sin" are only conquered—presupposing the help of divine grace—by a diametrically opposed attitude: a commitment to the good of one's neighbor with the readiness, in the gospel sense, to "lose oneself" for the sake of the other instead of exploiting him and to "serve him" instead of oppressing him for one's own advantage. (no. 38)

The Common Good Is Global

It is necessary today to situate the problems created by the modern economy in the widest possible context. As Richard A. Cohen teaches: "Humanism . . . is not merely the affirmation of the dignity of one person, of each individual alone; it is also an affirmation of the dignity of all humanity, the affirmation of an interhuman community, and social justice."[7] A new and more radical dimension of human solidarity is therefore demanded. In the early 1960s Lyndon B. Johnson beamed: "Don't forget, there are 200 million of us in a world of three billion. They want what we've got and we're not going to give it to them." Challenging this incorporated selfishness and arrogance, the Nobel Prize laureate and president of Costa Rica, Oscar Maria Sanchez, countered: "The challenge for the new millennium is to embrace . . . global citizenship."[8] Or as the Dalai Lama insists: "Human beings will have to develop a great sense of universal responsibility. Each of us must learn to work not just for his or her own self, family, or nation, but for the benefit of all mankind."[9] Today we can no longer be ignorant of the fact that in whole continents countless people are ravaged by hunger; whole regions of the world are destitute and are desperately trying to move up from misery and destitution to poverty, where at least the basic necessities of life are present.

The same duty of solidarity that rests on the individual exists also for nations. Therefore, every nation must today contribute to the common good of the human race. There is a need to establish greater justice in the sharing of goods both within the national communities and on the international level. Worldwide public authorities must tackle problems of an economic, political, social, and cultural nature that are posed by the universal common good. Is it not difficult to see what right the richer nations have to insist on their claims to increase their own material demands if the consequence is that other nations remain in misery?

Advanced nations have a very heavy obligation to help the poor nations. No country can rightfully keep its wealth for itself alone. The superfluous wealth of rich nations is called to be placed at the service of poor nations. The *1997 UN Human Development Report* stated that poverty is not inevitable, since the world has the material, natural resources, and know-how to make a poverty-free world in less than a generation. Eradicating poverty is therefore not just a moral imperative and commitment to human solidarity of the nations. It is also a practical possibility. The cost, it has been estimated, would be no more than 1 percent of global income and no more than 3 percent of US income.

The Centrality of Justice

If there is one distinguishing theme and central category of the Judeo-Christian vision for the world it is *sedaquah* or justice. God is not only committed to justice but is defined by it. The prophets, who were enraged by the absence of *sedaquah*, became obsessed with justice. As H. J. Kraus insists, "Amos, Hosea, Isaiah and Micah know only one decisive theme: justice."[10] Flowing from this fundamental understanding, it was believed that doing justice and not first and foremost *cultus*, was the primary sacrament of one's encounter with God. "Seek first the kingdom of God's justice, and all other things shall be added unto you" (Mt 6:33). Or as the *Westminster Shorter Catechism* states as the chief end of being human, "Being human is to share in God's justice and to enjoy it forever."[11] Social justice was what one owed to the common good. And if this justice is lacking, then the Judeo-Christian tradition predicts social and political collapse.

The understanding of justice has taken on a different meaning in Western secular society, for it establishes totally different priorities than those of the biblical understanding of justice. When we hear the word *justice* in our Western culture, we usually think in terms of litigation, bringing criminals to justice, and meting out their punishment. As one scripture scholar put it: "When God said, speaking through Amos, 'Let justice roll down like a mighty river,' the meaning is not, 'May prisons multiply and police forces expand. . . . May criminals writhe as they receive their just deserts.'"[12] Rather, in the biblical tradition the word *justice* immediately implies redistributive sharing and remedial systematic changes that address the needs of the poor. If retributive justice is the emphasis in Western secular society, redistributive justice is the central concern of biblical *sedaquah*. If the opposite of the Western idea of justice (that is, retributive justice or the delivery of punishment to the offender or sinner) is mercy, the opposite of biblical justice (conceived of as distributive justice) is human injustice. Marcus Borg insists, "Seeing the opposite of justice as mercy distorts what the bible means by justice."[13] Western justice posits a level playing field and therefore emphasizes impartiality with regards to the law. The biblical tradition, however, breaks from this self-serving "neutrality" and is decidedly biased in favor of the poor and critical of the rich. As Johann

Baptist Metz explains: "Messianic love is partisan. . . . There was certainly a privileged group around Jesus—those who were otherwise under-privileged."[14] If the modern idea of justice and law concerns itself with the ninety-nine, biblical justice goes off in search of the missing, excluded, or persecuted one. Thus biblical justice is that deep impulse to change and improve the law. It is that which continually spurs us on to a deeper, more inclusive, ever evolving humanity.

It is the bias of Western culture to blame the poor for their poverty (laziness, drugs, immoral sex, lack of intelligence, failure to "ratchet themselves upward by learning the skills necessary for success and how to acquire them," and so on), all the while saluting or envying the rich for their wealth. But the biblical conviction is that it is by and large the rich who are responsible for poverty, and therefore, if poverty is to be overcome, then the burden falls on those who have the means to effect change.

In Western culture criminals are mostly from the poor class and receive far harsher punishment than the "missteps" of the white-collar workers and rich folk who are afforded high-end punishment. This is just the opposite of the evaluation of biblical justice. A far harsher judgment is rendered to the rich and privileged than to the poor. If Western justice stresses individual rights and the sacrality of private property, biblical justice stresses the communal dimension of all rights and the sacredness of addressing the basic needs of the poor and disenfranchised. If Western culture is (opportunistically) pessimistic about eliminating poverty and tends to accept poverty as an enduring economic given, the biblical tradition hopes beyond hope that one day the kingdom will come.

Solidarity with the Poor

In almost every chapter of the Gospels, Jesus, in the tradition of the prophets, demands the social solidarity of the rich with the poor. Solidarity with the poor is not just some fanciful fad of an activist generation or some theological afterthought; it belongs to the very first thought of Jesus. When Jesus was asked, "Who is my neighbor?" he was in effect asked, What does it mean to be human? Who is the ideal, total human person? And his response was the parable of the good Samaritan. "The ideal human being, the complete human being, is the one who interiorizes, absorbs in her innards, the suffering of another."[15] The total human person is one who sees someone lying wounded in the ditch along the road and responds, helping the victim in every possible way. The parable does not tell us what was going through the Samaritan's mind, what he was feeling, what his beliefs were, or what his level of consciousness was. It simply states that he responded in solidarity with the wounded man.

If God is not God of the oppressed, then this God is not the God of the Judeo-Christian scriptures. The divine Mystery does not remain sealed up antiseptically in some heavenly realm, but rather is discovered in the struggle for new life among the oppressed and as a direct challenge to the affluent. This solidarity is an essential mark of Christian discipleship, since it was an essential mark of the praxis of Jesus and his disciples. It is the basic Christian ascesis; it is the way a Christian is redeemed. You will know they are Christians by their solidarity with the poor of the world. When Saint Paul recalled later the Council of Jerusalem, where the pillars of the Christian community formulated pastoral policy, he tells us that "their only request was that we remember the poor, which is the very thing I have spared no pain to do" (Gal 2:10). When Pope John XXIII announced the Second Vatican Council, he expressed his dream of a "church of all, especially the poor." It is this solidarity with the poor that the Christian offers the world as the foundation for humanization itself. Thus, José Comblin observes that "there is nothing more solid, more constant, or more evident in Christian anthropology than the special place of the poor. The entire bible is built on the historical role of the poor. Christian tradition takes up the theme again in every generation."[16]

In the Gospels we discover a gradual deepening of the praxis of solidarity with the poor. A disciple is first drawn into compassion for the poor. Then, there is the experience of communion, or of connectedness to the poor. This leads to collaboration, or working on behalf of the poor. And finally, at the deepest and most committed level, there emerges solidarity or an active taking up with the poor. This means that Christian communities are called not only to be *for* the poor, or working *on behalf of* the poor. At the most profound level they are invited to be also *of* the poor. This entails an exodus, a going out of one's place of perhaps privilege and entering into the world of the poor and accepting it as one's own. Praxis as a service *to* the poor transforms into a praxis *in the midst of* the poor because the world of the poor has become one's place of residence, not merely one's place of work. In this solidarity with the poor one begins to share in their lives, sorrows, joys, hopes, and fears. And in many instances this solidarity goes deeper and begins to take up the cross of Jesus. Archbishop Oscar Romero warned, "Those who commit themselves to the poor share the same fate of the poor."[17] This truth is amply testified to by those who have to face the same persecution of the poor expressed in unending criticism, fake accusations, insults, threats, pressures, plundering, arbitrary arrests, torture, and death squads. As the Asian bishops noted: "Opting to be with the poor involves risk of conflict with vested interests or 'establishments.'. . . It also involves for leaders of the Church especially loss of security, and that not only material but spiritual."[18] Archbishop Oscar Romero also believed that the church's ecclesiastical institution itself must be willing to risk everything for the poor. He witnessed the destruction of his archdiocese's radio and printing operations, and the torture and assassination of many of his priests and sisters, before he himself was assassinated.

The Witness of Alternative Communities

Although Jesus' focus was on the whole of Israel, traveling around in his ministry with his small band of twelve disciples (as in the twelve tribes of Israel, a kind of traveling mini-Israel), we see an inchoative communitarian form of the gospel rather than a strictly personal one. There is no such thing as private discipleship in the gospel, just as one cannot baptize oneself into the Christian community. When the early Christians found themselves in a diaspora situation until Christianity became a state religion, Christian life naturally took a more structured communitarian form that varied from the standard social system. Although the focus of the Gospels is on the kingdom and, therefore, on the whole of human society, witnessing communities have become essential components of gospel faithfulness.

Christian communities in diaspora situations are first of all "contrast societies,"[19] offering a concrete and livable alternative to existing social systems based on the gospel vision of Jesus. Through prayer and ministry these communities attempt to maintain a stance of freedom and independence in relation to the social structures of their day so as to be able to take liberating action in the interest of others, especially the "least of the brethren." But as Johann Baptist Metz warns, these communities should not establish themselves as "a 'micro-society' beside the 'great secular society.' Any separation of Church and State leading to a ghetto or to a micro society is fatal. The terminus a quo of the Christian mission should be the secular society in which it then becomes a new presence, a new alternative, and a new mobilization."[20]

On this society the "osmotic pressure" of Christian hope must be exerted. At the same time, these communities must try to face up to the difficulty of being in the midst of empire and at the same time struggling to be an absolute distance from it. As Emmanuel Levinas describes this tension from a Jewish perspective:

> Judaism . . . has always wished to be a simultaneous engagement and disengagement. The most deeply committed one who can never be silent, the prophet, is also the most separate being, and the person least capable of becoming an institution. Only the false prophet has an official function.[21]

Hence, it is necessary for these communities to live in some form of marginalization from society's central power structures and economic elites, in solidarity with people who in different ways live on the periphery in relation to those structures.

This marginalization, however, does not suppose the comfort of neutrality, or passive expectation, or the non-engagement of the ivory tower. Rather, it provides a necessary social space and distance that makes criticism and productive engagement possible. A vantage point arises that is external to culture and offers critical leverage. It allows the community to develop the skills of interpretation and discrimination sufficient to help recognize the possibilities and limits of building a humane society. It allows these contrast societies to be more capable of seeing rightly and developing their sociopolitical imagination, opening up space for more actions and social experiments that otherwise are too easily deemed unrealistic, inefficient, or ineffective (for example, nonviolence). It allows the community not only to dream dreams, but to begin to live out of the dream before it comes to pass and to embody the dream in its concrete actions and communal way of life, indicating what the world could be, but is not (yet).

The Judeo-Christian Vision of Life Is Necessarily Political

Jesus stood in the Hebrew tradition, in which religion is never separated from politics. No first-century Jews would suppose that their prayer and piety could be divorced from the vocation of Israel, since theirs was a corporate faith in every respect. The birth of Judaism was at once a political and a religious act; the liberating events of the Exodus resulted in Moses founding a nation (not a church or temple). But it was a nation that was inspired by the divine Mystery, YHWH, whom the Hebrews experienced in the making of a defense pact, a covenant with the poor against the agents of mammon. Their religion was necessarily expressed in terms of their national life. The Torah, for instance, was seen as divinely inspired and served as a kind of constitution embracing all their life, including not only what is commonly specified as religious life but also civil, criminal, and international law. What this really meant was that "religious" life was not relegated to such things as cult and prayer alone but also involved the purpose, structures, and destiny of the historic community of Israel. So the Hebrew ideal was never a separation of church and state but rather a theocratic nation that envisioned freedom from oppression—a time of justice, plenty, harmony, and peace.

Jesus, following in this tradition, never invited his followers to cultivate their own individual or communal piety, or to construct a separate ecclesial institution in isolation from or alongside their social, economic, and political life in Israel. We could even say that the ministry of Jesus was social and political from the beginning since Jesus' teachings continually addressed and challenged the social evils of his day. His teachings and parables on law, taxation, the juridical process, and so on were all challenges to the political leaders of his day. That is why Jesus warns his disciples when he sends them forth: "On my account you will be brought before governors and kings" (Mt 10:18).

He called for both an individual and a collective renewal of Israel. Jesus' very words and actions challenged the social arrangements of his day. He totally ignored the ordering of relationships based on class division, familial ties, or sexual hierarchy. No one was to be called rabbi or father. No one was to lord it over another. Those who were marginalized or ostracized by society, such as the sick, sinners, women, poor, even criminals, became his companions. Through Jesus' criticism of social arrangements and values of his day, his offering of an alternative way to live, and in the embodiment of that vision in the life of a community, we could conclude that "this is political in the broad sense of the word."[22] When Jesus came in conflict with his contemporaries, it had to do with which paradigm Israel was to be shaped by. Marcus Borg explains:

> For Jesus, compassion was more than a virtue of the individual. Compassion was also the paradigm or core value of his social vision. . . . It stood in sharp contrast to the core value of the social vision of elite [royal or temple] theology, which was a politics of holiness and purity centered in the temple and legitimating the social order. Compassion as a core political paradigm suggests a political order that is life-giving, nourishing, and inclusive.[23]

Because Jesus challenged and confronted these evils, and since he had attracted enough of a following to make him dangerous, he was executed by the state. Jesus' sacrifice on the cross was the climax of an open conflict. Walter Rauschenbusch's account of the forces that put Jesus to death included "religious bigotry, graft, political power, corruption of justice, mob spirit and action, militarism, and racial sin in class contempt."[24] He was not crucified because of some freak event in history, but because of his free choice to be in solidarity with the oppressed of society. Jesus hoisted on a tree outside the city limits became the quintessential despised outsider. As Monika Hellwig writes: "Jesus crucified is above all representative of the marginalized, despised and oppressed, of those who 'don't count' and are kept out of sight (socially invisible), of those who are outsiders and have no rights."[25]

But to insist that the way of Jesus had a political dimension does not imply that Jesus proposed any specific social blueprints. Jesus' teachings were not programmatic but rather visionary, foundational as well as confrontational. He offered standards by which social institutions should be judged, as did the prophets. The prophets judged rulers on the basis of how they enacted God's rule of justice and compassion. "May he [the king] defend the cause of the poor of the people, give deliverance to the needy" (Ps 72:2).

Jesus was thus political as all the pre-exilic prophets were political. He believed that God's blessing of the people of the covenant depended on their manifesting in the sociopolitical sphere the justice of God. As P. Steidl-Meier sums it up:

> It is important to distinguish between politics of struggle over legitimate authority and politics as a precise social agenda. I think that in the former sense Jesus was decidedly political, whereas in the latter he was only

> partially so. His politics can thus be called normative politics rather than prescriptive politics with a precise agenda. Thus the gospel does not present a precise program for all ages, but suggests criteria by which any precise program may be evaluated.[26]

The Christian is forever in danger of acquiescing to Jesus' insight that the children of this world are cleverer and more industrious than the children of light. (The rich are far more aggressive in pursuit of their agenda than the poor are in fighting for their human rights.) Realization of the kingdom, which Schillebeeckx concludes is, in the end, the attaining of the well-being of the human community,[27] must not be left up to some pitiful bowing to the facts or to hoped-for miracles from on high. The hope of Israel was never seen as basically a God-show, but rather as a covenant in which human participation was essential.

So we are not dealing here with salvation by miracle. If there is any miracle it is that human beings are made in the image of God and therefore have divine potential. As Pope John Paul II counsels:

> You must struggle for life, do everything to improve the conditions in which you live, to do so is a sacred duty because it is also the will of God. Do not say it is God's will that you remain in a condition of poverty, disease, unhealthy housing, that is contrary in many ways to your dignity as human persons.[28]

Christians are challenged to emerge from their passivity and reflexivity, to come out of their self-seclusion. They need not surrender to a merely negative evaluation of human potential or be defined exclusively by that to which they are opposed. This is what Gutiérrez calls "denunciation without annunciation."[29]

There might be good historical reasons to be pessimistic about the human potential for constructing a truly human polis, but this should not encourage us to become cynical about the potential for the political. All we have to do is remember that organized political action has been mainly responsible for almost every modern social advance, such as democracy, the end of slavery and of apartheid, universal suffrage, trade unions, civil rights, women's rights, gay rights, and almost every freedom we enjoy. Everything awaiting the human community must bear the stamp of human activity.

Human liberation will always demand responsible action. Pope Paul VI taught in *Populorum Progressio*, along with so many humanistic voices, that "man is only truly man insofar as he . . . is author of his own advancement" (no. 34). If the main threats against humanity are created by humanity, then it is through human action that humanity can create a better future. The South African author Alan Paton once wrote, "To give up the task of reforming society is to give up one's responsibility as a free man." Mahatma Gandhi affirmed this political reality in a most cogent way:

> To see the universal and all-pervading spirit of truth face to face, one must be able to love the meanest of creation as oneself, and a person who aspires after that cannot afford to keep out of any field of life. That is why my devotion to truth had drawn me into the field of politics, and I can say without the slightest hesitation, and yet in all humility, that those who say that religion has nothing to do with politics do not know what religion means.[30]

The Judeo-Christian Vision Addresses the Structures of Society

We do not find in the biblical vision any understanding that social structures are immune from the call to justice or that they operate under their own internal law system, sufficient unto themselves. Therefore, Jesus often attacked the authorities of his time as hypocrites, blind guides, blind fools, snakes, vipers, and so on when they were responsible for the glaring injustices as perpetrated in Israel. He also engaged the strategic institutions of his day, which were the centers of these authorities, such as the synagogue and temple. The temple in biblical times was close to what we would call today the system, and because this system was responsible for flagrant injustices, Jesus established his way outside this temple. "I assure you, there is something greater than the temple here" (Mt 12:6). When Jesus symbolically attacked the temple (Mt 21:12–13), he followed the path of the prophet Jeremiah, who challenged the corrupted temple, scorning the very word, crying out "this catchword of yours is a lie, put no trust in it" (Jer 7:4). Like Moses before them, the great social prophets of ancient Israel were God-intoxicated voices of religious social protest against the ruling elites of palace and temple.

In traditional Christian ascesis Christians were taught that personal sin was a result of giving in to concupiscence, and that they could overcome their sinfulness and reform their lives through effort and grace. This was strictly a personal affair between the person and God. But it is only in more recent times that we have become aware of the social and collective nature of experience, shaped in particular by cultural, economic, and political institutions that have the power to promote good or evil, human fulfillment or diminishment, liberation or bondage.

Evil and good are not only found in human hearts but also manifested in social structures. On the one hand, social sin derives from personal sin, but personal sins are also conditioned by social structures. They mutually strengthen and feed each other. Therefore, Pedro Arrupe, SJ, in 1975, while head of the Jesuit order, concluded: "What we must re-conquer and reform is our entire world. In other words, personal conversion and structural reform cannot be separated."[31]

When social structures ignore biblical justice, they become forms of social sin, or what Saint John designated as the world. As Arrupe once said, "The world is for the social dimension, what concupiscence is for the individual." This "social sin" of the world is not just the sum of the sins of individual sinners. "It becomes a world," explains Rosemary Ruether, "that we inherit and that biases our opportunities, either as oppressed people or as privileged, even before we have been able to make personal choices."[32]

Although people bring social structures to life in the course of history, these structures can become independent and take on a life of their own. Hence, Johann Baptist Metz warns of the "growing anonymous dictatorship of structures and processes,"[33] where legitimized injustices can become so diffuse that it becomes nearly impossible to identify any specific source of social evils. These structures can develop into objective forms of society that we find ourselves "in" and which can by osmosis influence even our inwardness, our personhood.

There was the belief after the Second World War that the economic growth of the corporate market economy would bring such a quantity of goods that as a byproduct to the increased wealth of rich nations, it would be possible to feed the hungry of the world and lift them out of poverty. Just give these corporate economic forces free reign, remove all interfering restraints, and accept the reality of an exclusive seeking of self-interest, and social progress for all will eventually take hold. How long eventually is, was never specified.

Both the wealthy and the deprived widely assumed that what had been achieved by the few could soon be achieved by the many. The problem is that no such eventuality has happened or promises to occur for any foreseeable generations to come. The world economy is not solving the problems of starvation and malnutrition; in fact, we have in the present international world order, in the analysis of Pope John Paul II, the parable of the rich man and Lazarus writ large (that is, globally) (*Redemptor Hominis*, no. 16).

The present economic structures, therefore, have proven incapable, Pope John Paul II continues, of "remedying the unjust social situations inherited from the past or of dealing with the urgent challenges and ethical demands of the present" (no. 16). The gap between the rich and poor is ever widening. As Hosni Mubarak told the World Economic Forum in Davos, Switzerland, the global free-market approach has failed the world's poor and needs to be rethought. Or, as Vicente Fox, Mexico's former president, concurred: "The world's industrial democracies need to acknowledge that the present methods of reaching out to the illiterate and the impoverished are simply not working. Instead of bridging the divide, the chasm between the rich and poor is only getting worse."

Super-development exists side by side with the miseries of underdevelopment. We have come to see that it has not been sufficient simply to increase overall wealth and the greater availability of goods for there to be an equitable or at least just distribution and consumption of the world's goods. Distributive justice is conveniently left out of the media's global market discussions. The main target of the justice question falls on the backs of the crimes of the poor. The goods of this world might be available for all, but what good is that to the majority if they do not have the means to avail themselves of them? As Pope Pius XII said in a radio address: "The economic prosperity of any people is to be measured less by the total amount of goods and riches there are than by the extent to which these are distributed according to the norms of justice."[34]

These massive, social worldwide problems we face today cannot be simply left up to individual good will. As Pope John Paul II taught:

> It is not merely a matter of "giving from one's surplus," but of helping entire peoples which are presently excluded or marginalized to enter the sphere of economic and human development. . . . This . . . requires above all a change of life-styles, of models of production and consumption and of *established structures of power* which today govern society. (no. 58, italics added)

The Absolute Belief in Hope

The God of the Jews was a God of promise: "For I know the thoughts and plans that I have for you, says the Lord, thoughts and plans for welfare and peace and not for evil, to give you hope in your final outcome" (Jer 29:11). The belief in a God of hope allowed the Jews to break through the pattern of divinized rulers and fixed class structures and believe that things can change, that we can live in a world where it is legitimate to hope. "Do not remember the former things; neither consider the things of old. . . . Behold I am doing a new thing in your life" (Is 43:18). Our culture persistently whispers in our ears: "Why refuse when everybody says adapt? Why negate when everybody affirms? Why be free for the future when everybody is domesticated to the present?"[35] This culture is confronted with the Judeo-Christian tradition that believes "where there is no vision, the people perish" (Prv 29:18). Just as Judaism and Christianity in biblical times looked at the world and found it wanting, so too can we find in this tradition a way to look at the present world situation and address those ways that are unacceptable and thus in need of transformation.

History has not ended. A better society is possible of being envisioned and enacted. Utopia does not necessarily conflict with reality but can disclose the potential and ideal dimensions of reality. We can expect more from history than the condemnation to exclusion and even death of the major part of the human community who live outside of any material standard of a decent human life. If poverty is socially caused, it is socially curable. The kingdom comes on earth as it is in heaven, in reality as it is in vision. Because of this possibility, it is necessary to reject any philosophy, ideology, or theology of inevitability that insists that this is the way things are, have been, and always will be. "The poor you will always have with you"—cynically coopting Jesus' words for totally opposite purposes. The Judeo-Christian tradition soundly rejects any approach, to paraphrase Daniel Berrigan, that baptizes the status quo as destined by nature, ordained by God, sanctioned by the Bible, sanctified by tradition, and greeted with Alleluias by those who are the beneficiaries of the unjust social arrangements.

When people are challenged to bring a new moral imagination into the world, utterly new, positive, and constructive things, never seen before, can actually happen in history. When, for example, American abolitionists dreamed of a society without slavery, or the suffragettes dreamed of the vote for women, or South Africans dreamed of the abolition of apartheid, although these dreams were dismissed as unrealistic and even laughable, such social advances with much human effort and suffering came into being. Far too often a call for political realism has been used as an ideological smoke screen to avoid facing and taking responsibility for what ethically is at stake in the current domination of market capitalism. "To say we have no choices is intellectual terrorism."[36] The appeal to realism and the ridicule of utopianism raises the question: "Who wants an end to utopian thought?" And as Johann Baptist Metz answers: "Those who dominate and enjoy and want to extend their present into the future and are afraid of any alternative future."[37] But the Judeo/Christian tradition is decidedly utopian. It calls people forth to "dream dreams" and to "see visions" (Jl 2:28). Utopia is both a denunciation of the injustices of the present social order and an annunciation that envisions through its creative imagination a society that has never been seen before. What must *be* takes priority over what *is*. Gutiérrez explains, "Utopias move forward; it is a projection into the future, a dynamic and mobilizing factor in history."[38]

Utopian thinking reminds us that political imagination and action do not need to be reduced to the pure business of planning. After all, all the great political theorists of history were well aware that they were injecting imagination into their theories. They were envisioning not so much political society as it is but as it could be. We live, however, at a time when the imagination has been hijacked, stultified, and colonized by consumerism. Disneyland, not the Promised Land, has captured the public's imagination. Public dreams are forever bigger (trophy) homes, more expensive cars, and more luxurious lifestyles. The crisis of imagination is so profound that the only measure we have for human progress and quality of life is the gross national product and the only measure of value is often reduced to what is efficient and profitable (for the few, the stockholders). As Pope John Paul II taught: "If injustices are to be overcome peacefully then there must be 'bold transformations,' in which the present order of things will be entirely renewed or rebuilt."[39] That is why Metz believes "that nothing is more urgently needed today than a moral and political imagination springing from a messianic Christianity and capable of being more than merely a copy of accepted political and economic strategies."[40] The prophetic imagination is not just some private daydream or inner mystic vision but rather a fully public imagination that inspires a commitment to the fullest vision of well-being. The Judeo-Christian imagination is not simply an abstract, fanciful, or solely internal activity but a creative expectancy, an embodied, energized social commitment, a passionate innovation in changing the world toward the kingdom of God.

Judeo-Christian Hope Comes with an Apocalyptic Warning

There is another aspect of the Judeo-Christian tradition that needs to be addressed at this point and that has to do with such biblical texts as Lamentations, the Book of Job, the Gospel of Mark, the Pauline Epistles, and the Book of Revelation. The New Testament ends not with a triumphalistic resurrection but with the apocalypse. There is a counter to a too facile hope. Not a disavowal but a warning, a profound caution, a pessimism confronts the optimism of the tradition. Good has to do intensive battle with evil. We are in no way assured of some grand evolutionary march to the Promised Land based on the reasonableness of social agendas. The apocalypse, for example, radically cautions and critiques the source of our hope and the "what is hoped for." It places the "what is hoped for," the promise, in the darkness of the abyss of the divine Mystery. Therefore, there must always be a continual critique of present social arrangements. *Neti, Neti!* Not just this. This is not yet it. Pragmatic, temporary solutions are far from what could and ultimately must be. There is no rest, no congratulations, no suspension of intense effort, no mollifying of critique, no failure to expose the many postures evil takes, often in sheep's clothing. There must always be an ever-demanding, never-ending, ever-creative hope that strives historically to uncover new possibilities of a reality that only the great Mystery can fully disclose.

This Judeo-Christian perspective resonates with such voices as Kierkegaard, Nietzsche, Schopenhauer, and Foucault, who radically critiqued Hegel's and Marx's optimistic belief in man's reasonable historical progress. This homogenous notion of time in which history and progress always go forward, hand in hand, endlessly and unstoppably is exposed as totally vacuous. "The apotheosis of banality!" cried Schopenhauer. They did not view history as the happy emergence of the harmonious freedom anticipated by Kant, Hegel, and Marx. History was for them nothing less than a calamity. After all, do we not have to conclude that the twentieth century, for all its scientific and technological achievements, was arguably the bloodiest in human history?

On the one hand, we can acknowledge that out of the morass of history there can be perceived the slow evolutionary emergence of human emancipation. Modernity as an emancipatory enterprise could even be seen as a political expression of the biblical promises of freedom, justice, and peace. But from another perspective we see only discordant interruptions, the out-of-nowhere incisions of the wholly new, the unexpected, leaps out of the blue. There has been calamity, chaos, disaster, mayhem, carnage, blood baths, crucified people. The apocalypse balances any too confident, optimistic hope. The cross comes before the resurrection not just in a temporal or evolutionary sequence, but in the always possible catastrophic irruptions that mark history also.

Hope Must Become Concrete

It is not enough simply to criticize the status quo or to wade through the great social issues of our times and hope for the best. Hope in the Judeo-Christian tradition is not some simple-minded optimism, pious presumption, or wishful thinking. It is necessary to take the crucial step of making concrete a social vision in terms of effective alternatives. Otherwise, all the insight in the world will suffer the fate of mere impotent idealism. The central question, therefore, is how we can begin to develop alternatives to a system that favors a few and in effect neglects the majority of the people. As John A. Coleman, SJ, suggests: To function as an effective guiding social force, "social Catholicism [for example] will need to engage in alternative model-thinking. It will not do to distance itself philosophically from both liberalism and socialism, if it is unable to embrace forms of institutional life which avoids the flaws of both systems." Principles must be thought through and specific choices have to be made in light of these principles that will determine the shape and character of social structures.

It has to be faced, however, that we are immersed in a culture where we are witnessing the "dumbing down" of America, or, as someone characterized it, the "modernization of stupidity," a stupidity that is harder to expose because it is so pervasive. It seems the dumber people get the more opinionated they become. People fancy themselves well informed, honest, and sincere without ever engaging in the very difficult process of truly intelligent analysis. That does not mean simply watching the news, reading the papers, and getting cues from the media's "talking heads." Wanting to do the right thing is not the same thing as knowing what the right thing to do is. To know is an arduous human process that involves hope not only in matters of the heart but in matters of the mind. We are not talking about some glib hope, but rather one that has its feet on the ground and devises concrete strategies. Otherwise, we simply end up, in Metz's words, with "pious gassing."[41] Jürgen Moltmann rightly concludes: "Without planning there can be no realistic hope. Hope without homework is sterile."[42] It is absolutely necessary, therefore, to work through the very difficult process of discovery and knowledge of a structural vision that includes practical proposals and a defined social agenda.

PART III

TOWARD A SPIRITUALITY OF INTEGRAL HUMANITY

14

The Self and the Other

Taoism long ago revealed that Reality is intrinsically dialectical. Polarity is an essential trait of all things. Yin/Yang is the double primordial condition of every manifest being that gives rise to every other polarity such as solitude/solidarity, masculine/feminine, silence/speech, stasis/vitality, and so on. God unmanifest or *narguna* (without properties) is at once God manifest or *sarguna* (with properties). The vision of the void/emptiness/*sunyata* is not the whole story. It is only half of the mystical understanding of Reality, which also blesses, participates in, and embraces the universe, time, history, others—a world filled with both bliss and suffering. Jesus proclaimed: "On earth as it is in heaven." Or as the Buddhists would say: "*Samsara* is like bread soaked in the milk of nirvana. You cannot eat *samsara* without eating nirvana and you cannot eat nirvana without eating *samsara*."[1]

Out of this dialectical Reality, which is immanent in human beings, we issue forth, have primal grounding, and have primal support. One essential human dynamic that emerges from this primordial Reality is the fundamental polarity of solitude and solidarity that is the focus of this study, which seeks to envision an integral humanity. There are other dialectics that could have been chosen or incorporated that are also essential in this quest. One such essential polarity that I am not addressing is the anthropological/cosmological axis or what could be termed the "I-It" relationship. I have chosen not to do so because I believe it would be attempting too much at the expense of adequately concentrating on one essential and fundamental dynamic. The interrelationship of solitude and solidarity can be explored through at least three corresponding dimensions: the self and the self, or the "I-I" relationship; the self and the other, or what Martin Buber calls the "I-Thou" relationship; and the self and community, or what Buber calls the "I-We" relationship. These distinctions will help clarify the increasing complexification of the self's relationship to all reality. We are going to begin first with the "I-I" dynamic.

At first we need to go down into the depths of our being and cling to our own essence and keep as close as possible to our being in our openness to our neighbor, the other, the "thou." As Howard Thurman counseled, "Each soul must learn to stand up in its own right and live." This is so because, as Thomas Berry proclaims: "Every being has its own role to fulfill, its own dignity, its inner spontaneity. Every being has its own . . . life principle, its own mode of self-expression, its own voice. . . . Every being declares itself to the entire universe."[2] However much we exist in relation to others, our identity is an absolute center in itself. "To be a person," teaches Romano Guardini, "means that I cannot be used by any other, but that I am an end in myself; I cannot be represented by any other, but must feel my own place."[3] Therefore, we must realize our autonomous reality, not outside of relationships, but on the other hand, not merely the sum total or the result of those relations. What is characteristic of a person is, therefore, that one lives oneself and decides about oneself. We must become autonomous agents of our lives and take the initiative for ourselves.

This emphasis on the dignity of the self or the "I-I" relationship takes on great significance in seeking solidarity with our brothers and sisters in the Third World. A proper self-regard should not be seen as the exclusive privilege afforded only to the leisure class of the First World. Peoples of the Third World who are oppressed by either totalitarian regimes or capitalist expansionism suffer not only economic poverty but also what has been called anthropological poverty. Human beings can be despoiled not only of those material goods that make life livable, but also of human identity and dignity. The corporate-sponsored media continually inculcates a powerful message to the people of the Two-thirds World: you are pitifully backward and inferior if you do not manage to dress, eat, act, and live like the modern Westerners that you see in movies, on TV, in magazines, or on the Internet. The resulting poor self-image and even self-loathing can be fostered not only by the market's propaganda that the good life entails consuming what they can never hope to obtain, but also by a spurious spirituality that preaches a humility that is not a virtue but rather a pietistic form of accepting subjugation. This negative self-image often leads the poor to turn in upon themselves rather than empowering them to deal with the powers that are oppressing them. The liberation process of the oppressed calls, therefore, for a "veritable resurrection of the self."[4] When Elizabeth Cady Stanton, a feminist in the nineteenth century, was faced with the patriarchal, self-serving rhetoric of self-sacrifice and pressured to stay in her place, she told a reporter to "put it down in capital letters: SELF-DEVELOPMENT IS A HIGHER DUTY THAN SELF-SACRIFICE."[5] We might at this point interject so as not to be misled that there are those who have been systematically deprived of their autonomy and subjectivity but there are also those of us who have been "overstuffed" with it.

Let us now move beyond the "I-I" to the "I-Thou." Although self-empowerment and self-realization are fundamental to human growth, this does not imply that it is possible to see the individual as the only "unit" of salvation and liberation, abstracted from or independent of the rest of the world. If encountering, embracing, and uniting with Reality is the deepest aspiration of spirituality, then any religious quest that goes off on its own, cut off from solidarity with the other, necessarily becomes self-absorbed. It ends up as merely encasing oneself in a religious cocoon of self-absorption. Lao Tzu taught: "A sound person's heart is not shut within itself."[6]

On the one hand, we have the autonomous self, which is our isolated solitariness, uniqueness, our *daimon*, our ontological enrootedness in being, or what the Jewish philosopher Franz Rosenzweig calls our character. But there is a greater destiny for the self. It is called to a higher vocation than autonomy alone. Character is not the only component of selfhood. Although we have our own inner form, we are also necessarily oriented or hard wired to the other. We cannot exist as a separate entity, but we are always an "I" oriented to another who constitutes a "thou." Coexistence is a constitutive aspect of a human person. "The other becomes present," Buber explains, "not merely in the imagination or feeling, but in the depths of one's substance, so that one experiences the mystery of the other being in the mystery of one's own. The two participate in one another's lives in very fact, not psychically, but ontically."[7]

Only when we open ourselves to a "thou," and when this opening is responded to by another, do we become fully realized and does our destiny as human beings fully begin. So we have two dialectical, interpenetrating components of the human person: the autonomous self and the corporate self. Rosenzweig calls this corporate self, or the responsible self of intersubjectivity, the soul. The soul breaks open the autonomous self's natural self-orientation. It draws consciousness beyond its immanent and independent tendencies. It is beyond the autonomous self and has the power to reorient it. It raises the self beyond its autonomy to greater responsibilities than those that revolve around the autonomous self alone. The other "steps before us and challenges us to yield the last thing, so hard fought for, the being at rest with one's own self, to breach the barriers of the self and to come out from ourselves to meet with essential otherness."[8]

If Buber points to the "thou" that engages the "I" in a fundamental dialogue, and if Emmanuel Levinas points to the "face" of the other that calls us forth into responsibility, Rosenzweig points to the power of intersubjectivity or personal love that awakens subjectivity. The self is introjected to a new realization, as a beloved being. The insular existence of the autonomous self is "overturned, pierced" by another's love. As Rosenzweig would have it: "Love, the excessive contact with the other person undergone in love, suffered in love, where one suffers for the other, feels for and with the other .. breaks the character of its isolation."[9] Love has the power to open up the "hard core, this hard nugget," the impenetrable, imperturbable, impermeable self-sufficiency of the autonomous self. The self is overwhelmed by love and henceforth learns the worth of loving others, the neighbor and even beyond the neighbor, the stranger.

Although the autonomous self is "pierced and disturbed" by the encounter with the other, it is not thereby dissipated or absorbed by that encounter. There emerges, in the words of Erich Fromm, a "paradoxical two-in-oneness" in which both separateness and togetherness prevail. In the language of Rosenzweig, the soul (or corporate self) does not allow the character (or *daimon*) to remain isolated in a complete monadic separation from the other, while the character does not allow the self to be devoured by the other or blended into "the mystical indifference of oblivion." Responding responsibly to the other does not relieve us of doing inner work when we are brought back to ourselves in solitude. We need all our inwardness, since it is an integral part of our wholeness as persons. In openness and meeting the other we need to be able to hold our own ground by being faithful to our own uniqueness all the while being faithful to the otherness of the other. We need not only to listen to our own inner voice but also to listen to the other's voice. As Fromm concludes: "To be open is the condition to enable me to become filled with him, to become soaked with him, as it were; but I need to be I, otherwise how could I be open? I need to be myself, i.e., my own authentic unique self."[10]

The Dalai Lama teaches that "loving others does not mean that we should forget about ourselves." Self-love is important because we not only affirm our own individual life but because this inner security points us away from the neediness of an insecure narcissistic ego-centeredness to ever wider expressions of love and responsibility for the other. Marc Gafni explains: "Only from a place of fullness of being can we reach out in love to others. The first step to love is always self-love."[11] Self-love and identity are not static but growth processes whereby we become increasingly aware of our membership in larger categories of life. We are integrated into a larger whole. Self-love also opens up the space for self-sacrifice. Big souls can more and more embrace and sacrifice for the other. "We attain selflessness," explains Maurice Friedman, "not by giving up the self . . . but by the totality of our response. In such totality we are taken out of our [autonomous] selves, called out by something to which we respond so fully and spontaneously that our self is neither our 'aim' nor our concern but only the self-understood and self-evident ground of our responding."[12]

When we seek to enter the deepest spiritual/human life, we discover, Raimon Panikkar points out, that the divine dimension both "shatters our isolation (solipsism) at the same time that it respects our solitude (identity)."[13] "We cannot achieve wholeness," Maurice Friedman insists, "by going inward and leaving the outward secondary and inessential, anymore than we can achieve it by going outward and neglecting the inward. If we have such a split between inner and outer, then our . . . inner, essential self is going to atrophy, and it will not be a real person at all."[14] In Albert Camus's story "The Artist at Work," no one can tell whether the word the dying artist writes on the canvas is *solitary* or *solidary* (at one with society).[15] That is because, in a full life, for the artist as for all of us, it is both. We have to be able to hold the polar tension of both dynamics. As José Comblin combines primal distancing with primal relation:

> The person is an autonomous, isolated, inaccessible, incomprehensible being, who must withdraw in self-affirmation, in an assertion of self-sufficiency, maintaining a sufficient distance from others. In order to be

> a person, one must be one's own person. On the other hand, personhood arises from a cognitive identity, on a visceral level, with other persons. It arises from the contemplation of another person, from love, from physical contact with another.[16]

I am called, therefore, to at once retain my autonomy as I correspondingly foster the existential space of others so they can attain the aim to which they are destined. I remain a "thou" for the other, and the other is a "thou" for me. A person, therefore, means at once to-be-oneself and to-be-in-relationship. The ideal is as simple as this:

> To live like a tree, single and free and
> In brotherliness among the trees of the forest
> That is our dream.
>
> —Nazim Hikmet

15

Autonomy and Community

In the last chapter we looked at the relationship of "I-I" and "I-Thou." We are now going to turn our attention to the "I-We" relationship. In this further dynamic let us continue with what Rosenzweig calls the soul. At this point the soul of the autonomous self allows itself to be grasped and incorporated into increasingly wider and concrete contexts. This deepens the process first experienced in personal love to a life of moral and social demands. The autonomous self is subjected or overwhelmed not only by the beloved other but also by all others. One is not only in the society of two but of three, four . . . the whole human community. Schillebeeckx insists that an intrinsic part of Jesus' ministry not only was found in the midst of the poor but also was aimed at the "transformation of the world to a 'higher humanity.'"[1] The soul directs us to an "alterization" far more complex and far-reaching than its initial impact. Even more is demanded than responsibility for the beloved or the immediate other (that is, ethics); one must aid all humanity (justice). Just as the shift from autonomy to being "pierced" by the other is transformative, so too the shift from two persons to the whole human community is a transformative (sociopolitical) experience.

In seeking to understand this "I-We" relationship, a certain light can be shed by what we have discovered in our exploration of the Buddhist and Judeo-Christian traditions. Every person is primordially oriented to both the mystical transformation of the inner self and to an active participation in the transformation of the world. If Buddhism, which emphasizes the solitary spiritual process, is dominated by a mystical approach of a disengaged gnosis or salvific wisdom, the Judeo-Christian tradition emphasizes the prophetic stance of solidarity with the world that is impelled by a mystical thrust of engaged agape. Out of this dialogue emerge gnosis and agape as two distinct and irreducible instincts arising out of the deepest zones of every person. They are two primordial tropisms converging on a single Reality.

Each pole of the human spirit needs to be allowed its full range of distinctiveness and mature growth all the while realizing it is a dialectical counterpart to the other. One pole, therefore, needs to be complemented and fed by the other in order to express adequately the total human encounter with life. Any valid human spirituality, whether of the East or West, North or South, will necessarily incorporate both poles of the human/religious experience. The receptive, contemplative, solitary, Gnostic pole must be intrinsically wedded to the initiating, active, social, solidarity pole. The ideal of personal transformation necessitates social liberation and vice versa.

On the one hand, Andrew Harvey warns us that any "states of consciousness," however exalted and with whatever distinguished a pedigree, that do not simultaneously radically expose us to the full brutality of the historical situation and lead us to an active response are frivolous. Outside reality there is no salvation. A spirituality that devolves into a type of religious solipsism, devoid of any responsible social concern or praxis, remains not only inadequate and unconvincing but is maimed and can even become dangerous. It can lead (and has led) to scandalous a-moral irresponsibility, which in turn can even end up, in effect, in complicity with evil.

But it is also necessary to understand that energy must be generated before it can be dispersed. If it is true that contemplative gnosis or wisdom can become inhuman without engaged love, it is also true that engaged love without wisdom can be blind and fruitless. It can become merely the blind leading the blind. If the West has acquired an attitude of disdain for gnosis or the mystical and has supplanted wisdom with instrumental knowledge and an obsession with information, the result has been an inability to "revitalize the withered half of its own soul."[2] As the mystic of liberation, Bishop Pedro Casaldaliga, wrote: "Without a profound mysticism, without a new people, the best social reforms and the best revolutions will not get anywhere."[3] We can neither say the person is before the community nor the community is before the person. Rather, persons and communities necessitate, condition, and complement each other. Social transformation, therefore, exists in a dialectical tension with personal transformation. Marx was mistaken to assume that material conditions alone, without attention to inward liberation, were sufficient for human emancipation. When it is posited that it is our genes or early childhood or human instinct or, as with Marx, our social class, that determines what we do, the human will and the responsible self is abrogated. This disastrously diminishes human life and has far-reaching negative consequences. Marx did not foresee that reducing human consciousness to instrumental reason alone could produce a new kind of bondage, for example, the stultifying technocratic consciousness of the "one-dimensional man."[4]

Dietrich Bonhoeffer believed that no one can fruitfully live alone who cannot live in community and no one can maturely live in community who cannot live alone.[5] Autonomy and community are two complementary energy systems destined for coexisting, confronting each other, blending in a dynamic interplay. These are two essential aspects of a synthesis in which human beings can at last actualize all the resources of their complex nature. Therefore, the great challenge is to strengthen subjectivity and communion simultaneously.

Fritjof Capra points out two seemingly opposite yet nevertheless essential aspects of living systems: the self-assertive and the integrative.[6] Every living organism is a self-organizing system that has a self-assertive tendency to create and preserve its individual autonomy. Every living system aims at its own self-creation. The order of its structure is not imposed by its environment but is established by the system itself. Therefore, self-organizing systems exhibit a certain degree of autonomy. This, however, does not imply that living systems are isolated or independent from their environment. On the contrary, living organisms also have an integrative tendency to participate, bond, and function as part of a larger whole. By way of analogy, we can say that through self-assertion we preserve our essential integrity and uniqueness and make our impression on the future, and yet such self-assertion and self-expression will devolve into mere fruitless ego assertion going nowhere without cooperation and integration into the larger community. David Korten offers the human body as perhaps the most vivid example of this intrinsic interplay: "For the body to work, each cell needs to maintain its integrity as an independent being, yet be devoted to the health of the whole. So it's constantly balancing the individual interest with the collective interest."[7]

Capra further explains that the two principal dynamic phenomena of the self-organization of a living system are self-renewal and self-transcendence. Self-renewal is the ability of living systems continuously to renew and recycle their components while maintaining the integrity of their overall structure. As Ken Wilber explains, living systems "do not simply reflect a pregiven world. Rather, according to their capacity, they select, organize, give form to, the multiplicity of stimuli cascading around them. Their responses *never* simply 'correspond' to something 'out there,' they *register* (and thus *respond to*) only that which fits the *coherency* of their *regime*."[8] Self-transcendence, on the other hand, is the ability of this same system to reach out creatively beyond its physical and psychical boundaries in the process of learning, development, and evolution. Using this distinction as a human metaphor, we could conclude that every person is called to preserve and enhance his or her own autonomy all the while transcending that autonomy in the creative, evolving, and transformative encounter with the human community.

Raimon Panikkar reflects: "I understand a person as a knot in a net of relationships. These threads connect us with our fellow man, the earth and divinity. The more conscious the person is the more he realizes that his person reaches out to the confines of the world. That is the realized man."[9] These relationships, however, do not destroy our individual autonomy; rather, "greater complexity leads to greater interiority, which, in turn, leads to more creative unions. . . . The more 'other' they become in conjunction, the more they find themselves as 'self.'"[10] Although our mission is for the other, the other cannot determine what our mission should or will be. We have to "be active in the world as an outcome of our own being."[11] This is what the Hindus call *svadharma* or the choice of a vocation that is in harmony with our own personal nature and that allows us to be faithful to our own being.[12]

"Life consists," Thomas Merton believed, "in learning to live on one's own, spontaneous, freewheeling: to do this one must recognize what is one's own—

be familiar and at home with oneself . . . learning who one is and learning what one has to offer to the contemporary world and then learning how to make it valid."[13] Precisely how we engage ourselves in community must not be primarily determined by utilitarian or ideological concerns. Our first responsibility is to do what we are called to do, are able to do, what we can best do. And this determination is not the domain of some outside, objective, impersonal decision of some collective body but what our deepest soul insists on. In fact, action determined solely by circumstances or social needs can be a temptation to be unfaithful to our unique mission in the world. It can absolve us of all inner work. When Gil Baille was seeking advice from Howard Thurman about what needed to be done in the world, Thurman responded: "Don't ask yourself what the world needs. Ask yourself what makes you come alive, and go do that, because what the world needs is people who have come alive."[14] Or, as Frederick Buechner defined vocation: "Neither the hair shirt nor the soft berth will do. The place God calls you to is the place where your deep gladness and the world's deep hunger meet."[15]

Thomas Merton also made the observation that "before we can become prophetic, we have to become authentic human beings."[16] Or, as Thich Nhat Hahn once warned: "To work for peace, you must have a peaceful heart. . . . But many who work for peace are not at peace. They still have anger and frustration and their work is not really peaceful."[17] If we fail to do intensive inner work of both a psychological and a spiritual nature, we can deceive ourselves into thinking that our pursuit of peace and justice is motivated by a sense of fairness when all the while we might in fact be motivated by, for example, anger or some unresolved conflicts in our personal lives. As one social activist admitted, "I was disillusioned to discover the extent to which my behavior is often motivated by the need for recognition and not just pure humanitarian ideals." Franciscan friar Richard Rohr, who has spent years ministering with social activists, had to conclude sadly that our culture and frankly much of peace and justice work is "dominated by very fragile egos, superficial intellectual and emotional lives, knee-jerk reactions that are often politically correct but nowhere close to the Gospel."[18]

As the social activist Jeff Dietrich admits: "I recognize that I am compulsively drawn to combative situations with authority figures; that I seek public adulation by positioning myself as the 'Heroic Underdog-Advocate for the Poor.' The David and Goliath story is a perennial favorite and I know how to exploit it."[19] Jim Wallis, the evangelical Christian leader, once noted that there are very serious problems found among social justice activists, such as hidden aggression, manipulation, an assertive ego, a divisive spirit, a desire for provocation that can work beneath the surface of moral platitudes or ideology.[20] Moral rhetoric can be used to hide the will to power. A desire to win over others, to defeat the enemy, or to humiliate the opposition flies in the face of the gospel they purport to be following. This is why June Singer concludes:

> The person who will be most effective in his strivings toward social justice is the one who is most critical of himself, who takes care to differentiate his own flaws and to take responsibility for them before he goes out to correct his neighbor's. He will make his impact more effective by setting an example, than by bludgeoning his opponent into submission.[21]

If we merely plunge into the world with a whirlwind of activities and projects, trying to save it and reconstruct it without ever deepening our self-awareness, compassion, or wisdom, we might very well end up doing nothing of enduring value or even doing more harm than good. We might, for example, prove quite articulate in our ruthless examination of the social conditions but be curiously mute when it comes to a ruthless self-examination. "Liberation theology cannot be a theology concerned solely about liberation from oppressive sociopolitical structures," counsels Felix Wilfred. "Such a project will not yield fruit, will not move in the direction of greater humanization, unless it is accompanied simultaneously by a process of personal conversion, liberation, and transformation of the subject."[22]

Howard Thurman taught a "mystical activism" in which periods of withdrawal are not just a preference of a particular type of personality but necessary for making worthwhile contributions to social reconstruction. He called for "lulls in the rhythm of doing" because reflection and self-examination can only be done in solitude. Withdrawal is not necessarily an escape from social responsibility but a necessary preparation to address social arrangements significantly. There is always a danger that without profound reflection we might not focus on the real problems, let alone the real questions, let alone the real answers.

Ken Wilber makes an important point when he insists that these two corresponding tendencies of a person both to secure one's own autonomy and to be in communion with larger realities are absolutely crucial and equally important; an excess of either will stunt human potential. Even a moderate imbalance can lead to personal deformity or pathology.

> Too much individuality leads to a severing (repression and alienation) of the rich networks of communion that sustain individuality in the first place; and too much communion leads to a loss of individual integrity, leads to fusion with others, to indissociation, to a blurring of boundaries and a meltdown and loss of autonomy.[23]

Although human beings need to participate for their nurture and growth in a communion with larger and more comprehensive realities than themselves, they must first realize that "before communion can begin, entities have to be differentiated in the first place."[24] A similar conclusion is reached by Maurice Friedman, who maintains that

We must distinguish between holding our ground and rigidity, even as we must distinguish between going out to meet the other and dissolving the boundaries, between person and person in a symbiotic clinging, or what the Gestalt therapists call "confluence." To live means to venture, but it does not mean to give up one's ground in doing so.[25]

16

Being and Becoming

At this point I would like to introduce the primordial philosophical dynamic of being and becoming. I have touched on this dynamic to some extent elsewhere, but I would like to explore it now in a little more depth because I believe it has such a profound effect on perceiving an integral vision of life. I actually could have begun this study by introducing this essential dynamic of existence as a prelude to the solitude/solidarity dialectic, but I prefer to introduce it now because I think at this point we can better understand how this dynamic affects the understanding of the solitude/solidarity dynamic. If you examine any spiritual vision that is proffered today, you could ask the question: does this vision unite the dynamics of being and becoming or does it prioritize one side of the polarity while relegating to a secondary position, ignoring, or trivializing the other side? In other words, is the spiritual vision all being and no becoming or vice versa? An emphasis on being, for example, tends to prioritize the present over the past and the future, the a-historical over the historical. If the emphasis is on becoming, the priority will be the future and the historical dimension of human existence. If the solitude dynamic tends to emphasize being/the eternal present/the Now/contemplation/ the a-historical, the solidarity dynamic emphasizes becoming/hope/the future/ engagement/the historical.

Being

First, let us look at the "being" pole of this dynamic. Certain philosophies, spiritualities, perspectives, and lifestyles prioritize being over becoming. Classical science beginning with the ancient Greeks up until the twentieth century presented a static view of the world in which all changes in physical phenomena were regarded as mere illusions. What we had was a static, timeless understanding of the universe where deterministic laws of physics were the only acceptable laws. Philosophers such as Plato, Aristotle, and Plotinus pointed to this same prioritization. These philosophers tended to depreciate becoming and exalt mere being, to depreciate relativity and exalt the independence and absoluteness of the Good or the One. Aristotle summed up this tendency when he taught that what was immutable and unchangeable was infinitely superior to that which was changeable or capable of being influenced or affected by any other being (the impassibility of God).

For these philosophers the highest goal for human beings was contemplation of the eternal and immutable "One," which transcends the "many." These philosophers had great influence on Christian spirituality, which almost unanimously counseled the spiritual aspirant to rise above the transitory "many things," to move upward, vertically, toward the contemplation of the transcendent realm beyond matter and time, the spiritual and eternal sphere. This created a spirituality that became the "house of the transcendent," which in turn became the stable and fixed amid the flux of time and history. This spirituality resulted in a consciousness that was basically a-historical.

Buddhism, in a wholly different way, is found on this side of the being/becoming polarity and hence is a-historical. In the Buddhist approach human life is not viewed as moving from life to death in any temporal or historical sequence but rather is seen as enveloped in the unchanging process of living-dying. There is neither creation nor some final human or historic fulfillment in time but rather endless *samsara* (flux) or transiency, in the midst of which nirvana (total realization) can be realized.

For the Buddhist, the process of time is totally concentrated in each moment. Each "now" is the "Eternal Now," the absolute present. But the unawakened are not aware of this basic reality. The Now, however, can become a place of action specifically when those who are awake help emancipate the spiritual sleepers from their slumber or from their karmic transmigration in *samsara*. The important point, however, is that the unawakened are not emancipated to any sort of future historical responsibility in building what the Judeo-Christian tradition calls the kingdom, but rather are awakened to a completely realized time in the here and now. The unawakened are released from their karmic dross of the past and the uncertainty and anxiety over the illusionary future. In the light of the Buddhist approach, we could ask two important questions: "If Buddhism knows the pure simultaneity of time, or a time that is present, past, and future at once, does this preclude the possibility of a truly new or future time? Does such a simultaneity of time foreclose the possibility of a truly forward historical movement, and foreclose it by its envisionment of a time that is forward and backward at once?"[1]

We could at this point note that certain present-day spiritualities adopt this very perception. Eckhart Tolle, for example, in *The Power of Now*, asks:

> Why is the (now) . . . the most precious thing? Firstly, because it is the *only* thing. It's all there is. The eternal present is the space within which your whole life unfolds, the one factor that remains constant. Life is now. There was never a time when your life was *not* now, nor will there ever be. Secondly, the Now is the only point that can take you beyond the limited confines of the mind. It is your only point of access into the timeless and formless realm of *Being*. (italics added)[2]

Genpo Roshi further explains this state: "In this state of mind, there isn't anything to take care of. There isn't anything to do. There are no problems. . . . There is no self."[3]

Another fundamental perspective that would prioritize being over becoming, the transcendent over the historical, the absolute over the transient, is that of Protestant theologian Karl Barth. I investigate Barth because of his immense influence on Christian theological thinking in the past century and because he still represents the tendency in many Christian spiritualities to posit an a-historical, transcendent spirituality. For Barth, human history is not the bearer of anything positive but rather its "gift" is despair, frustration, and the destruction of humankind. Fulfillment does not come from any historical initiative on humanity's part but from beyond history, from the totally transcendent God. There was, for Barth, an "infinite qualitative difference" between God and the human, eternity and time. Transcendence does not penetrate into history but rather stands over against it. The cross represents what humanity does on its own. *Homo creator* always ends up as a "Titan."

But the cross is not the last word. The resurrection of Jesus Christ is the impossible possibility—impossible because the possibilities of human history were exhausted on the cross. God creates in history and in the Godly person a "horror of history." Human beings' transcendent possibilities come only from God as a gift of grace. Therefore, "the Christian must not allow himself to be distracted by changes in the political order or by the relative struggles for power in history from the primary task of proclaiming the resurrection of man and God in Christ."[4] Hence, Easter time is the time par excellence: "It is time without any future . . . an eternal presence of God in time [nirvana in *samsara*]. As such it cannot become past, neither needs any future, a time purely present."[5] "The epiphany of the eternally present" liberates one from the transitoriness of history and integrates one into the truth of that which is. Here we have a clear statement on the prioritization of Being/the Now/timelessness/futurelessness/the a-historical.

Becoming

If the Eternal Now is the hallmark of the being polarity, the future is the hallmark of the becoming polarity. If the being polarity invites us to contemplative lingering, in the becoming polarity there is an urge and yearning for a time "to come." Becoming suggests process, transition, incompleteness, act and potency, fact and possibility.[6] Eternity cannot equal timelessness. John Macquarrie asks: "What need is there for a historical incarnation if the ebb and flow of history go on forever, while the unseen reality remains unchanged and unaffected?"[7] Rather, the becoming polarity points to, in Heidegger's words, a "primordial temporality."

Probably the most representative thinker who expresses the becoming polarity of existence is process philosopher Alfred North Whitehead. For Whitehead, God has a primordial and consequent nature. God's primordial nature is the ground of actuality (a primordial envisagement of pure possibilities) but God's consequent nature is ever self-creating and incarnating into creation. For Whitehead, creative becoming is the universal category, and he sums up his whole philosophy by claiming that creativity is the "category of the ultimate," the "universal of universals." This new perspective sees the divine Reality as living, active, constantly creative, infinitely related, ceaselessly operative. As Raimon Panikkar writes: "Being explodes itself into being . . . into something that goes its own way. . . . What is most important is the process, the dance, the whole thing expanding. . . . Being is just . . . explosion!"[8]

Whitehead's philosophy is in harmony with the more dynamic view of the new science, which emphasizes the becoming, evolutionary, unrepeatable, open-to-surprise nature of reality over the traditional static view. In Thomas Berry's words, we are now beginning to understand that "we live not so much in a *cosmos* but in a *cosmogenesis*, a universe ever coming into being."[9] Whitehead's perspective, according to Norman Pittenger, sees God as ever "incarnating himself in his creation, which means he is ever entering it—not as if he were absent from it or intervenes now and again in it, but in the deeper sense that he who is unexhausted in himself, ever energizes in nature and in history, and above all in the lives of man, expressing himself more fully, until the whole created order becomes, in some sense, 'the body of God.'"[10] This means that "all phenomena—all things and events, people, animals, minerals, plants—all are manifestations of the superabundance and plenitude of the Spirit, so that Spirit is woven intrinsically into each and all, and thus even the entire material and natural world was, as Plato put it, 'a visible, sensible God.'"[11]

And further, within all creation God "is there as the omnipresent lure, the omnipresent aim, the omnipresent agency for affecting love in the world."[12] Or, as Raimon Panikkar says, "The divine reality is not there to 'swallow up' beings. It is there to '*potentiate*' them from within."[13] What this implies is that there is something in each living organism, in every human being, an aim, an attraction, a telos, a purposeful aspect, a historical responsibility, a miniature omega point, whereby the person is headed in the direction of a realized fullness not only for self but for all others. God, in a sense, calls humanity forward to actualize unrealized opportunities, opening for humanity a space of freedom and self-creativity. That is why Whitehead believed that "the pure conservative is fighting against the essence of the universe."[14] Therefore, humankind's historical project is a response to the divine initiative. We can see in the historical process certain moments of fullness, an evolutionary development, in response to the agency of a divine attraction. Certain historical events involve the actualization of totally new possibilities. Whitehead once wrote that Christianity, unlike Buddhism, is a faith based on certain historical events seen as crucial in disclosing "what God is up to." For the Christian community, one such disclosure was the historical appearance of Jesus of Nazareth.

Out of Whitehead's process philosophy emerged what has been called process theology. In this theology God is no longer thought of as utterly unchangeable and empty of all temporal distinctions. Rather, God is understood (in God's consequent nature) as being continually in the process of self-creation. God who is infinitely self-sufficient continually surpasses God-Self in expression and activity because there is a plenitude of possibility as yet unrealized. Therefore, there is a certain incompleteness in all things. As Emmanuel Levinas states concerning the phenomenon of love: "Incompleteness is the law of love: it is the future itself, the coming of the world that never ceases coming, but also the excellence of that coming compared to presence as persistence in being and in what has always been."[15] Indeed, all creation becomes the arena of the divine activity, divine self-creation, and divine incarnation in creation. Every time there is a "creative transformation," whether among molecules, human beings and their consciousness, or societies, God, in differing degrees, has taken flesh.[16]

Therefore, whatever happens in the world as a result of God's lure, the agency of God's aim, the impetus of God's love, contributes to God's satisfaction, enriches God's possibilities in further self-expression, and provides new opportunities to manifest divine loving care. If God is supreme self-creativity in creation, humans participate in this reality. Human beings are not simply *in* the world, but they come into being *with* the world. There is a "metabolism" that goes on between them and the world. This metabolism in the deepest way goes on with the divine Reality, which is self-creating in the world, and therefore human beings can be understood as self-created creatures and the makers of themselves through their own decisions. In this way the human person in a real sense is a creator of something in God.

Human beings are part of a changing, moving, living, active world in which they are no longer dealing with inert substances but with dynamic processes. To use the words of Johann Baptist Metz: "The world appears on this horizon not as a fixed and sacrosanct reality in a pre-established harmony, but as an *arising* reality, which can be innovated toward its future through the historically free actions of men."[17] The force of becoming prevents the present from closing in on us, from closing us up. The force of becoming "rises up from present to provocation, ascending from being at present to the promise that insinuates itself into being and makes being restless."[18] Human beings, therefore, in their own historical decisions and finite processes of creative becoming create certain historical realities that somehow take on permanent significance because human acts can in a real way participate in the creative becoming of God. Thomas Berry teaches us that "history is governed by those overarching movements that give shape and meaning to life by relating the human adventure to the larger destinies of the universe."[19] These human decisions, these historical choices, these overarching movements are fundamental to human life. Human consciousness has now become historical.

Synthesis

In order to attempt to hold these two polarities together in a fruitful synthesis, I suggest a few preliminary proposals. First, I believe that both the dynamics of being present to the Now and being involved in the historical project of humanity are essential in envisioning an integral humanity. One way of having a synthetic vision that incorporates both dynamics is to understand that there is no such thing as a totally realized fullness of Reality that we have seen posited in various perspectives. Since Reality is both being and becoming, at any given moment of the Now, there are infinite potentials yet to be realized. There is within the Now the lure of God to move in history in increasingly creative and fruitful ways. There is both a kind of stasis as well as a dynamic activity in any given Now. We could posit here a *relative fullness* whereby the contemplative moment of being totally present to what is at hand is at the heart of an integral humanity. But there is also a caution. Because if there are potentials to reality that are awaiting our historical and responsible response, then at any given moment we are called to be both totally present and also listening ahead and awaiting the call of the future, which places an urgent demand upon us at this moment.

Second, in response to those theologies represented by Karl Barth that make an infinite divide between the divine and the human and for whom there is no becoming, I believe Karl Rahner's thought on the *supernatural existential* is very helpful here. On the one hand, theologians like Karl Barth proclaim that any historical advance of humanity is the total work of God by grace; on the other hand, political humanists such as Marx insist that creating a future for humanity is an achievement totally in the hands of humanity. Liberation comes from humanity alone.

Karl Rahner taught that grace, offered to all, is not given as an extrinsic addition to human nature. We do not receive grace as we put on a new coat. Rather, grace infuses and becomes part of human nature, part of the psychological structures of human consciousness. We are born with a "supernatural horizon." A "fundamental act of transcendence constitutes the essence of man."[20] Therefore, there is no such thing as a God above or over against "mere or only nature." Our very existence is more than just human nature. It is by its very nature also divine. Therefore, we could say that the responsibility for constructing an increasingly human future is in the hands of both God and humanity. God is infusing us with the divine lure and divine aim, and we are constructing reality with God. Humanity possesses within itself the impetus and vision for a new future because the lure and aim of God is at work in the very nature of the human person. This would bring together in a sense both Karl Barth and Karl Marx, but in a totally unique way through Karl Rahner. The future of humanity is in the hands of both the Divine and the human. Whereas Marx equated humanity's highest capacity as instrumental reason, this new vision understands that humanity also has a divine dimension. And whereas Barth saw humanity as cut off from the Divine, this new vision sees the Divine as part of humanity's very nature.

Last, I would like to point to the polarity in Jesus' teaching between the kingdom that is in our midst ("the kingdom is in your midst,") and the prayer of Jesus for the kingdom to come ("thy kingdom come"). If the kingdom is in our midst then it must not be so fully, otherwise how can the kingdom come (in the future)? For Jesus, as the whole Hebrew tradition, there is a belief in the reality of time. Maurice Friedman explains:

> The response of Biblical man has not taken the form of cyclical order of time or an unchanging absolute, like the Greek, nor of the dismissal of time and change as *maya*, or illusion, like the Hindu, nor of the notion that one may flow with time, like the Taoist. He stands face to face with the changing creation and receives each new moment as an address of God—the revelation that comes to him through the unique present.[21]

Therefore, if the Buddhist emphasis is on the emptiness/the Divine unmanifest/being here now/contemplative side of the polarity, the Judeo-Christian tradition emphasizes the Divine manifest/form/becoming/creativity/time/history. The great challenge is to construct praxes that holds these polarities—being present to the Now and alert to our historical responsibilities—in a dynamic union.

17

Serenity and Struggle

Within the solitude/solidarity dialectic, there is a subtext of serenity/struggle. We find in the Gospels that Jesus says two contrasting things: "Peace be with you" (Jn 20:19b) and "Do not suppose that my mission on earth is to spread peace. My mission is to spread not peace, but division" (Mt 10:34). In the book of Job we find a profound mixture of trust and contending. Although Job ultimately places his trust in God, he stands his ground: "He may slay me, I await it. But I will argue my ways before him" (Jb 13:15). The East emphasizes serenity and considers the attainment of inner peace or tranquility the fundamental sign of spiritual maturity. Esteem for others is primarily based not on what they say, or what they own, or what they have accomplished, but rather on the quality and degree of their inner serenity and composure. "Flying off the handle" might be excused because of youth, but it is a deep disgrace if one is an adult. This is quite different, however, than the "quiet life" that comes about when we secure a lifestyle no longer bothered by anyone or anything or any challenge to our comfortable stasis. Nor are we talking of developing a "thick skin" so as not to become a "bleeding heart." We are even less pointing to the natural indifference of a phlegmatic personality. The body, soul, and mind do not become imbued with tranquility from an acquired idleness but through inner work of the most difficult kind. It involves the slow process of moving from living life from the periphery to living life from our center, where we uncover a profound, primordial inner stillness. The ego and monkey mind can no longer be given free reign. Rather, a frame of mind gradually emerges that is rooted in our deepest core, where we are freed from the constant turbulence that the ego-mind can evoke.

Seeking a serene state of soul first of all involves "learning to see" or "accustoming the eyes to calmness, to patience, to letting things come up to it, postponing judgment, learning to go around and grasp each individual thing from all sides."[1] This is the first preliminary schooling for spirituality. This kind of discipline is practiced not only during periods of sitting meditation but "every single act must be permeated by the composure it produces."[2] Every act of daily life is made the subject of praxis. As soon as we find ourselves getting upset, disturbed, or annoyed by something, the Dalai Lama counsels, Stop! Before saying a word, before instant reaction, take a breath, then two.

You must struggle back to inner composure. Let the best part of you look at the situation and decide if any word or act is necessary or is just useless venting. Chogyam Trungpa counsels:

> You must not make an impulsive move into any situation. Let the situation come, then look at it, chew it properly, digest it, and sit on it. The sudden move is unhealthy, impulsive and frivolous rather than spontaneous. Whenever there is an impulse to do something you should not just do it; you should work with the impulse. Frivolousness means reacting according to reflex.[3]

Finally, at the deepest level, serenity comes from a fundamental cosmic trust that the universe is basically friendly. There is this primordial confidence that all is well, that everything in the universe is working for our good, that all life is perfect and luminous and infinitely generous just as it is. As Joseph Campbell explains this vision, at least from an Eastern perspective, the world is "great just the way it is. And you are not going to fix it up. Nobody has ever made it better. It is never going to be any better. This is it, take it or leave it. You are not going to correct or improve it. . . . You've got to say yes to life and see it as magnificent this way; for this is surely the way God intended it. . . . It is joyful just as it is."[4]

But since every value is in a dialectical relationship to a contrasting one, this serenity must hold itself together with an inner tension or struggle. The praxis of tranquility is not self-complacency or an attempt to eliminate from our life all pain and suffering, but is at once called forth and challenged by realities that cannot be "swallowed up into one's soul." Such an attempt would manage to produce only a kind of "flaccid peace" totally lacking in any creative tension with life. Albert Camus makes a relevant point in his notebooks: "Peace would be loving in silence. But there is conscience and the person; you have to speak. To love becomes hell."[5] Heraclitus's dictum was "harmony is contrarity." Radical trust goes hand in hand with radical struggle. There is an intrinsic agonistic quality to all reality. That is why José Comblin insists: "True human beings will be found in a state not of truce, but of combat. The human condition is delineated by struggle. From birth to death we are caught up in struggle and this is what constitutes the substance of human dignity. A person who does not struggle can have no dignity."[6] But we must not confuse this striving and struggle with discord and dispute or see it as disorder and destruction. In essential struggle the opponents raise each other not only into the self-assertion of their natures but also beyond themselves into a new, more complex, more variegated unity.[7] Authentic inner peace, therefore, never attains a state of "having arrived" but is always in a state of becoming. "Do not escape from struggle," counsels Kenji Myazawa. "Go straight into it. . . . Burn all struggle as your fuel."[8] As Meister Eckhart reminds us: "The wood does not surrender to the fire without a struggle. . . . The soul must be in labor to give birth to the son."[9] Life continually offers us challenges to surpass ourselves and thus a new tension arises. We can either attempt to kill or to respond to these challenges. When peace of mind at all costs silences all struggle, it is a clear sign of backsliding and stagnation. But if we accept life's challenges, we will be brought to an ever-deepening, authentic, life-giving peace. In a vital, integrated life there is an ongoing struggle between the given present reality and that which yearns to be created; there is a never-ending conflict between the existent and the not-yet-existent. As Whitehead insisted: "If there is to be progress beyond limited ideals, the course of history . . . must venture along the borders of chaos in its substitution of higher for lower types of order."[10] In the end, we have to be able to reconcile the lightning and the rainbow.

In the Judeo-Christian scheme of things, however, there is a hierarchy of human challenges. Not all challenges to our stasis have the same ontological weight. The biblical God is not only the infinite source of transcendent peace but also of unending passion and pathos. Or, as Rumi described the Godhead, "infinite passion arising out of infinite peace." And this pathos manifests itself in a very concrete and prioritized form, that is, a promised involvement in humanity's misery and enslavement. If Huston Smith could say, "I am a Buddhist, in the sense of the Buddha's opening gambit: 'How are things going?' If the answer is 'Quite well,' he said, 'I am very happy, I have nothing to say to you,'"[11] the Judeo-Christian response would be: "That's all well and good but how is your neighbor, and what is the condition of the world?" We have, therefore, not only an ontology of Being or Being beyond Being but also a "being-as-involvement" or "being-as-compassion."

But as Albert Nolan has noted,[12] *compassion* has become a rather weak word that doesn't convey what the Greek word *(splagchnizomai)*[13] really implies. English translations of the Greek verb for compassion use such expressions as "he felt sorry for" or "his heart went out to them." Yet none of these rather bland attempts convey the gut-wrenching reaction, the movement or impulse that wells up from one's depths that the Greek word demands. Out of the depths of an infinite divine peace roars a wail over human injustices like that of a mother over the death of her child. In the Hebrew scriptures Moses was the symbol of a person attuned to the voice of God. And this attunement led Moses to be radically disturbed over the servitude and suffering of his oppressed people in Egypt. His whole being rebelled against the unjust treatment meted out to the Israelites in an alien land. It was this unquiet heart/mind of Moses that the Hebrew tradition presents as the most appropriate receptacle for the self-manifestation of God.

If the divine Mystery is called Love, then we have to see in the dynamics of love the very heart of our relationship to the real. Love can be understood as an abiding, contemplative dalliance in the presence of the beloved. Much of Christian mysticism is an experience of this profound peace and ecstatic savor of the divine Presence. But there is a corresponding experience of love. As Daniel Day Williams explains: "Love does not put everything at rest; it puts everything in motion. Love does not end all risk; it accepts every risk which is necessary for its work. Love does not resolve every conflict; it accepts conflict as the arena in which the work of love is to be done."[14]

Our personality might tend to share the desire of those mystics and idealists who wish to secure a serene and tensionless existence. But if we are so hidebound to achieve this that we flee any social responsibility, we might find our lives merely dozing off into some kind of stupefying bliss or vapidity. But if we are naturally led to social engagement, there might be so much harping and obsessing on responsibility, social justice, the historical moment, programs for progress, and so on, that we lose any inner focus and cut ourselves off from any meaningful circumspection. And in the process we are in danger of shaving off whole parts of human life such as beauty, art, leisure, wonder, intellectual life—possibly the best part of what it means to be alive. As the New York anarchist Emma Goldman once commented: "If I can't dance, I don't want to be in your revolution." Reuben Alvez, a liberation theologian, reminds the most active activist that there is something beyond all our work and toil, and it is found in the garden: "In the garden his life work is finished. In the garden he finds pleasure. He rests from work. He becomes pure contemplation, pure play, pure enjoyment. Nothing else is to be done. No ethics, no commandment, no politics: there is a fruit to be eaten."[15] Whitehead once wrote, "God's purpose in the creative advance is the evocation of intensities."[16] Our human nature calls us to embrace the whole panorama of life, all the intensities of life: both the surge of power and will and the tranquility of contemplation; both ecstatic bliss as well as profound grief and pain; both the serenity of Buddha and the anguish of Jesus on the cross. In the end, every peace is disturbed and every disturbance is brought peace. "Peace I bring to you but not as the world brings peace" (Jn 14:27).

18

The Spirituality of Subtraction

Perhaps one of the most fundamental praxes, that address the vital concerns of solitude and solidarity, wedding the two together in the most intimate of bonds, is the praxis of voluntary poverty, or what Richard Rohr refers to more broadly as "the spirituality of subtraction."[1] If Buddhism emphasizes the relief of personal suffering by seeking a Gnostic detachment from material goods, the Judeo-Christian tradition emphasizes relieving the suffering of others often caused by those individuals and social classes that hoard material goods. Voluntary poverty stands at the crossroads between the primarily inner ascesis of Buddhism and the primarily other-oriented ascesis of Judeo-Christianity. Voluntary poverty, which embraces both an inner transformation as well as a radical alteration of one's lifestyle, has both personal as well as social consequences of great magnitude. Maybe there are few other praxes that could enable both East and West, both solitary and solidarity aspects of human transformation, to converge, join forces, become personal, local, and global at the same time and to create a new day for humanity and indeed the whole creation.

The two sins that the Hebrew people considered most grievous were unfaithfulness to their covenant with God through idolatry and failure to seek social justice for their neighbor. Idolatry and injustice are intrinsically linked because they believed that it was primarily through greed that one is led to idolatry. The biblical God demands justice for the oppressed and poor. Nowhere do we find that the rich are raised up, favored, praised, or accorded special honor except when they are engaged in the act of helping the needy. The great Mosaic vision was "he that gathers much had nothing over and he that gathers little had no lack; each gathered according to what he could eat" (Ex 16:18). In the Synoptics, Jesus talks more about the question of wealth and poverty than any other single topic. In one out of every ten verses (one out of seven in the Gospel of Luke), Jesus addresses this issue. One could not possibly surmise that his concern, indeed preoccupation, over the dangers of affluence was occasional, casual, or tangential. Although a case could be made that Jesus appeared somewhat ambiguous about other complex questions, in this case Jesus is direct, loud and clear. If Jesus saw this problem as so central in an agrarian society where money was not a national mania, how much more central is this question in our money culture? Jesus knew that money and possessions form one of the most central dynamics of human experience and reveal more about an individual's soul than almost any other single aspect of human life. This is a deeply spiritual issue that closely affects the core of a person. That is why Jesus, as Karl Barth sums up in *The Call of Discipleship*, calls for five "breaks" if we are to follow him in discipleship: possessions, reputation, violence, family, and religion.

Robert Bellah observed that the menace of Soviet totalitarianism has been replaced today by "market totalitarianism," in which life is reduced more and more to its market value as a commodity. Whereas *wealth* originally meant well-being, it has been degraded and reduced to simply the possession of money. Quality of life now is equated with our standard of living. The ideal becomes, according to Thomas Berry,

> to take the greatest possible amount of natural resources, process these resources, put them through the consumer economy as quickly as possible, then on to the waste heap. This we consider progress—even though the immense accumulation of junk is overwhelming the landscape, saturating the skies, and filling the oceans.[2]

Since the name of the game has become profits and increased conspicuous consumption, many of our most talented citizens are conscripted to search into every corner of the human psyche to find the most effective ways to stir up and cultivate among consumers the desire for some bankable product. And, of course, advertisers have been enormously successful in convincing us that if we only enter more completely into increased patterns of consumption, we will attain a certain blessed contentment. So we have ended up with an economy that is not only based on the satisfaction of desires but, more important, on the creation of desires. All this has produced a people who have more clothes than they can wear, more food than they can or should eat, while over one billion of our brothers and sister in the world live in destitution.

According to Thomas Merton, the idolatrous are those who give "metaphysical significance to that which is hollow." Since consumption has assumed such an inordinate place in our lives as North Americans, we are guilty of idolatry. We have embraced money as our most central reality, our source of meaning, the object of our veneration. What used to be done for the sake of God is now done for the sake of money. Market affluence, privilege, and security have been raised to a sacral level. Ever increased consumption continues to be fueled by a personal, almost godlike force, which rules us as an active agent, becoming a rival to God. As Ambrose Bierce wrote almost one hundred years ago in *The Devil's Dictionary*, the word formerly spelled G-o-d has had an *L* added to it and it is now spelled G-o-l-d.

It would be a mistake, however, to conclude that we are a materialistic people as opposed to a spiritual people. More accurately, we are neither materialistic nor spiritual but consumptive. We have been engineered into a lifestyle that equates satisfaction with *throughput* (the rate and quantity of things used up).

There is no stopping to relish and enjoy things but rather a rush to collect more and more of them. The dictums of this throughput are these: Thou shall not pay attention. Thou shall not linger. Thou shall not enjoy. Thou shall keep moving. What has become "normal" as a way of life has been characterized by Ellen Goodman as "getting dressed in clothes that you buy for work, driving through traffic in a car that you are still paying for, in order to get to the job that you need so you can pay for the clothes, car and house that you leave empty all day long in order to afford to live in it."[3] Once you get to the office the pace is dizzying and the hours are mind numbing. You work long hours into the evening because if you leave at five o'clock the boss will notice and your co-workers will ridicule you. Corporations hire the best and the brightest from the universities and offer them a deal as they are treated to an open bar overlooking the city skyline. All this world of corporate luxury, ritzy hotel, first class on jets, and all the rest can be yours if you sign on with us. We will pay you big bucks if you are prepared to work seventy, eighty, ninety hours a week through the best years of your life. Leave your bed at home and bring your sleeping bag to the office. And these conditions are agreed upon because you accept financial rewards as a substitute for inner harmony and achievement as a substitute for completeness. You learn to set aside all other human goods, such as family life, friendships, leisure, ministry, in pursuit of the trophy home existence. If this has become the blessed life, then why are the three most frequently prescribed drugs in the United States an ulcer medication, a hypertension reliever, and a tranquilizer? And why has stress management become one of the nation's fastest-growing industries? A director of behavioral medicine at the University of Louisville has observed: "Our mode of life itself, the way we live, is emerging as today's principal cause of illness."

Plato reflected the belief of most great religious and philosophical teachers when he stated: "The greatest wealth is to live content with little." Or as the Tao Te Ching taught: "He who knows he has enough is rich." It was Aristotle's contention that for each successive increment of income, you get less and less value, and that beyond a certain point, the attachment to money destroys you. Or as the psychologist Jonathan Freeman concluded after surveying people's subjective mood of well-being: "Once some minimal income is attained, the amount of money you have matters little in terms of bringing happiness. Above the poverty level, the relationship between income and happiness is remarkably small."[4] The proper role of money is to provide a foundation upon which we can build a good life. But we will never find the good life within the economic realm alone. The purpose of enough money is to get us to the point where we can turn away from it, so that we can seek what really does bring about the good life. When the Earth Summit was held in Rio de Janeiro in 1992 it made the point that "beyond meeting basic physical needs, the quality of human life depends more on the development of social relationships, creativity and artistic expression, spirituality, and the opportunity to be a productive member of the community than on the ever increasing consumption of material goods."[5] We need, therefore, to learn to distinguish between the necessary and the superfluous, the useful and the wasteful, the beautiful and the vulgar, the cultured and the banal.

Jacob Needleman noted that in other times and places not everyone wanted money more than anything else.[6] The good life has also embraced such values as love, romance, leisure, friendship, conversation, contemplation, creativity, sport, and more. If we have more than enough, yet hunger for still more, we will not find any remedy in more money because our problem is not that we lack anything, but that we've acquired a tapeworm in our mind called insatiability. John D. Rockefeller Sr., when asked, "How much money does it take to make a person happy?" is said to have responded, "Just a little bit more." Money addiction goes way beyond the vital function it can perform and grows inside the personality like a cancer cell to such an extent that all the faculties of the personality become devoted to its service. Bit by bit it corrupts every faculty we have. It twists our priorities and distorts our view of reality. In the end we forsake any authentic path to human fulfillment. We find ourselves slipping ever deeper into the emptiness from which the advertisers promise their products will rescue us.

Our lifestyles radically affect not only us but also our brothers and sisters in the world. Our insatiability has not only corrupted our inner psychic and spiritual center but, as John Woolman, the famous Quaker, maintained, it is the "underlying force that gives rise to oppression and injustice." Our economic life and standard of living are not purely private matters but have enormous worldwide consequences. In America there have always been two dreams; one dream is of riches, and the other is of simple living. Ronald Reagan characterized the first dream when he said, "What I want to see above all is that this country remains a country where someone can always get rich." On the other hand, in the political vision of both Jefferson and Adams, sometimes called Republican simplicity, there was a serious concern that the pursuit of money would corrupt the virtues needed for democracy. There would develop a lack of concern for public well-being if all individuals were merely scurrying about pursuing their economic interests. If the pursuit of money fuels the capitalist economy, a life of simplicity would challenge it and foster and nurture a more human and creation-centered society.

19

The Spirituality of Universal Embrace

In seeking praxes that draw solitude and solidarity together in a mutual fecundity, voluntary poverty both helps cleanse the soul of its insatiability and situates one's lifestyle in solidarity with the global community. It demands both intensive inner work and a challenging generosity of one's whole life for the sake of all others. It works, in a sense, by subtraction, by elimination, by learning to say no, enough is enough. But as encompassing a praxis as it is, it needs to be complemented by the integrative praxis of universal embrace, the spirituality of addition or the mysticism of integration. In this form of mysticism the person's whole being is rooted in a wider, more inclusive reality. In this spirituality one learns continually to say yes. If the spirituality of subtraction learns what to reject, the spirituality of addition learns how to accept. It seeks not to strip itself of everything but to assimilate it all. It necessitates, therefore, the gift of elasticity. "The more" can be seen, on the one hand, as a greedy impulse to have and to possess, but it can also be seen as an expansion of life's horizons. As Paolo Soleri puts it: "In any given system, the most complex quantum is also the liveliest."[1] Solitude tends toward the spirituality of subtraction, climbing up the mountain to be alone with the Alone, freeing oneself from every distraction and attachment. But the spirituality of addition moves us in the direction of the other, all others, or, as Buber describes this approach: "the lived multiplicity of all for the sake of a unity of all that is to be experienced."[2] Therefore, the spirituality of subtraction, or voluntary poverty, needs to be complemented by the spirituality of addition or of universal embrace, which seeks to embrace more and more of every aspect of life. This is in sync with tantric spirituality, since the Sanskrit word *tantra* means "to expand." It seeks to live life like the poet Rilke, who said, "I live my life in growing orbits which move out over the things of the world." Saint Paul wrote: "I give no thought to what lies behind but push on *(epekteinomenos)* to what is ahead" (Phil 3:13). In other words: "I strive, I stretch, I tend toward something ever before me, ever beyond, something ever unreachable and unseizable."[3] From Saint Paul's idea arose the concept of *epextasis*, or a continuous tension without arrival, ever transcending ourselves. The Ultimate is the abyss that never ceases in motion, proceeding "from beginning to beginning . . . without end."[4] As Raimon Panikkar concludes:

> *Epextasis* is not only precisely the human condition, but the symbol of the very structure of ultimate reality, as well. We do not have to emerge from ourselves into a transcendent ecstasy in order to reach ultimate reality. It will suffice to adopt this attitude of continuous tension without arrival, ever transcending ourselves. . . . For the end, God, the ultimate, is precisely the abyss that never ceases its motion, proceeding "from beginning to beginning."[5]

This approach to life is not so much seeking a single path or the middle path but rather a total path. Bernard Loomer initiates us into this spirituality by calling us to "size":

> By size I mean the stature of a person's soul, the range and depth of his or her love, his or her capacity for relationships. I mean the volume of life you can take into your being and still maintain your integrity and individuality; the intensity and variety of outlook you can entertain in the unity of your being without feeling defensive or insecure. I mean the power to sustain more complex and enriching tensions. I mean the magnanimity of concern to provide conditions that enable others to increase in stature.[6]

The great virtue of this spirituality is magnanimity, which Saint Thomas Aquinas called the greatest of all the virtues. It comes from two Latin words, *magna* and *anima*, and it means "a large soul." It is the expansion of the soul to great things. It is an abundance within that is called forth from without. And the great sin from this spiritual perspective is pusillanimity, a small soul, a "constriction of awareness," a settling for puniness in the midst of divine Vastness. It is living a mediocre existence in the world that becomes for us an unfocused and directionless multiplicity.

This spirituality calls us to cross the horizon of the known, safe, and comfortable and to expose ourselves to new people, new perspectives, and new ways of life. "The idea," as Chogyam Trungpa points out, is "not so much to make things harmonious and less active and more manageable . . . but . . . to allow one's plate to be full. . . . We will be dead soon enough; we will experience the peace of the coffin sooner than we think; now there's living to be done."[7] The goal of this path, therefore, is to become what could be called a universal person, one who experiences all the manifold qualities of life: ordinary human existence, immersion into nature, social life, intellectual life, creative life, sensuous life, contemplative life, and so forth. "Universal human beings," described Piero Ferruci,

> are at ease with the whole cosmos, and nothing in all creation is alien to them. They are inwardly open to any experience, ready to adapt to any situation because they are available and will not let themselves be limited by roles, history, or creed. They have access to every possible experience

> and recognize in themselves the many different aspects of life, male and female, rational and irrational, dark and light. They are also universal because they find the capacity to suffer and rejoice with all other living beings the ultimate affirmation of their humanness.[8]

Thomas Berry distinguishes between the "wild" or authentically spontaneous person and the "disciplined" person. He sees these two polarities as inhering in the two constitutive forces of the universe: the *expansive force* and the *containing force*. He points out that Mars turned into rock and therefore nothing fluid can exist there. Jupiter, on the other hand, remained a fiery mass of gases and therefore nothing firm can live there.[9] He sees a universal lesson here. An excess of discipline suppresses the wildness and spontaneity of the person, while an excess of wildness forecloses any personal stability. Whitehead made a similar point when he spoke of "the contrast between order as the condition for excellence, and order as stifling the freshness of living." He concludes that the "art of progress is to preserve order amid change, and to preserve change amid order."[10]

The spirituality of subtraction rightly warns us of an aimless availability to life where our being has no clear boundaries to give our life shape; where our personhood leaks out all over the place with no proper container; where we never choose where we stand and hence never commit ourselves fully to anyone or anything. Heraclitus said: "It is death to the soul to become water." We must be on guard against losing our individual form and becoming dissolved in the flux. There is, as Emmanuel Levinas points out, an open-mindedness that turns out to be nothing more than a sophisticated form of close-mindedness. As Richard A. Cohen characterizes Levinas's thought:

> Open to everything, nothing would count more than anything else. Open to all possibilities, such approaches would be closed to self-implication, to responsibility. A safe openness, untouched, "free" . . . mere free-floating "possibility," the possible divorced from the actual, leading not to life but to a "phantom" life.[11]

Chogyam Trungpa teaches: "In order to extend your boundary, you have to have a boundary."[12] We have to be able to determine out of life's myriad possibilities, those that are intrinsic to our own nature. There is the danger of never limiting or committing ourselves, in cultivating ever-fresh potentialities without the necessity of choosing which to actualize and which to leave undeveloped. Jose Ortega y Gasset believed: "Life consists in giving up the state of availability. Mere availability is the characteristic of youth faced with maturity. The youth, because he is not yet anything determinate and irrevocable, is everything potentially. Herein lay his charm and his insolence. Feeling that he is everything potentially he supposes that he is everything actually."[13] If we accept the path opened up by our unique potentials, then we will have the centeredness and strength gradually to hold together everything fruitfully.

On the other hand, the spirituality of universal embrace warns us of the opposite danger: the continual constriction of life. As Raimon Panikkar warned: "Simplification of a complicated lifestyle is one thing and utter simplicity taken to its final consequences quite another. Total simplicity i.e. a specialization in simplicity may lead to inhuman practices. . . . Simplicity cannot be the only principle governing human life, for if it is, it will destroy that very life."[14] Universal people are not mere chameleons, changing colors wherever they may be, but large souls whose identities are not threatened by the other or the new or the unfamiliar but are completed by them all. Universal people are supremely conscious of Heraclitus's dictum: "You would not find out the boundaries of the soul, even by traveling along every path: so deep a measure does it have."[15] The universal person, according to Raimon Panikkar, is, as Saint Thomas said, *capax universi*, or capable of the universe, where "nothing is despised, nothing left over, everything is integrated, assumed, transfigured."[16] Therefore, universal people are not only expansive people who allow their horizons a wider and wider circumference but also encompassing people who learn to embrace all to which they have become exposed. As the great Sufi mystic Ibn al Arabi proclaimed:

> My heart has become capable of all forms.
> It is a meadow for gazelles and a monastery for Christian
> monks,
> A temple for idols and the pilgrim's Ka'aba,
> the Tables of the Law and the book of the Koran.
> I profess the religion of Love, and whatever direction
> its steed may take, Love is my religion and my faith.[17]

In embracing the world, universal people are not only open and expansive but also responsible. They take responsibility for all that they embrace. In opening their eyes to the world, they become aware of the many forms of bondage people find themselves. So in embracing the world, they join in the liberation of the world. Big souls, however, do not simply focus on one form of liberation but take responsibility for what could be called a seamless web of liberations. Little souls, for example, might rail out against abortion but enthusiastically advocate capital punishment, which, in effect, baptizes revenge. Little souls might powerfully preach black liberation while denouncing gay rights. They might promote women's rights with such gusto that they ignore the world's poor. They might promote gay rights while eagerly embracing a consumptive lifestyle. The liberation theologians were at one point criticized because in advocating human liberation they failed to address the liberation of creation. After all, if the planet becomes uninhabitable, there will be no human liberation possible. Anthropology relies on cosmology. All the social structures that have produced the great divide between rich and poor have also ravaged the earth. The universal person not only embraces human liberation but also the liberation of the planet earth. Magnanimous people have the vision of an "integral liberation," where rights of life, rights of the earth, rights of the unborn, racial and ethnic harmony, woman and gay rights, all the great movements for freedom and the fullest flowering of all peoples, indeed all creation, are at the heart of their total concern, advocacy, and responsible action.

Perhaps the reason the Catholic monk Thomas Merton has such enduring popularity years after his death in 1968 is because he was a universal person. Those closest to Merton described him as someone who was totally open to everything, who always wanted to know more and more. As one friend described him: "Merton . . . a natural born hound . . . joyous (always) with expectation and surprise. Welcoming 'open-souled'—without check, reservations, qualifications, without fear of who he was—a wide-mouthed, gulping of the 'mystery unknown.'"[18] Merton had an incredible capacity for authentic dialogue, asking a million questions and then listening, never trying to convert anyone to anything. As he would have it: "If I insist on my truth and never stop to receive your truth, then there can be no truth between us."[19] He was continually responsive and vulnerable to the hiddenness and mystery of the other. He was unflinchingly open to everything that might enlarge, give texture to, and deepen the existential choice of being a Christian. His ideas were always changing, although always moving around one center, from an inner ground that was at once universal and yet entirely his own. Yet he was always seeking this center from the vantage point of somewhere else. He became very vocal regarding race relations, the peace effort, and the ecological question. One of his fellow monks described Merton: "He was a global man, a cosmic person. As long as he lived he reached and reached, to other classes, to other races, to other creeds, to other nations, other cultures. This reaching would lead him to die in a faraway Bangkok, on a journey with ever-widening horizons."[20]

One of the most transforming experiences in Merton's life happened in Louisville, Kentucky, on the corner of Fourth and Walnut, in the center of the shopping district where he was suddenly overwhelmed with the realization that "I loved all those people, that they were mine, and I theirs, that we could not be alien to one another even though we were total strangers. It was like awakening from a dream of separateness, of spurious self isolation."[21] Merton came to realize in the core of his being that we are all children of the same family; that the whole human adventure on this planet is one single adventure of human life. To paraphrase Merton, if our vision is the tribe, then we will work to defend our people against other tribes. But if our aim is the world, then there is nothing to attack; there is instead our common humanity to be discovered and affirmed. Borrowing from the Persian psychologist Dr. Reza Arasteh, Merton saw this new openness of his as a sign of what Arasteh called the "final integration." This is an experience of self-discovery and self-maturation by which we assume a new transcultural identity, becoming a cosmic or universal person. We are no longer simply identified with our ego-self in isolation but in a very real sense with "everybody."

It was in this spirit that Merton undertook a trip to the East, a pilgrimage to the surviving sources of Asian wisdom. "I come," said Merton, "as a pilgrim who is anxious to obtain not just information, not just 'facts,' but to drink from ancient sources."[22] Merton did not go to the East merely to store up experiences to enrich his cultural and intellectual horizons. Nor did he go as a kind of spiritual tourist, simply sharing notes with Eastern gurus. Rather, he believed in a "lived-out theology" whereby he sought to encounter Asian wisdom in his heart. He sought to realize within himself a universal consciousness, where all the divided world of humanity could "co-inhere" within his being. He sought to be a universal person in the sense of sharing in some deep way the experience of the Buddhist, the Hindu, the Muslim, the Jew, the other. It was an attempt to apprehend the power, the living experience that creates, animates, and sustains these foreign forms of the human experience, and entrust himself to its dynamism. I am able to understand my neighbors as they understand themselves because I discover they are part of me. As Raimon Panikkar cautions: "If I do not discover in myself the terrain where the Hindu, the Muslim, the Jew and the atheist may have a place—in my heart, in my intelligence, in my life—I will never be able to enter into a genuine dialogue with him."[23]

"At the daybreak of its third millennium," suggests Armand Veilleux, abbot of the Abbey of Scourmont in Belgium, "humanity is just now passing through a crisis which historians and sociologists unanimously look upon as the most acute one known in history. At bottom it is neither a social crisis, nor a political or an economic one, but in fact an anthropological crisis. It is the appearance of a new kind of civilization, the birth of a new type of man. . . . New relational forms between men, and original modes of regrouping." Beyond the universal person there emerges what some have called a mutational person. Mutational persons are cross-cultural, multidimensional individuals who appropriate within themselves complex forms of consciousness, realization, and the whole diversity of human experiences. In mutational persons both East and West, North and South, masculine and feminine, science and mysticism, solitude and relationships, autonomy and responsibility, the political and the aesthetic converge. Out of this convergence a new synthesis, even a global mutation can occur, and it will be made concrete in the consciousness and lifestyles of these mutational people. The result is that these global persons anticipate a new age in their being and praxis, which may also have historical repercussions when the time is ripe. They can become mediators of the future, witnessing to all of us what we are all capable of, as we struggle to make the passage from the past into the in-breaking future. They are prototypes of a new humanity.

Besides the important witness of Thomas Merton, we could look to such figures as Raimon Panikkar and Thomas Berry to give us hints as to what mutational people are like. Ewert Cousins considers Raimon Panikkar a mutational and multidimensional person because in his life there is a convergence of great cultural and spiritual traditions of diverse origin.[24] He holds together the polarities of East and West, science and mysticism, mythic and rational thinking, outer and inner consciousness, pragmatic involvement in the world and a necessary spiritual detachment. When Panikkar returned to Europe after fifteen years as a pilgrim traveling through Asia, he could make the statement: "I 'left' as a Christian, I 'found' myself a Hindu and I 'return' a Buddhist, without ceasing to be a Christian."[25] Once Thomas Berry, the geologian, was at a seminar and was talking about his Buddhist soul, and his Hindu soul, and his Chinese soul. But as he spoke he was infuriating a woman philosopher who finally pounded the table and demanded, "What do you believe?" It was as if she was insisting that to believe one thing negated all else; as if our soul can only contain one form of revelation and not another. And Thomas Berry answered: "I believe everything. . . . I am a believer and I like to believe. Why should I limit my belief? As St. Paul says: 'Believe all things' (1 Cor 13:7)."[26]

In listening to this encounter with Thomas Berry and the woman philosopher, we can discern two types of approaches to life. Emmanuel Levinas posits the distinction between "totalizers" and "infinitizers" in his most famous work entitled "Totality and Infinity." Totalizers attempt to contain all reality in a given system, whether philosophical, psychological, scientific, religious, ideological, political, or economic. Outside the system there is no reality. So their way of life is to organize all reality within their given system. Infinitizers, on the other hand, are not satisfied with any given systemic totalization of reality and are always open for the "more." If the totalizers strive for order and security, infinitizers strive for freedom and creative advance. If totalizers seek power and control, infinitizers seek a higher quality of life. Many examples can be found in history of those persons and those political and religious conglomerates that seek totalization. How few and far between are persons and institutions given to continual creative advance!

Certainly Jesus Christ was a mutational person who encountered the systemization of reality by the Jewish/Roman and Greek realities of his day. The whole thrust of his ministry was taking all that was best in Judaism to a new level. Jesus extended the reign of God, the kingdom, in the most inclusive way possible. And Jesus enacted this inclusion in the most radical way possible. It was not simply in the theoretical terms of a scholar, or in the private cloistered domains of a monk or nun, or in the solitary experiences of a mystic, or in the institutionalized function of clerics and apologists, or in the discussions and analyses of workshops. This radical inclusion was enacted like the Jewish prophets in the streets and alleyways and marketplaces of the world. There is always the danger that, for example, monk-hood becomes nothing more that comfortable bachelorhood or convenient spinsterhood, never opening the cloistered doors to the realities of humanity. Or the danger that religious liturgies that celebrate the mystical body of Christ serve as a holy smoke screen behind which the faithful avoid, perhaps unconsciously, the harsh realities of poverty, injustice, and exploitation—and their own complicity in such realities. Or that mere enthusiastic talk about forms of universal embrace can substitute for a praxis that brings this into reality. Jesus sought to reconcile all that was torn apart in the world, and in order to do that he assumed the condition of those who were most radically excluded from society. This radically inclusive embrace of Jesus is thus realized not primarily in the private domains of solitary religious experience, not in communal enclaves, not in institutional formalities and juridicism, but in the radical inclusive praxis of relational mysticism that characterized the ministry of Jesus. And the final entrance into the Jesus Christ experience is on the other side of the cross, which is not only the inevitable upshot of the Jesus praxis but the passageway into the final integration.

20

The Highest Teaching

Dostoyevsky once wrote to his friend Maikov: "There is a thought that has haunted me for a long time. . . . It is to portray a wholly good man. Nothing is more difficult . . . especially in our time." Perhaps today the word *good* is so worn out that it might seem a bit prosaic or lacking of any profound content. But I believe that Dostoyevsky is talking about a goodness that goes all the way down. We are not dealing here with a goodness that is a mere polite "shut-up-ness," a kind of benign blur or an inoffensive petrification of the human spirit. Dostoyevsky is talking about a good-as-God goodness, a good beyond being, a radical self-giftedness, a radical *diakonia,* a goodness that overwhelms and transforms. In *Crime and Punishment* Dostoyevsky uses the remarkable phrase "insatiable compassion." This is a desire that continually deepens itself, fueling one with a hunger forever new. However much I take upon myself responsibility for others, I am still infinitely more responsible. Levinas refers to this as the "infinition" of goodness. In the end, I believe that both the solitude and solidarity human dimensions forge into a fusion of goodness that is perhaps a simpler way of talking about compassion and love. The question I would like to raise at the end of this exploration is this: In the eager pursuit of important, high teachings in both the domains of solitude and solidarity, what might emerge and merge as the highest or ultimate teaching that would lead to this goodness/compassion/wisdom/love/justice?

Joining Dostoyevsky in his quest for a wholly good man, where should we look for insight, inspiration, example, indeed imperative "command," for the highest teachings? Who teaches us to live ultimately not only by what we proclaim but how we live? Human history has presented us with an extraordinary variety of exemplary human lives. In the West, at least, we have come to call a wholly good person a saint. Who is a saint? Edith Wyschogrod offers a definition of a saint that I find helpful: "one whose adult life in its entirety is devoted to the alleviation of sorrow (psychological suffering) and pain (the physical suffering) that afflicts other persons without distinction to rank or group . . . whatever the cost to the saint in pain and sorrow."[1] The other, however, is not only the personal other but can also be the collective other, those who have been called the "wretched of the earth." That is why it is necessary to add to Wyschogrod's definition what Robert Ellsberg does: "There are countless saints who exhibit charity, but we also need those with a prophetic thirst for justice."[2] Compassion and justice will be fundamental anchors of what the human community will henceforth envision as a saint.

The great power of the saints comes first of all from the fact that they were real human beings, although often their hagiographies are tweaked according to ingrained, specific religious assumptions and contexts. Nevertheless, historical plausibility is the first step in evoking and validating an authentic human/religious life. Their lives invite us to realize the highest human potential and hence to "live forward" what they have lived. To lead a fully human life does not necessitate a theory about how one should live but flesh-and-blood persons who actually have lived extraordinary lives and who offer us biographies exhibiting the compelling force of their lives, which takes on an imperative power. Saints empower us to reach and become higher or better than we presently are.

Robert Ellsberg asks a key question: "Did anyone ever become better from reading a handbook on ethics? Yet most of us, at one time or another, have felt our hearts respond to an example of courage, goodness or spiritual nobility that inspired us to a higher path."[3] Or as Brother David Steindl-Rast insists: "Nothing has as much power to change our lives as the example of others. No theory, not even higher experience, has as much power as when it is embodied in a human person." This is what is crucial about saints: "Their lives were organized around higher principles—the human capacity for love, for sacrifice, for generosity."[4] They applied themselves to the great task of being human. The truth of their lives is verified in their living witness. The saint says to us all, "Here I am," and turns to us and invites and empowers us by a historical imperative, "Come, follow me!"

Saints, in all the world's religious traditions, have committed themselves to the wretched of the earth, but we have to keep in mind the historical and religious contexts in which a particular saint operated. Saints do not arise out of only one historical or religious context but are formed out of a broad spectrum of belief systems and institutional practices. Interestingly though, many of the world's saints often mature in tension with "institutional frameworks that may nevertheless later absorb them."[5] Historically, we have often seen how institutional norms can seek to thwart saintly intentions. Saints frequently impinge on entrenched religious customs as veritable "moral insurgents." Therefore, saints do not always transmit standard theological discourse. What legitimizes their sometimes antinomian practices is not theological concepts but the absolute imperative that emerges in the moral vortex of their lives.

Edith Wyschogrod makes a very important distinction between a saint and a mystic. As she says: "Not all saints are mystics, and not all mystics are saints." I believe this is an important distinction, but it must be based on a specific understanding of what we might mean by *mystic*. I would affirm this statement of Wyschogrod if by *mystic* we are referring to the traditional sense where there is evidence that a person has achieved high stages of consciousness or has passed through the successive stages of purgation, illumination, and union as described by the great Christian mystics. In this sense of the word *mystic*, we can affirm that not all saints are mystics and not all mystics are saints. However, we could adopt a broader, more flexible use of the term *mystic*. We could point, for example, to the saint's life visibly transformed by a radical service to the wretched of the earth that necessarily springs from an intense inner fire. A saint, in this broader understanding, could be considered a mystic.

But the point that Wyschogrod is making, I believe, is crucial in light of certain religious trends in contemporary spirituality. Questions naturally arise from this distinction: Is the goal of the human person enlightenment or the attainment of specific stages of consciousness or unitive experiences? Is spiritual development seen as the goal of a religious life? Is our life in the world the mere context of mystical or non-dual realizations or as the field where we manifest or radiate our spiritual actualizations? The answers, I believe, should be no. Is it not in the end narcissistic, even if it is of a more rarified variety, to be primarily preoccupied with one's own spiritual progress? This is not in the least to denigrate or belittle the inner life. Nor is it to claim that all who seek to realize higher stages of consciousness are thereby narcissists. But the important point, I believe, is what Maurice Friedman insists on: "The issue here is not whether inwardness may be dispensed with . . . but whether one aims at it as one's ultimate goal."[6]

In this discussion of the distinction between a saint and a mystic, I would like to bring up the witness of Jesus, which we will subsequently discuss more directly. Andrew Harvey points out that in reference to perhaps the greatest religious figure in human history, we do not have any reliable records of the inner spiritual development of Jesus. Jesus "spoke rarely, if ever, of his own [spiritual] experiences; it was an inherent part of his message that actions . . . should speak louder than any words or metaphysical explanations, however inspiring."[7] And yet Harvey often refers to Jesus as an "awakened, empowered mystic" who lived in the midst of the human community with his fierce visionary presence and passion for justice. Jesus, in other words, was a mystic in a broad sense.

Although we do not know what went on in Jesus' interior life, we know he had one. Geza Vermes points out that Jesus is never presented in the Synoptic Gospels as participating in acts of worship. Although we find Jesus in both temple and synagogue in the role of a teacher, we do not find him in any sense a temple or liturgical officiando. Rather, the Synoptics present Jesus as chiefly interested in non-communal prayer. We mostly find Jesus addressing God in solitary places, or at least some distance from other people: in the desert (Mk 1:35; Lk 5:15), on a mountain (Mk 6:46; Mt 14:23; Lk 6:12), in the garden of Gethsemane away from his disciples (Mk 14:32–41; Mt 26:36–44; Lk 22:41–45). As Vermez concludes: "This consistent omission of cultic worship is attributable to Jesus' stress on the private, unostentatious and even secret character of prayer (Mt 6:5–6; Mk 12:40; Lk 20:47)."[8] We are presented, in other words, with a great religious figure for whom we have no evidence of what stage of union he reached, but we have abundant evidence that Jesus had a very profound inner, solitary life that consistently opened up to the way of compassion.

Although human history has provided us with incredible saints and teachers, I am choosing to concentrate on two: Buddha and Jesus. And the question I wish to ask is this: From these two great religious teachers, what might be the highest teachings that will remain as the bedrock foundation for the ongoing development and maturation of humanity? Let us first turn to Buddha. Although this will be a rather cursory approach, I would like to zero in on only what I perceive to be perhaps Buddha's highest teachings that will have everlasting validity. As one of Buddha's disciples characterizes Buddha's teachings: "The most noble truth is silence."[9] Buddhist tradition recalls the Buddha's love for silence, his concern for his own silence, and his recommendation of silence to his disciples. Noble silence is part and parcel of the Buddhist spirit. Silence is the ground, the core of reality, and all else relates to it and emanates from it. Silence suffuses the core of our being. Silence is the primal and necessary human atmosphere that gives birth to all that is precious in becoming human. The more profound and embracing the silence, the greater the human actualization.

There are three types of silence: that of the body, that of the mouth, and that of the mind. The greatest silence, the silence that Buddha is referring to, is the silence of the mind. We live in an age in which we can no longer bear being alone, in which we can no longer stand the silence. Agitated individuals "run after the crowd. They hope they can drown their terror by embracing the din, blare, uproar."[10] The silence that the Buddha offers is not only for the purpose of liberating us from the external din within and without, but also to calm us and to reconcile us with all the factors that displace us from our center of gravity. It is like a fasting of the mind that lets us taste everything as it really is once more. Silence turns out to be not only the absence of sound but a living, palpable presence in its own right, filled with boundless vitality. This silence is also seen in some quarters of the Western, Christian tradition as a privileged entry into the realm of God. Meister Eckhart called silence the "nearest thing to God." Thomas Merton viewed silence as the deepest manifestation of God's presence. We could almost define the essence of an authentic human inner life by one word: silence. From this perspective it could further be asserted that there is nothing in the world that resembles God as much as silence. That is why we may dare to assert that silence is God. In the Christian spiritual tradition there has been discovered an intrinsic connection between silence and love, as every lover knows. The upshot is that the silence of God and the silence of love are one and the same thing. We have now arrived at the heart of the solitude polarity.

But then the Lord Buddha presents us with a corresponding, equally essential teaching: "If one teaching is grasped and known, all my teachings will be in the palm of your hand. What is this one teaching? It is altruism."[11] Further articulating this fundamental viewpoint, the current Dalai Lama has stated: "The highest perfection is altruism, the ultimate altruism is *Bodhicitta*. . . . The aspiration to bring about the welfare of all sentient beings and to attain Buddhahood for their sake—[this] is really the *distilled essence*, the *squeezed juice* of all Buddhism's teachings."[12] And then, the Dalai Lama, in his own inimitable way of presenting very complex matters in a disarmingly simple, almost homespun way combines the Buddha's teaching on silence and altruism by making this very condensed statement: "Compassion, born out of the quiet and reflective moments of silence, is the most powerful force in the world."[13] Or as the Dalai Lama says elsewhere: "Spiritual practice . . . involves, on the one hand, acting out of concern for others' well being [solidarity]. On the other, it entails transforming ourselves so that we become more readily disposed to do so [solitude]."[14]

I believe it is helpful here to interject what Thomas Merton, a Christian monk who developed intimate ties with the Buddhist tradition, had to say on this matter, since it so closely allies and affirms what the Dalai Lama is teaching. Thomas Merton, in one of his last talks before he died, entitled "Silence and Contemplation," made precisely the point that the Dalai Lama has presented. Merton said that the deeper we go into the heart the more connected we become with the wider earth community. To go inward is at once to move outward to all living beings, especially those who struggle for the basic necessities of life. What emerges from this solitude/solidarity dialectic is the fundamental point that the spiritual life is not a goal we set out to attain but rather the byproduct of the way, out of the silence of our minds and hearts *(Bodhicitta)*, we meet and expose ourselves to others in their need. Fully human persons are measured not only or even primarily by the stages of consciousness they have realized but to what extent they surrender themselves in service to sentient beings. Meister Eckhart articulates this prioritization quite starkly: "If a person were in such rapturous state as St. Paul once entered, and knew of a sick man who wanted a cup of soup, it would be far better to withdraw from that rapture for love's sake and serve him who is in need."[15]

After this brief summary and affirmation of Buddha's essential teachings, let us now turn to Jesus. The first point I believe to be essential to this search for the high teachings of Jesus is the question of his historicity. As Geza Vermes concludes: "Of course, the Gospels fall far short of the requirements needed for a real biography of Jesus, or for a full, detailed and systematic account of his teachings. But this is a far cry [from saying that] . . . we can know 'almost nothing' concerning him. The sensible question to ask is whether we can grasp *something significant and central* about his life and message."[16] Swami Prahavananda and Christopher Isherwood both have claimed that it does not matter whether Jesus really lived because we have his teachings, which are universal. But as Maurice Friedman points out, they "miss the central reality from which all religious teachings spring and to which they again point back: the image of the human."[17] A one-time historical figure stands behind these teachings. It is not irrelevant whether Jesus lived or not just as it is not irrelevant if a saint is a purely fictional construct or is a concrete witness to human potential. That is why, for example, records of athletes are so important to us, because they demonstrate what the human being is capable of. Exceptional human beings confirm with their lives that as they have lived, so others may live.

In the Christian scriptures and tradition we can find a multitude of Jesuses: the mythological Jesus, the heavenly Jesus of John, the Christ of Paul, the Constantinian Jesus Christ, the "Euro-ecclesiastical Christ of the official church,"[18] the eschatological Jesus of Schweitzer, the revolutionary Jesus of liberation theology, and so on. But as Vermes posits: "A great challenge, perhaps the greatest of all, which traditional Christianity of the Pauline-Johannine variety has . . . still to confront does not come from atheism or agnosticism, or sheer materialism, but from within, from the ancient witnesses, Mark, Matthew and Luke, through whom speaks the chief challenge, Jesus the Jew."[19] Or as Andrew Harvey believes: "Paying attention to how Jesus acted and in what context and to what he really said—and not on the dogmas surrounding his divinity—can have a paradoxical effect of making us take him and his actions and words even more seriously and, above all, and in the highest, most urgent sense, practically."[20] It is this historical figure of Jesus that most concerns us here.

One of the first things to understand about Jesus is that he was a Torah-observing Jewish rabbi, and as such he was a highly influential teacher. He was a popular rather than a professional figure, "an itinerant master who did not deliver his message in a fixed location such as a 'school' or a particular synagogue."[21] Jesus marched in the footsteps of the great prophets of Israel. "He adopted, intensified and sought boldly to inject into the Judaism of ordinary people the magnificent prophetic teaching of the religion of the heart (Is 29:13)."[22] As a popular, charismatic teacher and healer, his ministry finds great resonance with the biblical prophets such as Elijah and Elisha, who cured diseases and fed the hungry. Joseph Klausner concludes: Jesus was "the outstanding Galilean Hasid who, thanks to the sublimity, distinctiveness and originality of his ethical teaching stood head and shoulders above the known representatives of this class of spiritual personality."[23]

In order to grasp the teachings of Jesus in all their height, profundity, and extremity, I would like to use as a guide along the way perhaps an unlikely choice, the great Jewish philosopher Emmanuel Levinas. If mystics like Saint John of the Cross and Saint Teresa of Avila present us with a phenomenology of the interior spiritual states and stages, Emmanuel Levinas presents us with the phenomenology of the radical transition from ego-concern to concern for others. In this Emmanuel Levinas helps us to understand the "too muchness" of Jesus. "He was too much for them" (Mk 6:3; Mt 13:37). One of the complaints about Jesus, leveled against all the great prophets (and we should note also against Levinas), is that Jesus was too extreme; he demanded the impossible. Harold Bloom, for example, makes a comment heard often in different ways: "Jesus . . . emulates Yahweh in the hyperbolic demands of his teachings, with insistence on perfections mere humans scarcely can achieve."[24]

Andrew Harvey makes an important observation concerning those who critique Jesus' extremism. He believes that the reason why commentators might patronize Jesus' teachings as utopian or extreme is because they are operating out of a lower level of awareness or from a more constricted heart.[25] Jesus' radical teachings, as exemplified in his call to love our enemies, is not the call of a utopian dreamer but the announcement of a law of transformation, a way of mystical evolution. "Jesus," Harvey insists, "is always realistic, but his realism is that of an awakened heart; it is the realism of the highest dimension of reality and so the most astute and demanding realism imaginable."[26] The position of this study is that it is the very extremity of not only Jesus' teachings but the extreme conclusion of his life that presents to the human community not only *his* highest teaching but perhaps *the* highest teaching of all.

Jesus sums up his path to his disciples: "Whoever wishes to come after me must deny himself, take up his cross, and follow me" (Mt 16:24). He further instructs his disciples: "Whoever wishes to be first among you shall be your slave. Just so, the Son of Man did not come to be served but to serve and to give his life as a ransom for many" (Mt 20:26–28). Then Jesus finalizes his teaching in John: "No greater love than this, than a person lay down his life for his friends" (Jn 15:13). As John concludes in his epistle: "The way we come to know love was that he laid down his life for us; so we ought to lay down our lives for our brothers. If someone who has worldly means sees a brother in need and refuses him compassion, how can the love of God remain in him?" (1 Jn 3:16–17). Richard of St. Victor, in his "The Four Degrees of Passionate Charity," made a relevant point here. Reflecting the witness of Jesus, he taught that beyond the mystical states of purgation, illumination, and union, a further unfolding of love is required. The highest degree of charity cannot be a "resting" but rather this: "For greater love has no man but this, than a man lay down his life for his friends. Those who are able to lay down their lives for their friends have reached the highest peak of charity."[27] This is precisely the upshot of Jesus' life and the life he calls us to. He was executed on the cross by the state because he provocatively espoused the cause of the wretched of the earth, which was perceived as a direct challenge to the political and religious stasis. This is the "too muchness" of Jesus that prompted his disciples to ask: "Will only a few people be saved?" And Jesus responded: "Because strait is the gate, and narrow is the way, which leads unto life, few there are that find it" (Mt 7:14).

What Emmanuel Levinas does so profoundly is to provide for us a phenomenological dissection of what the poet Theodore Roethke calls "the long journey out of the self" unto a radical service to the other(s) in need. But his is not a call to deny the existence of the autonomous self or a call to destroy the self; it is, rather, a path of self-transcendence. This transcendence does not lift the person out of the world into the Elysian fields of some heavenly abode, but to the "height" of the suffering other. In other words, the site of transcendence is the other person. This is why Jean Wahl replaced the word *transcendence* with the word *transascendence*. As Andrew Harvey notes in this context: "A mystic who concentrates 'only' on personal development and purification and a cultivation of the so called 'higher' mystical states cannot begin to imagine, let alone embody, the fullness of [Jesus' way] which demands at every stage . . . an ever-more abandoned service of the other beings and an ever-more critically engaged and transformatory commitment to justice and the works of love within the world."[28] What Emmanuel Levinas describes is this ascension of the self to a responsibility for the suffering other or what he calls the "humanism of the suffering servant."[29] It is this *transascendence* or ascension that raises humanity to its highest dignity, its highest destiny, its highest calling.

Perhaps the parable of Jesus that best characterizes two contrary responses to life's exigencies is the parable of the good Samaritan. On the one hand, we have the so-called religious folk, either the professional clergy or the common churchgoer, who on their way to Sunday service are confronted with a person in the ditch of destitution. Levinas gives us a very detailed description of this precarious exposure or encounter. Levinas first describes the folks off to church. We could note here that the encounter of Jesus with the rich young man has the same dynamics. Both the church folks and the rich young man are confronted by the challenge to sacrifice their self-absorption for the sake of the man in need. As Levinas describes a typically self-absorbed person: "[the] for-another arises in the enjoyment in which the ego is affirmed, is complacent, and posits itself."[30] To come upon the other is to come upon the otherness of one who has needs outside the range of my concern with my own needs. I am disturbed in my reverie. I am awakened from the quiet slumber of my egotism. I am contested in my claims to autonomy.[31] But rather than respond generously and radically to the call of the other, the rich young man, like the priest and Levite in the good Samaritan parable, "complacently returns to the self, overlooking, ignoring, neglecting, abandoning, escaping, otherwise refusing the priority of [his] . . . moral responsibility to and for the other person."[32]

But if I allow myself to be pierced by the cry of another, to be "penetrated-by-another,"[33] the pain of the other will interrupt my enjoyment in its very isolation and tear me from myself. My ego-shell is shattered and I am expelled from my psychic cocoon, from my being-at-home-with-myself. I am extradited from myself to another.[34] I am "brought out of my invisibility, my hiddenness, my privacy, out of the shadows where my responsibility could have been avoided."[35] I quit the "clandestiness" of myself as subject.[36] In my exposure to the other I neglect my natural defenses. A pure withdrawal from myself is demanded whereby I abandon all shelter, where no quiet slipping stealthily away is any longer possible. I thereby become a "hostage" to the other, delivered over as a gift. (Jesus calls himself a "ransom for many" [Mk 10:43–45].) All escape routes are closed, and no immersion in a pleasurable or at least safe inner life is any longer justifiable.

This exposure to the other is a risky business. It is "a painful wisdom"[37] whereby my skin is turned inside out in pure vulnerability. This is a far more precarious proposition than any mere being "present" to the other. In a presence to the other I can still maintain a relatively safe psychic distance and preserve my space and self-possession. But in self-exposure, in this "denuclearization" of my selfhood, I offer myself as a pure susceptiveness. I will be afflicted with a closeness, a most extreme immediacy, a "never-enough" proximity which will continually disturb my peace. ("I have not come to bring peace," Jesus said.)[38] We are told, for example, of a Hassidic rabbi, Moshe Leib of Sasov, who used to nurse all the sick boys in town. Moshe Leib said: "He who is not willing to suck the pus from the sore of a child sick with the plague has not climbed even halfway up the mountain of love."[39] This radical and traumatic exposure to the other in turn becomes a for-another as a "despite oneself, a non-coinciding with oneself, a non repose in oneself."[40] Hence, I willingly "lose my place." Jesus said, "The son of man has no place to lay his head" (Lk 9:58). Levinas then posits, I will be "emptied into a no-ground."[41] Jesus had no decent place to be born (Lk 2:7), no reputable place to live and work (Jn 1:46), no safe place in his own country to hide from oppressive rulers (Mt 2:13–14), no honorable place to die (Lk 23:23), and no place of his own to be buried (Mt 27:59).

As Dostoyevsky's great saintly figure Alyosha exclaimed: "Each of us is guilty before everyone, and I more than others."[42] Because I am guilty before everyone I am responsible for everyone. "Everything becomes incumbent on me."[43] "I am my brother's keeper all the way."[44] I am called to bear the burden of another's existence and supply for the other's needs like the good Samaritan. This responsibility is enacted not only in offering one's property ("Go, sell what you have, give to the poor, and come follow me"), but in giving of one's substance ("Can you be bathed in the same pain that I am bathed in?" [Mk 10.38]).[45] I am called to "give to another the bread from my mouth."[46] I will provide food for the other that I could enjoy eating; clothing to another that I could enjoy wearing; money to the other that I could enjoy spending; peace to another that I could have rested in.[47]

Jesus lived and moved amid the masses, the crowds of people, the "mob." But when we speak of the "crowds," we are not speaking of them in the derisive or dismissive sense of, for example, Kierkegaard, who once cried "the crowd is untruth!" Rather, we are speaking of the crowds in the sense of what Asian liberation theologians call the *dalits* (those broken or trampled upon) or the *minjung* (the suffering multitude, the destitute majority). Jesus did not stow away and live his spiritual life in some idyllic remote retreat or squeeze his spirituality into the narrow confines of a pious liturgical functionary at a local synagogue. Jesus did not "withdraw from the world and pray for deliverance on the fringes of catastrophe; he had to act at the heart of the world."[48] To be with Jesus was to be an itinerant, moving in the midst of the people, always in the direction of those most in need.

One of the things that marks Jesus as unique among the great spiritual figures in history is the extent, the radical nature of, and fervor with which Jesus applied his vision of the kingdom of God to the society of his time. We find no division in Jesus' teachings or way of life between the social and the spiritual, between his deep inner life and a focused, critical, transformative activity within Israel. When Jesus said "My kingdom is not of this world" (Jn 18:36), he did not mean that it belonged to some purely ethereal realm. He was not in any way an escapist or a quietist. What Jesus meant was that the kingdom of God had nothing to do with the banal, violent world created by human greed, power grabs, petty intrigues, ignorance, and frivolousness.

Jesus' message was socially provocative and it was not lost on the powers in Jerusalem who found it continually necessary for the smooth functioning of state to eliminate any potential disruption to the status quo. But it was to the transformation of this status quo that Jesus dedicated all his considerable skills and powers. And it was this passionate focus that made Jesus "*lethal* to the ruling political powers of his day and that *ensured his death*."[49] The upshot of Jesus' ministry came to a head when Jesus "steadfastly set out for Jerusalem" (Lk 9:5), the center of the storm. A whole lifetime of the most passionate love and sacrifice had prepared Jesus to take this journey on behalf of the people. No sooner did Jesus arrive in Jerusalem than "the passion of his vision of the Kingdom and the agony of tenderness for all beings that propelled it, propelled him to the moment when he crystallized all his angry hope, prayerfulness, and social and political ideals in one symbolic iconoclastic act he knew would risk his life."[50] By driving out the moneychangers from the temple, Jesus sealed his fate.

This Jesus who embodied the immensity of compassion and the demands of divine justice in his life praxis, who embodied human solidarity, the sufferings of others, their needs of liberation, their eschatological hopes—this Jesus was crucified on their behalf. Martin Buber concludes: "Jesus' witness was perfected in death, the sole absolute man has to offer." We have seen that the highest goal of Buddhism is to become a Bodhisattva or one who hands over his or her life for others. We have seen that for Levinas, one of the greatest of all Jewish teachers in our time, "to be for the other . . . (right up to dying for the other)[51] . . . to serve the other morally and to serve others in justice—here lies the *ultimate exigency* of the meaning and dignity of human kind."[52] We have seen in the witness of Jesus that one can have no greater love than to lay down one's life for the life of the world. Perhaps in this sweeping vision of human solidarity emerging from an unimaginable solitude, which culminates with Jesus executed on the cross, we have arrived at the highest teaching of all. Is it not this radical giftedness, this profligate love, that was and continues to be vindicated by a continual resurrecting hope?

Notes

PART I
SOLITUDE

1 The Solitude/Solidarity Dynamic

1. Carl Jung, quoted in June Singer, *Boundaries of the Soul* (Garden City, NY: Anchor Books, 1973), 187.
2. John Cowper Powys, *A Philosophy of Solitude* (New York: Simon and Schuster, 1930), 37–38.
3. Ibid., 38.
4. Jean Rostand, *Pensieri di un biologo* (Milan: Edizioni del Borghese, 1968), 87.
5. Carl Jung, *Psychology and Alchemy*, Collected Works, vol. 12, Bollingen Series 20, trans. R. F. C. Hull (New York: Pantheon, 1953), 28.
6. Henry David Thoreau, *Walden* (New York: New American Library, 1960), 95.
7. Archbishop Desmond Tutu, in *What Does It Mean to Be Human?* (New York: St. Martin's Press, 2000), 271.
8. D. H. Lawrence, *Apocalypse and the Writing on Revelations*, ed. Mara Palnins (Cambridge: Cambridge University Press, 2002), 149.
9. Jean Paul Sartre, "Une idée fondamentale de la phenomenologie de Husserl: L'intentionnalite," *La Nouvelle Revue Francais 304* (January 1939), 131.
10. Interview with Ken Wilber on "Integral Naked," 2008.
11. Raimon Panikkar, *The Cosmotheandric Experience* (Maryknoll, NY: Orbis Books, 1993), 18.
12. Arthur O. Lovejoy, *The Great Chain of Being* (Cambridge: Harvard University Press, 1964), 49.
13. Beatrice Bruteau, *God's Ecstasy* (New York: Crossroad, 1997), 84.
14. Chogyam Trungpa, *Crazy Wisdom* (Boston: Shambhala, 1991), 96.
15. Ram Dass, *One Liners* (New York: Bell Tower, 2002), 10.
16. Raimon Panikkar, *Myth, Faith and Hermeneutics* (New York: Paulist Press, 1979), 72.
17. Dionysius the Areopagite, quoted in Leo D. Lefebure, *The Buddha and the Christ* (Maryknoll, NY: Orbis Books, 1993), 96.
18. Raimon Panikkar, *Christophany: The Fullness of Man* (Maryknoll, NY: Orbis Books, 2004), 103.
19. Martin Buber, *I and Thou*, trans. Walter Kaufmann (New York: Simon and Schuster, 1970), 69.
20. Panikkar, *Christophany*, xii.

21. Beatrice Bruteau, *The Grand Option* (Notre Dame, IN: University of Notre Dame Press, 2001), 66.
22. Ibid., 66–67.
23. Panikkar, *Christophany*, 64.
24. Ken Wilber, *Sex, Ecology, Spirituality* (Boston: Shambhala, 1995).
25. Saint Augustine, quoted in *J. L. Mehta on Heidegger, Hermeneutics and Indian Tradition*, ed. William J. Jackson (Leiden: E. J. Brill, 1992), 78.
26. Thomas Merton, *A Search for Solitude* (San Francisco: HarperSanFrancisco, 1966), 28.
27. Pierre Teilhard de Chardin, *Hymn of the Universe* (New York: Harper and Row, 1961), 64.
28. Martin Buber, "With a Monist," in *Pointing the Way: Collected Essays*, translated from the German and edited by Maurice Friedman (New York: Harper, 1957), 28.
29. Martin Buber, quoted in *Encounter on the Narrow Ridge* by Maurice Friedman (New York: Paragon House, 1993), 81.
30. Leonardo Boff, *Ecology and Liberation* (Maryknoll, NY: Orbis Books, 1995), 161.
31. Huston Smith, in *Doors of Understanding: Conversations on Global Spirituality in Honor of Ewert Cousins*, ed. Ewert H. Cousins and Steven Chase (Quincy, IL: Franciscan Press, 1970), 161.
32. Pierre Hayat, "Preface," in Emmanuel Levinas, *Alterity and Transcendence* (New York: Columbia University Press, 1999), x.
33. Pierre Teilhard de Chardin, *Toward the Future*, trans. Rene Hague (London: Collins, 1975), 86–87. This was written in Peking in 1934.
34. Huston Smith, *Why Religion Matters* (San Francisco: HarperSanFrancisco, 2001), 211.
35. Arnold Toynbee, *A Study of History*, Somerville abridged edition (London: Oxford University Press, 1960), 217.
36. Martin Buber, *The Eclipse of God*, trans. Maurice Friedman et al. (Atlantic Highlands, NJ: Humanities Press, 1988), 102.
37. Pierre Teilhard de Chardin, *Human Energy* (London: Collins, 1969), 33.
38. Jon Sobrino, *The Principle of Mercy* (Maryknoll, NY: Orbis Books, 1994), 38.
39. *Leggenda Perugina*, 74. Quoted in Raimon Panikkar, *Cultural Disarmament: The Way to Peace* (Louisville, KY: Westminster John Knox Press, 1995), 39.
40. Rabbi Haninah ben Dosa, quoted in Salomon Malka, *Emmanuel Levinas: His Life and Legacy* (Pittsburgh: Duquesne University Press, 2002), xxvi.
41. Emmanuel Levinas, quoted in Richard A. Cohen, *Elevations: The Height of the Good in Rosenzweig and Levinas* (Chicago: University of Chicago Press, 1994), 125.
42. Emmanuel Levinas, quoted in Malka, *Emmanuel Levinas*, 216.
43. Aloysius Pieris, SJ, *An Asian Theology of Liberation* (Maryknoll, NY: Orbis Books, 1992), 86.
44. Quoted in Leonardo Boff, *Faith on the Edge* (San Francisco: HarperSanFrancisco, 1989), 58.
45. Martin Buber, *The Legend of the Baal-Shem*, trans. Maurice Friedman (New York: Harper Bros., 1956), 50.

2 Buddhist and Judeo-Christian Approaches

1. Chogyam Trungpa, *The Path Is the Goal: A Basic Handbook of Buddhism Meditation* (Boston: Shambhala, 1995).
2. Aloysius Pieris, SJ, *Love Meets Wisdom* (Maryknoll, NY: Orbis Books, 1988), 61.
3. Emmanuel Levinas, *Otherwise than Being or Beyond Essence*, trans. Alphonso Lingis (The Hague: Martinus Nyhoff, 1981), 161.
4. William Johnston, *The Still Point* (New York: Harper and Row, 1970), 33.
5. Meister Eckhart, quoted in James Matthew Ashley, *Interruptions: Mysticism, Politics, and Theology in the Work of Johann Baptist Metz* (Notre Dame, IN: University of Notre Dame Press, 1998), 248.
6. Buber, *I and Thou*, 141, 128.
7. "The ancient story of the Samaritan was the Council's model of spirituality" (Pope Paul VI, *Concilio Vaticano II* [Madrid, 1965], 816).
8. Peter Hans Koehnbach, SJ, video message to the World Assembly of Christian Live Community, Hong Kong, *Progressios* 2–4 (1994), 40.
9. Johann Baptist Metz, *Love's Strategy: The Political Theology of Johann Baptist Metz*, ed. John K. Downey (Harrisburg, PA: Trinity Press International, 1999), 169.
10. Emmanuel Levinas, *Difficult Freedom*, trans. Sean Hand (Oxford: Blackwell, 1996), 191.
11. Johann Baptist Metz, *The Theology of the World* (New York: Herder, 1969), 104.
12. Ceslas Spicq, *Agape in the New Testament*, vol. 1, *Agape in the Synoptic Gospels* (St. Louis: Herder, 1963), 28.
13. Michael Amaladoss, *The Asian Jesus* (Maryknoll, NY: Orbis Books, 2006), 61.
14. Thich Nhat Hahn, *Going Home: Jesus and Buddha as Brothers* (New York: Penguin Putnam, 1999).
15. Smith, *Why Religion Matters*, 254.
16. Thomas Merton, "Wisdom in Emptiness: A Dialogue by Daisetz T. Suzuki and Thomas Merton," New Directions 17 (New York: A New Directions Book, 1961), 82.
17. Ken Wilber, *One Taste* (Boston: Shambhala, 1999), 113.
18. Johannes Scotus Eriugena, quoted in Friedman, *Encounter on the Narrow Ridge*, 68.
19. Rabbi Hayim ben Isaac of Volozshin, *The Soul of Life (Nefesh Hayayim)* (1824), chap. 1, sec. 9.
20. Ibid., chap. 1, sec. 12.
21. Gustavo Gutiérrez, *Gustavo Gutiérrez: Essential Writings*, ed. James B. Nickoloff (Maryknoll, NY: Orbis Books, 1996), 80.
22. Emmanuel Levinas, quoted in Edith Wyshogrod, *Emmanuel Levinas: The Problem of Ethical Metaphysics* (New York: Fordham University Press, 2000), 50.

3 What to Do?

1. Thoreau, *Walden*, 54.
2. Ralph Waldo Emerson, "Self-Reliance."

3. Anna Silvas, *The Asketikon of St. Basil the Great*, no. 5 (London: Oxford University Press, 2005), 181.
4. Friedman, *Encounter on the Narrow Ridge*, 85.
5. Joseph Campbell, *A Joseph Campbell Companion*, ed. Diane K. Osbon (New York: Harper Collins, 1991), 151.
6. Dag Hammarskjöld, *Markings* (New York: Ballantine Books, 1964), 46.
7. Andrew Harvey, *The Return of the Mother* (Berkeley, CA: Frog, 1995), 101.
8. Jürgen Moltmann, *The Church in the Power of the Spirit* (New York: Harper and Row, 1977), 283.

4 On Entering Solitude

1. Huston Smith, in *God, the Self, and Nothingness*, ed. Robert E. Carter (New York: Paragon House, 1990), 14.
2. Mircea Eliade, *Journal 1, 1945–1955* (Chicago: University of Chicago Press, 1990), 61.
3. Rosemary Ruether, quoted in Monica Furlong, *Merton: A Biography* (San Francisco: Harper and Row, 1980), 300.
4. Panikkar, *The Cosmotheandric Experience*, 131.
5. Ibid., 85.
6. Chogyam Trungpa, *Orderly Chaos* (Boston: Shambhala, 1991), 61.
7. Elie Wiesel, quoted in Raimon Panikkar, *Invisible Harmony* (Minneapolis: Fortress Press, 1995), xii.
8. Thomas Merton, *Disputed Questions* (New York: Harcourt Brace and Co., 1960), 179.
9. George Gurdjieff, *All and Everything* (London: Routledge and Kegan Paul, 1950), 1183.
10. P. D. Ouspensky, *In Search of the Miraculous* (Orlando, FL: Harcourt, 1949), 76.
11. Joseph Campbell, *The Power of Myth with Bill Moyers* (New York: Doubleday, 1998), 58.
12. Walter Brueggemann, *The Prophetic Imagination*, 2nd ed. (Minneapolis: Fortress Press, 2001), xvii.
13. Trungpa, *The Path Is the Goal*, 293.
14. Hammarskjöld, *Markings*, 52.
15. Martin Buber, quoted in Friedman, *Encounter on the Narrow Ridge*, 363.
16. Quoted in Rollo May, *Man's Search for Himself* (New York: A Delta Book, 1953), 15.
17. Luigi Pirandello, *Naked Masks*, ed. Eric Bentley (New York: E. P. Dutton, 1952), 102, 122, 138.
18. Quoted in Joseph Chilton Pearce, *Exploring the Crack in the Cosmic Egg* (New York: Julian Press, 1974), 116.
19. Thomas Merton, *The Hidden Ground of Love* (New York: Farrar, Strauss, Giroux, 1985), 93.
20. Abraham Maslow, *The Farther Reaches of Human Nature* (New York: Penguin Books, 1972), 34.

21. Graham Greene, *A Burnt-Out Case* (London: Penguin Books, 1975).
22. Pierre Teilhard de Chardin, *The Divine Milieu* (New York: Harper Colophon Books, 1968), 71.
23. Emmanuel Levinas, *Existents and Existence* (The Hague: M. Nijhoff, 1978), 35.
24. Merton, *Disputed Questions*, 164.
25. Sebastian Moore, *Jesus, the Liberator of Desire* (New York: Crossroad, 1989), 32.
26. Angela West, *Deadly Innocence: Feminist Theology and the Mythology of Sin* (London: Wellington House, 1995), 109.
27. Thoreau, *Walden*, 40.
28. Friedrich Nietszche, *Thus Spake Zarathustra* (Mineola, NY: Dover Publications, 1999), 80.
29. Max Picard, *The World of Silence* (Chicago: Henry Regnery Company, 1952), 50.
30. Aldous Huxley, quoted in Anthony Robbins, *Awake the Giant Within* (New York: Free Press, 1991), 172.
31. Emmanuel Levinas, *Is It Right to Be? Interviews with Emmanuel Levinas*, ed. Jill Robbins (Stanford, CA: Stanford University Press, 2001), 97.
32. Jerry Mander, *Four Arguments for the Elimination of Television* (New York: Quill, 1978), 152.
33. James Baldwin, quoted in Harvey, *The Return of the Mother*, 14.

5 A Second Education from Within

1. Thomas Merton, *The Asian Journal* (New York: New Directions, 1968), 117.
2. David Fideler, "Stranger in Flatland," *Gnosis Magazine* (Summer 1994), 11.
3. Huston Smith, *The Way Things Are* (Berkeley and Los Angeles: University of California Press, 2003), 11.
4. Clark Kerr, quoted in Rubem A. Alves, *A Theology of Hope* (Washington, DC: Corpus Books, 1969), 9.
5. Thomas Merton, *Love and Living* (New York: Harcourt Brace and Company, 1979), 11.
6. Steven Miller, quoted in Smith, *The Way Things Are*, 124.
7. Blaise Pascal, referred to in Boff, *Ecology and Liberation*, 145.
8. Paul Tillich, *The Courage to Be* (New York: Yale University Press, 1952), 51f.
9. Meister Eckhart, quoted in Matthew Fox, *Breakthrough: Meister Eckhart's Creation Spirituality in New Translations* (New York: Doubleday, 1980), 407.
10. Chogyam Trungpa, *Born in Tibet* (Baltimore: Penguin Books, 1972), 116.
11. Martin Luther, referred to in Rollo May, *Freedom and Destiny* (New York: W. W. Norton, 1981), 99.
12. Abraham Heschel, in Matthew Fox, *Sins of the Spirit, Blessings of the Flesh* (New York: Harmony Books, 1999), 4.
13. Carl Jung, *Modern Man in Search of a Soul* (London: Routledge and Kegan Paul, 1933), 236.
14. Friedrich Nietzsche, *Portable Nietzsche*, ed. Walter Kaufman (New York: Penguin Books, 1976), 138.

15. Ralph Waldo Emerson, *Nature, Addresses, Lectures: The Complete Works of Ralph Waldo Emerson* (Boston: Houghton Mifflin, 1903), 131–32.
16. Friedrich Nietzsche, in Kaufman, *Portable Nietszche*, 351.
17. Chogyam Trungpa, *The Myth of Freedom* (Berkeley, CA: Shambhala, 1976), 6.
18. Marcel Legaut, *True Humanity* (New York: Paulist Press, 1982), 191.
19. Chogyam Trungpa, *The Essential Chogyam Trungpa*, ed. Carolyn Rose Gimian (Boston: Shambhala, 1999), 185.
20. Thoreau, *Walden*, 66.
21. Brother David Steindl-Rast, OSB, interview with John Loudon, "Become What You Are," *Parabola* 7, no. 4 (1982), 60–67.
22. Shin'ichi Hisamatsu, *Zen and the Fine Arts* (Japan: Koshanda International, 1971), 84.
23. Raimon Panikkar, *Blessed Simplicity* (New York: Seabury Press, 1982), 34.
24. Chogyam Trungpa, in Gimian, *The Essential Chogyam Trungpa*, 89.
25. Thoreau, *Walden*, 65.
26. Chogyam Trungpa, in Gimian, *The Essential Chogyam Trungpa*, 66.
27. Thomas Merton, *Conjectures of a Guilty Bystander* (Garden City, NY: Doubleday, 1966), 64.
28. Dalai Lama, *Ethics for a New Millenium* (New York: Riverhead Books, 1999), 98.
29. Harvey, *The Return of the Mother*, 101.
30. William James, quoted in Allan Combs, *The Radiance of Being* (St. Paul, MN: Paragon House, 2002), 8.
31. Anais Nin, "The All Seeing," in *Under a Glass Bell* (New York: E. P. Dutton, 1948).
32. Erich Neumann, C. G. Jung, and R. F. C. Hull, *Origins and History of Consciousness*, Bollingen Paperback (Princeton, NJ: Princeton University Press, 1970).
33. Rabbi Jack Bemporad, *The Inner Journey: Views from the Jewish Tradition*, Parabola Anthology Series (Sandpoint, ID: Morning Light Press, 2007), 143–44.

6 Self-discovery

1. Howard Thurman, quoted in Sam Keen, *Hymns to an Unknown God* (New York: Bantam Books, 1994), 7.
2. Thomas Berry, *The Dream of the Earth* (San Francisco: Sierra Club Books, 1988), 201.
3. Thomas Merton, *Day of a Stranger* (Salt Lake City, UT: Gibbs M. Smith, 1981), 31–32.
4. Walt Whitman, *Leaves of Grass* (Garden City, NY: Doubleday, 1926), 349–50.
5. Panikkar, *The Cosmotheandric Experience*, 74.
6. Panikkar, *Christophany*, 23.
7. Bruteau, *The Grand Option*, 30.
8. Raimon Panikkar, *A Dwelling Place for Wisdom* (Louisville, KY: Westminster/John Knox Press, 1993), 68.
9. Gershom Scholem, *Major Trends in Jewish Mysticism* (New York: Schocken Books, 1967), 55.

10. Carl Jung, quoted in Singer, *Boundaries of the Soul*, 375.
11. Jean Houston, *The Search for the Beloved* (Los Angeles: Jeremy P. Tarcher, 1987), 126.
12. Sogal Rinpoche, *The Tibetan Book of Living and Dying* (New York: HarperCollins Publishers, 2002).
13. Ibn Al Arabi, quoted in Henry Corbin, *Creative Imagination in the Sufism of Ibn 'Arabi* (Princeton, NJ: Princeton University Press, 1981), 62, 94.
14. Buber, *I and Thou*, 109.
15. Joseph Campbell, *Transformations of Myth through Time* (New York: Harper and Row, 1990), 188.
16. Socrates, *Defense* or *Apology*.
17. Pindar, quoted in David L. Norton, *Personal Destinies: A Philosophy of Ethical Individualism* (Princeton, NJ: Princeton University Press, 1976), 16.
18. Trungpa, *Crazy Wisdom*, 13.
19. William Butler Yeats, *Mythologies* (New York: Macmillan, 1961), 336.
20. Arthur Schopenhauer, in Rudiger Safranski and Ewald Osers, *Shopenhauer and the Wild Years of Philosophy* (Cambridge: Harvard University Press, 1991).
21. Michael Ventura, *We've Had a Hundred Years of Psychotherapy and the World Is Getting Worse* (San Francisco: HarperSanFrancisco, 1992), 21.

7 Working with Our Inner Alchemy

1. Kular nava Tantra, quoted in E. F. Schumacher, *A Guide for the Perplexed* (New York: Harper and Row, 1977), 131.
2. Harvey, *The Return of the Mother*, 26.
3. Parker Palmer, "A Spirituality of Public Life," in *Action Information* (November/December 1989), 3.
4. Aldo Caretenunto, *Psyche and Pathos: Shades of Love and Suffering* (Toronto: Inner City Books, 1987), 100.
5. The Gospel of Thomas (11,2), #70, in *The Nag Hammadi Library*, gen. ed. James M. Robinson (New York: Harper and Row, 1977), 126.
6. Buber, *I and Thou*, 137.
7. Trungpa, in Gimian, *The Essential Chogyam Trungpa*, 105.
8. Albert Camus, *Lyrical and Critical Essays* (New York: Vintage Books, 1970), 7.
9. Rainer Maria Rilke, quoted in Edward Hirsch, *The Demon and the Angel* (New York: Harcourt, 2002), 157.
10. M. C. Richards, *Centering* (Middletown, CT.: Wesleyan University Press, 1964), 40.
11. The Bhagavad Gita (The Song of the Blessed), vs. 35.
12. Panikkar, *Blessed Simplicity*, 125.
13. Raimon Panikkar, "The New Monk," *Monastic Interreligious Dialogue Bulletin* 72 (April 2004).
14. Joseph Campbell, in Osbon, *A Joseph Campbell Companion*, 135.
15. Thomas Merton, "Poetry and Contemplation: A Reappraisal," *Commonweal* 70 (1965), 137.

8 The Further Journey

1. Thomas Merton, *New Seeds of Contemplation* (New York: New Directions, 1961), 64.

2. Saint Augustine, *In Johannis epistulam*, tract 9.0.

3. Daisetz Teitaro Suzuki, *Outline of Mahayana Buddhism* (London: Luzae and Co., 1907), 238.

4. Hillel, quoted in Harold Bloom, *Where Shall Wisdom Be Found?* (New York: Riverhead Books, 2004), 5.

PART II
COMPASSIONATE SOLIDARITY

9 Solidarity Mysticism

1. Raimon Panikkar, quoted in Camilia Gangasingh MacPherson, *A Critical Reading of the Development of Raimon Panikkar's Thought on the Trinity* (Lanham, MD: University Press of America, 1996), 51.

2. Karl Rahner, *Foundations of Christian Faith: An Introduction to the Idea of Christianity* (New York: Seabury Press, 1978), 222.

3. Emmanuel Levinas, *Entre-Vous* (New York: Columbia University Press, 1998), 3.

4. Abraham Heschel, quoted in Maurice Friedman, *Abraham Joshua Heschel and Elie Wiesel: You Are My Witnesses* (New York: Farrar, Straus, Giroux, 1987), 70.

5. Alfred North Whitehead, "Religion in the Making," in *Alfred North Whitehead: An Anthology*, selected by F. S. C. Northrop and Mason W. Gross (New York: Macmillan, 1953), 472.

6. Franz Rosenzweig, *The Star of Redemption* (Madison: University of Wisconsin Press, 2005), 223.

7. Robert Wuthnow, *God and Mammon in America* (New York: The Free Press, 1994), 58.

8. Dorothee Soelle, *The Silent Cry: Mysticism and Resistance* (Minneapolis: Fortress Press, 2001), 3.

9. Martin Buber, *Hasidism and Modern Man*, ed. Maurice Friedman (New York: Harper Torchbooks, 1966), 180f.

10. Sarvepalli Radhakrishnan, quoted by Richard A. Cohen, "Introduction," in Emmanuel Levinas, *Humanism of the Other* (Chicago: University of Illinois Press, 1972), vii.

11. Harvey, *The Return of the Mother*, 101.

12. *The Cambridge Translations of Medieval Philosophical Texts*, vol. 2, *Ethics and Political Philosophy*, ed. Arthur Stephen McGrade, John Kilcullen, and Matthew Kempshall (Cambridge: Cambridge University Press, 2000), 187.

13. Bruteau, *The Grand Option*, 41.

14. Martin Buber, quoted in Friedman, *Encounter on the Narrow Ridge*, 137.

15. Leon Brunschvicg, *De le vrai et de la fausse conversion, suivi de la querelle de L'Atheisme* (Paris: Presses Universiteraires de France), quoted in Levinas, *Difficult Freedom*, 48.

16. Dalai Lama, quoted in Lama Surya Das, *Buddha Is As Buddha Does* (San Francisco: HarperSanFrancisco, 2007), xxii.

17. Emmanuel Levinas, "Eternite a domicle," *Evidences* 28 (November 1952): 35–36.

18. Abraham Heschel, quoted in Friedman, *Abraham Joshua Heschel and Elie Wiesel*, 48.

19. Metz, *Love's Strategy*, 165.

20. Fyodor Dostoyevsky, *The Brothers Karamazov* (New York: Penguin Classics, 1993).

21. Cohen, "Introduction," in Levinas, *Humanism of the Other*, xviii.

22. Cohen, *Elevations*, 188.

23. Ibid.

24. Edward Schillebeeckx, *The Schillebeeckx Reader*, ed. Robert J. Schreiter (New York: Crossroad, 1985), 273.

25. Smith, *Why Religion Matters*, 211–12.

26. Pius IX, quoted in Joe Holland, *Modern Catholic Social Teaching: The Popes Confront the Industrial Age* (Mahwah, NJ: Paulist Press, 2003), 92.

27. Robert McAfee Brown, "What Every North American Should Know about Liberation Theology," editor's interview, *U.S. Catholic* (April 1989), 22.

28. Boff, *Faith on the Edge*, 70.

29. Chogyam Trungpa, "Foreword," in Osel Tendzin, *Buddha in the Palm of Your Hand* (Boston: Shambhala Publications, 1982).

30. Raimon Panikkar, "The New Innocence: Interview with Raimon Panikkar," *Share International* (October 1996), 3.

10 Engaged Buddhism

1. Matthieu Richard, *The Monk and the Philosopher* (New York: Schocken Books, 1999), 143.

2. Saint Augustine, quoted in H. A. Reinhold, ed., *The Spear of Gold: Revelations of the Mystics* (London: Burns Oates, 1947), 174.

3. Thich Nhat Hahn, *Heart of Understanding: Commentaries on the Prajnaparamita Heart Sutra*, ed. Peter Levitt (Berkeley, CA.: Parallax Press), 4.

4. Chogyam Trungpa, *The Heart of the Buddha* (Boston: Shambhala, 1991), 118.

5. Ibid., 108–9.

6. Ibid.. 125.

7. Ibid., 119.

8. Ibid., 113.

9. Tibetan Buddhist monk, quoted in Harvey, *The Return of the Mother*, 212.

10. Thich Nhat Hahn, *Interbeing: Commentaries on the Tiep Hien Precepts*, ed. Fred Eppsteiner (Berkeley, CA: Parallax Press, 1987), 35.

11. Harvey, *The Return of the Mother*, 408.

11 The Hebrew Tradition

1. Emmanuel Levinas, “L’inspiration religieuse de l’Alliance,” *Pais et Droit* 15, no. 8 (October 1935): 4.
2. Jack Nelson-Pallmeyer, *Is Religion Killing Us?* (Harrisburg, PA: Trinity Press International, 2003).
3. Vanessa Baird, “In the Name of God,” *New International* 370 (August 2004): 10.
4. Elise Boulding, *Cultures of Peace: The Hidden Side of History* (New York: Syracuse University Press, 2000).
5. Nelson-Pallmeyer, *Is Religion Killing Us?* xii.
6. Ibid., 54.
7. Thomas Cahill, *The Gift of the Jews* (New York: Nan A. Talese/Anchor Books, 1998), 5.
8. William J. Jackson, ed., *J. L. Mehta on Heidegger, Hermeneutics, and the Indian Tradition* (Leiden: E. J. Brill, 1992), 108.
9. Cahill, *The Gift of the Jews*, 239.
10. Ibid., 237–38.
11. Jack Miles, *God: A Biography* (New York: Vintage Books, 1995), 99.
12. Karl Barth, *Church Dogmatics*, 11/1 (Edinburgh: T&T Clark, 1956), 386.
13. N. H. Snaith, *The Distinctive Ideas of the Old Testament* (London: Epworth Press, 1944), 48.
14. Chogyam Trungpa, *Cutting through Spiritual Materialism* (Berkeley, CA: Shambhala, 1973).
15. Martin Buber, quoted in Friedman, *Encounter on the Narrow Ridge*, 357.
16. Ibid., 137.
17. Martin Buber, *Between Man and Man* (New York: Macmillan, 1965), 52.
18. Shlomo Malka, quoted in *The Levinas Reader*, ed. Sean Hand (Malden, MA: Blackwell, 1989), 289.
19. Emanuel Levinas, *Proper Names* (Standford, CA: Stanford University Press, 1996), 72.
20. Dostoyevsky, *The Brothers Karamzov*, Book V1, Part 11a, cited in Levinas, *Otherwise than Being or Beyond Essence*, 146.
21. Levinas, *Proper Names*, 70.
22. Ibid., 76.
23. Michael Purcell, *Levinas and Theology* (Cambridge: Cambridge University Press, 2006), 51.
24. Levinas, *Difficult Freedom*, 275.
25. Levinas, *Proper Names*, 89, 86.
26. Levinas, *Difficult Freedom*, 248.
27. Ibid., 17.
28. Ibid., 195
29. Levinas, *Is It Righteous to Be?* 109.
30. Emmanuel Levinas, *Totality and Infinity*, trans. Alphonso Lingis (Pittsburgh: Duquesne University Press, 1969), 78.

31. Cohen, *Elevations*, 107–8.
32. Ibid., 245.
33. Levinas, *Entre-Nous*, 63.
34. Emmanuel Levinas, quoted in Hand, *The Levinas Reader*, 6.
35. Levinas, *Difficult Freedom*, 17.
36. John D. Caputo, "The Question of God," in *The Face of the Other and the Trace of God: Essays on the Philosophy of Emmanuel Levinas*, ed. Jeffrey Bloechl (New York: Fordham University Press, 2000), 302–3.

12 Jesus and His Radical Gospel

1. J. P. Nail, "The Role and Problems of Private Enterprise in Education," *The Christian College and National Development* (Madras: CSL, 1967), 134.
2. Metz, *Love's Strategy*, 121.
3. Sebastian Kappen, *Jesus and Freedom* (Maryknoll, NY: Orbis Books, 1977), 18.
4. Levinas, *Difficult Freedom*, 246.
5. Kappen, *Jesus and Freedom*, 25.
6. E. Lohmeyer, *The Lord of the Temple* (Edinburgh: Oliver and Boyd, 1961), 47.
7. Ibid., 72.
8. Kappen, *Jesus and Freedom*, 25.
9. Ibid., 18.
10. Ibid., 19.
11. Paul F. Knitter, ed., *Pluralism and Oppression* (New York: University Press of America, 1991), 170.
12. Emmanuel Levinas, "The Pact," in *Beyond the Verse*, trans. Gary D. Mole (Bloomington: Indiana University Press, 1994), 79.
13. Kappen, *Jesus and Freedom*, 21.
14. W. D. Davies, *The Sermon on the Mount* (Cambridge: Cambridge University Press, 1966), 151.
15. Kappen, *Jesus and Freedom*, 23.
16. Metz, *Love's Strategy*, 144.
17. Sobrino, *The Principle of Mercy*, 1.
18. Metz, *Love's Strategy*, 33.
19. Ignacio Ellacuría, *Freedom Made Flesh* (Maryknoll, NY: Orbis Books, 1976), 114.
20. Kazoh Kitamori, *Theology of the Pain of God* (Richmond, VA: John Knox Press, 1965), 98.
21. Karl Rahner and W. Thurssing, *Christologie Systematisch und Exegetich* (Freiburg: Herder, 1972), 29.
22. Leonardo Boff, quoted in G. E. Ladd, *The Presence of the Future: A Revised and Updated Version of Jesus and the Kingdom* (Grand Rapids, MI: Eerdmanns, 1974), 101.
23. John Fuellenbach, *The Kingdom of God* (Maryknoll, NY: Orbis Books, 1995), 36.
24. Sobrino, *The Principle of Mercy*, 20.
25. Aloysius Pieris, SJ, *God's Reign for God's Poor: A Return to the Jesus Formula* (Kelaniya: Tulana Research Centre, 1999), 42.

26. Aloysius Pieris, SJ, *An Asian Theology of Liberation* (Maryknoll, NY: Orbis Books, 1992), 18.
27. Aloysius Pieris, SJ, *Fire and Water* (Maryknoll, NY: Orbis Books, 1996), 134.
28. Saint Basil, Sixth Homily against Wealth, cited in John Ryan, *Alleged Socialism of the Church Fathers* (St. Louis: Herder. 1913), 9.
29. Leonardo Boff, "The Need for Political Saints," *Cross Currents* (Winter 1980–81), 372.
30. Johann Baptist Metz, quoted in Gerhard M. Kirk, "Sensitivity for the Wrong of Others," Baden newspaper (March 1999).
31. Edward Schillebeeckx, *Jesus: An Experiment in Christology* (New York: Crossroad/Seabury Press, 1979), 203.
32. Ibid., 139.
33. Albert Nolan, *Jesus before Christianity* (Maryknoll, NY: Orbis Books, 1991), 113.
34. Robert McAfee Brown, "Toward a Just and Compassionate Society: A Christian View," *Cross Currents* (Summer 1995), 168.
35. Pieris, *An Asian Theology of Liberation*, 122.
36. Edward Schillebeeckx, interview, *Creation* (September/October 1990), 23.
37. Johann Baptist Metz, *The Emergent Church* (New York: Crossroad, 1981), 27.
38. Pieris, *Fire and Water*, 128.
39. Pedro Casaldaliga, *In Pursuit of the Kingdom* (Maryknoll, NY: Orbis Books, 1990), 247.
40. Pieris, *An Asian Theology of Liberation*, 107.
41. Bhagwan Shree Rajneesh, *The Book of Wisdom: Discourses on Atisha's Seven Points of Mind Training* (Osho International, 2001), 86.
42. Ulrich Luz and Axel Michaels, *Encountering Jesus and Buddha* (Minneapolis: Fortress Press, 2006), 72.
43. Schillebeeckx, *Jesus*, 210.
44. Virgil Elizondo, *The Future Is Mestizo* (Bloomington, IN: Meyer Stone Books, 1988), 79.
45. Dietrich Bonhoeffer, *The Cost of Discipleship* (New York: Macmillan, 1965), 7.
46. Walter Wink, *Naming the Powers: The Language of Power in the New Testament*, vol. 1 (Philadelphia: Fortress Press, 1984), 140.
47. Nolan, *Jesus before Christianity*, 100.
48. Metz, *Love's Strategy*, 30.
49. Thorwald Lorenzen, *Resurrection and Discipleship* (Maryknoll, NY: Orbis Books, 1995), 89.
50. *Christ* is a compendious title that has absorbed all that Christian believers have attributed to Jesus ever since the Easter experience (Aloysius Pieris, SJ).
51. Jon Sobrino, *La Fe en Jesu Cristo: Ensayo desde las victimas* (Madrid: Editorial Trotta, 1999).
52. Romano Guardini, quoted in Pedro Casaldaliga and Jose Maria Vigil, *The Spirituality of Liberation* (New York: Hyperion Books, 1994), 58.
53. Jon Sobrino and Ignacio Ellacuría, eds., *Systematic Theology* (Maryknoll, NY: Orbis Books, 1993), 69, 282.

13 Toward a Judeo-Christian Future Vision

1. José Comblin, *Retrieving the Human: A Christian Anthropology* (Eugene, OR: WIPF and Stock Publishers, 2003), 45.

2. U.S. Catholic Bishops, *Economic Justice for All: Pastoral Letter on Catholic Social Teaching and the U.S. Economy* (Washington, DC: National Conference of Catholic Bishops, 1986), no. 13.

3. Frederick Herzog, *Justice Church* (Maryknoll, NY: Orbis Books, 1981), 43–44.

4. Thomas Merton, *The Inner Experience* (San Francisco: HarperSanFrancisco: 2003), 22.

5. Martin Heidegger, *Being and Time* (New York: Harper and Row, 1962), 220.

6. Pope John XXIII, quoted in *Economic Justice for All*, no. 17.

7. Cohen, "Introduction," in Levinas, *Humanism of the Other*, xviii.

8. Oscar Maria Sanchez, quoted in Helena Cobban, *The Moral Architecture of World Peace* (Charlottesville: University Press of Virginia, 2000), 157.

9. Dalai Lama, quoted in Das, *Buddha Is As Buddha Does*, xxi.

10. H. J. Kraus, quoted in Jose Porfirio Miranda, *Marx and the Bible: A Critique of the Philosophy of Oppression* (Maryknoll, NY: Orbis Books, 1974), 78.

11. *Westminster Shorter Catechism*, quoted in Frederick Herzog's *Justice Church*, 84.

12. Nicholas Wolterstorff, "Justice as a Condition of Authentic Liturgy," *Theology Today* 48, no. 1 (April 1991).

13. Marcus Borg, *The Heart of Christianity* (San Francisco: HarperSanFrancisco, 1995), 127.

14. Metz, *Love's Strategy*, 24.

15. Sobrino, *The Principle of Mercy*, 17.

16. Comblin, *Retrieving the Human*, 35.

17. Oscar Romero, quoted in Casaldaliga and Vigil, *The Spirituality of Liberation*, 153.

18. First Bishops' Institute of Social Action, BISA 1 (Novaliches, 1974), in *For All the Peoples of Asia*, vol. 1, ed. Gaudencio Rosales and C. G. Arévalo (Quezon City, Philippines: Claretian Publications, 1997), 200.

19. Gerhard Lohfink, *Jesus and Community* (Philadelphia: Fortress Press, 1982), 122.

20. Metz, *Love's Strategy*, 24.

21. Emmanuel Levinas, quoted in Hand, *The Levinas Reader*, 257.

22. Marcus Borg, *Jesus in Contemporary Scholarship* (Valley Forge, PA: Trinity Press International, 1994), 98.

23. Marcus Borg, *The God We Never Knew* (San Francisco: HarperSanFrancisco, 1998), 143.

24. Walter Rauschenbusch, quoted in Stanley Hauerwas, *A Community of Character: Toward a Constructive Social Ethic* (Notre Dame, IN: University of Notre Dame Press, 1981), 57.

25. Monika Hellwig, quoted in John A. Coleman, "How the Eucharist Proclaims Social Justice," *Church* (Winter 2000), 7.

26. P. Steindl-Meier, *Social Justice Ministry, Foundation, and Concerns* (New York: Le Jacq Publishing, 1988), 15.

27. Edward Schillebeeckx, referenced in Paul F. Knitter, *Jesus and the Other Names* (Maryknoll, NY: Orbis Books, 1996), 116.
28. Pope John Paul II, quoted in Donald Dorr, *Option for the Poor: A Hundred Years of Catholic Social Teaching* (Maryknoll, NY: Orbis Books, 1983), 283.
29. Gustavo Gutiérrez, *A Theology of Liberation* (Maryknoll, NY: Orbis Books, 1971), 233.
30. M. K. Gandhi, *The Story of My Experiment with Truth* (Ahmedabad: Navajivan, 1966), 282–83.
31. Pedro Arrupe, SJ, quoted in Robert McAfee Brown, *Spirituality and Liberation* (Louisville, KY: Westminster Press, 1988), 34.
32. Rosemary Ruether, *Liberation Theology* (New York: Paulist Press, 1972), 8.
33. Johann Baptist Metz and Jürgen Moltmann, *Faith and the Future* (Maryknoll, NY: Orbis Books, 1995), 11.
34. Pope Pius XII, *La sollentina della Pentecoste*, radio message June 1, 1941 (*AAS* 33), 200.
35. Alves, *A Theology of Hope*, 75.
36. Maude Barlow, "Globalization and the Dismantling of Canadian Democracy, Values, and Society," PCD forum article no. 17 (June 1, 1996).
37. Johann Baptist Metz, in Metz and Moltmann, *Faith and the Future*, 203.
38. Gutiérrez, *Essential Writings*, 202.
39. Pope John Paul II, speaking in the industrial city of Monterey, Mexico (*AAS* 242).
40. Johann Baptist Metz, in Metz and Moltmann, *Faith and the Future*, 203.
41. Metz, *Love's Strategy*, 1.
42. Jürgen Moltmann, *Hope and Planning* (London: SCM Press, 1971), 178.

PART III
TOWARD A SPIRITUALITY OF INTEGRAL HUMANITY

14 The Self and the Other

1. Harvey, *The Return of the Mother*, 253.
2. Thomas Berry, *The Great Work: Our Way into the Future* (New York: Bell Tower, 1999), 4, 22.
3. Romano Guardini, quoted in Marian Jaworski, *The Human Person from a Transcendental Perspective*. Available on the www.crvp.org website.
4. Rosemary Ruether, *Liberation Theology*, 12.
5. Elizabeth Cady Stanton, quoted in Carol Gilligan, *In a Different Voice* (Cambridge: Harvard University Press, 1982), 129.
6. Lao Tzu, *Tao Teh Ching*, chap. 49, quoted in Philip Koch, *Solitude: A Philosophical Encounter* (Peru, IL: Open Court, 1994), 289.
7. Buber, *Between Man and Man*, 202.
8. Ibid., 212.
9. Franz Rosenzweig, quoted in Cohen, *Elevations*, 62.
10. Erich Fromm, *Beyond the Chains of Illusion: My Encounter with Marx and Freud*, The Credo Series (New York: Simon and Schuster, 1962), 149.

11. Marc Gafni, *The Mystery of Love* (New York: Atria Books, 2003), 31.
12. Maurice Friedman, *The Human Way* (Chambersburg, PA: Anima Books, 1982), 34.
13. Raimon Panikkar, *The Experience of God: Icons of the Mystery* (Minneapolis: Fortress Press, 2006), 44–45.
14. Maurice Friedman, *A Heart of Wisdom* (Albany: State University of New York Press, 1992), 198.
15. Albert Camus, *Exile and the Kingdom* (New York: Vintage Books, 1957), 158.
16. Comblin, *Retrieving the Human*, 84.

15 Autonomy and Community

1. Edward Schillebeeckx, *Church: The Human Story of God* (New York: Crossroad, 1991), 170.
2. Aloysius Pieris, SJ, "Christ beyond Dogma: Doing Christology in the Context of the Religion of the Poor," *Louvain Studies* 25 (2000), 220.
3. Pedro Casaldaliga, in Casaldaliga and Vigil, *The Spirituality of Liberation*, 158.
4. Herbert Marcuse, *One Dimensional Man* (London: Routlege and Kegan Paul, 1964).
5. Dietrich Bonhoeffer, *Life Together* (Minneapolis: Augsburg Fortress, 1996).
6. Fritjof Capra, *Turning Point* (New York: Bantam, 1982), chap. 8.
7. David Korten, in an interview with Arnie Cooper, "Everybody Wants to Rule the World," *The Sun* (September 2007), 8.
8. Wilber, *Sex, Ecology, Spirituality*, 59.
9. Raimon Panikkar, "The New Innocence—An Interview with Raimon Panikkar," *Share International* (October 1966), 3.
10. Pierre Teilhard de Chardin, *The Phenomenon of Man*, trans. Bernard Wall (New York: Harper and Row, 1965), 262.
11. Panikkar, *Blessed Simplicity*, 47.
12. See *Baghavad Gita*, XVIII, 47.
13. Merton, *Love and Living*, 3.
14. Gil Bailie, *Violence Unveiled* (New York: Crossroad, 1995), xv.
15. Frederick Buechner, *Wishful Thinking: A Seeker's ABC* (San Francisco: HarperSanFrancisco, 1993), 119.
16. Thomas Merton, *The Springs of Contemplation* (New York: Farrar, Straus, Giroux, 1992), 136.
17. Thich Nhat Hahn, *Living Buddha, Living Jesus* (New York: Riverhead Books, 1995), 74.
18. Richard Rohr, "A Clandestine Christian," *Radical Grace* (August/September 1999), 8.
19. Jeff Dietrich, *Catholic Agitator* (September 2002), 4.
20. Jim Wallis, in Ronald Rolheiser, *The Holy Longing* (New York: Doubleday, 1999), 4.
21. Singer, *Boundaries of the Soul*, 227.
22. Felix Wilfred, in *Leave the Temple: Indian Paths to Liberation*, ed. Felix Wilfred (Maryknoll, NY: Orbis Books, 1992), 6–7.
23. Wilber, *Sex, Ecology, Spirituality*, 45–46.

24. Ibid., 69.
25. Friedman, *The Human Way*, 98.

16 Being and Becoming

1. Thomas J. J. Altizer, "Buddhist Emptiness and the Crucifixion of God," in *The Emptying God*, ed. John B. Cobb, Jr., and Christopher Ives (Maryknoll, NY: Orbis Books, 1991), 76.
2. Eckhart Tolle, *The Power of Now* (Novato, CA: New World Library, 1999), 40–41.
3. Genpo Roshi, online interview, www.masteringthepowerofnow.com.
4. Karl Barth, quoted in Charles C. West, *Communism and the Theologians* (New York: Macmillan 1958), 269.
5. Barth, *Church Dogmatics* 1/2, 114.
6. John Macquarrie, *In Search of Humanity* (New York: Crossroad, 1983), 2.
7. John Macquarrie, *In Search of Deity* (New York: Crossroad, 1985), 97.
8. Panikkar, *Blessed Simplicity*, 123.
9. Berry, *The Great Work*, 163–64.
10. Norman Pittenger, *God in Process* (London: SCM Press, 1967), 19–20.
11. Ken Wilber, *Sex, Ecology, Spirituality*, 8.
12. Alfred North Whitehead, *Process and Reality* (New York: Macmillan, 1929), 522.
13. Raimon Panikkar, *The Silence of God* (Maryknoll, NY: Orbis Books, 1989), 144.
14. Alfred North Whitehead, *Adventure of Ideas* (New York: Macmillan, 1933), 354.
15. Emmanuel Levinas, "Contempt for the Torah as Idolatry," in *In the Time of the Nations*, trans. Michael B. Smith (Bloomington: Indiana University Press, 1994), 58–59.
16. John B. Cobb, *Christ in a Pluralistic World* (Philadelphia: Westminster Press, 1975), 62–94.
17. Metz, *Love's Strategy*, 20.
18. John D. Caputo, *The Weakness of God: A Theology of the Event* (Bloomington: Indiana University Press, 2006), 121.
19. Berry, *The Great Work*, 1.
20. Karl Rahner, *Sacramentum Mundi*, vol. 3 (New York: Seabury Press, 1969), 116.
21. Maurice Friedman, *Problematic Rebel* (Chicago: University of Chicago Press, 1970), 8.

17 Serenity and Struggle

1. Friedrich Nietszche, *Twilight of the Idols* (1888).
2. Karlfried Durkheim, *The Japanese Cult of Tranquility* (York Beach, ME: Samuel Weisner, 1991), 40.
3. Trungpa, in Gillian, *The Essential Chogyam Trungpa*, 185.
4. Campbell, *The Power of Myth with Bill Moyers*, 65.

5. Albert Camus, quoted in Thomas Merton, *The Literary Essays of Thomas Merton* (New York: New Directions Books, 1985), 276.
6. Comblin, *Retrieving the Human*, 169.
7. Martin Heidegger, *Poetry, Language, Thought*, trans. and intro. Albert Hofstadter (New York: Perennial Classics, 2001), 47.
8. Kenji Myazawa, quoted in Matthew Fox, *A Spirituality Named Compassion* (Minneapolis: Winston Press, 1979), 120–21.
9. Meister Eckhart, quoted in John D. Caputo, *The Mystical Element in Heidegger's Thought* (New York: Fordham Press, 1986), 137.
10. Whitehead, *Process and Reality*, 169.
11. Smith, *Why Religion Matters*, 253.
12. Nolan, *Jesus before Christianity*, 28.
13. The Greek word *splagchnizomai* (compassion) is derived from the noun *splagchnon*, which means "intestines, bowels, entrails, or heart."
14. Daniel Day Williams, "God and Man," in *Process Theology*, ed. Ewert H. Cousins (New York: Newman Press, 1971), 182.
15. Rubem A. Alves, *The Poet, The Warrior, The Prophet* (Philadelphia: Trinity Press International, 1990), 129.
16. Whitehead, *Process and Reality*, 161.

18 The Spirituality of Subtraction

1. Richard Rohr, *Letting Go: A Spirituality of Subtraction*, eight talks on tape (Cincinnati: St. Anthony Messenger Press, 2005).
2. Berry, *The Great Work*, 76.
3. Ellen Goodman, quoted in Joe Dominguez and Vicki Robin, "Introduction," in Jaqueiline Blix and David Heitmiller, *Getting a Life: Real Lives Transformed by Your Money or Your Life* (New York: Viking, 1991), xiii.
4. Jonathan Freedman, *Happy People* (New York: Harcourt Brace Jovanovich, 1978), 136.
5. Earth Council, *The Earth Summit, ECO 92: Different Visions* (San Jose, Costa Rica: Inter-American Institute for Cooperation of Agriculture, 1994), 181.
6. Jacob Needleman, *Money and the Meaning of Life* (New York: Currency Doubleday, 1991).

19 The Spirituality of Universal Embrace

1. Paolo Soleri, "Techno/Logy/Theo/Logy," in Panikkar, *Blessed Simplicity*, 173.
2. Buber, *The Legend of the Baal-Shem*, 50.
3. Panikkar, *The Silence of God*, 142.
4. Gregory of Nyssa, *De Vita Moysis* (PG, 44:941).
5. Panikkar, *The Silence of God*, 143.
6. Bernard Loomer, "S-I-Z-E," *Criterion* 13, no. 3 (Spring 1974): 21.
7. Trungpa, *Orderly Chaos*, 16.
8. Piero Ferucci, *Inevitable Grace* (Los Angeles: Jeremy P. Tarcher, 1990), 32.

9. See Berry, *The Great Work*, 52.
10. Whitehead, *Process and Reality*, 514, 515.
11. Richard A. Cohen, *Ethics, Exegesis, and Philosophy* (New York: Cambridge University Press, 2001), 225.
12. Trungpa, *Orderly Chaos*, 156.
13. Jose Ortega y Gasset, "In Search of Goethe from Within," trans. Willard Trash, in *The New Partisan Reader, 1945–1953*, ed. William Phillips and Philip Rahv, 289–313 (New York: Andre Deutsch, 1953).
14. Panikkar, *Blessed Simplicity*, 124.
15. Heraclitus, quoted in Singer, *Boundaries of the Soul*, epigraph.
16. Panikkar, *The Cosmotheandric Experience*, 1.
17. Ibn al Arabi, quoted in Corbin, *Creative Imagination in the Sufism of Ibn 'Arabi*, 135.
18. Ron Seitz, *Song for Nobody* (Liguori, MO: Triumph Books, 1993), 32.
19. Thomas Merton, *Emblems on a Season of Fury* (New York: Image Books, 1968), 81.
20. M. Basil Pennington, OCSO, *Thomas Merton, Brother Monk* (San Francisco: Harper and Row, 1987), 155.
21. Merton, *Conjectures of a Guilty Bystander*, 156.
22. Merton, *Asian Journal*, 216.
23. Raimon Panikkar, quoted in Walter H. Capps, "Toward a Christian Theology of the World Religions," *Crosscurrents* 29, no. 2 (1953), 161.
24. See Ewert Cousins, "Raimon Panikkar and the Christian Systematic Theology of the Future," in *Crosscurrents* 29 (1974), 143.
25. Raimon Panikkar, quoted in Walter H. Capps, "Toward a Christian Theology of the World's Religions," 161.
26. Thomas Berry, CP, with Thomas Clarke, SJ, *Befriending the Earth* (Mystic, CT: Twenty-Third Publications, 1991), 18.

20 The Highest Teaching

1. Edith Wyschogrod, *Saints and Postmodernism* (Chicago: University of Chicago Press, 1990), 34.
2. Robert Ellsberg, *All Saints* (New York: Crossroad, 1997), 4.
3. Ibid., 5.
4. Brother David Steindl-Rast, interview with Richard Smoley, "Heroic Virtue: An Interview with Bro. David Steindl-Rast O.S.B.," *Gnosis* (Summer 1992), 6.
5. Wyschogrod, *Saints and Postmodernism*, xxiii.
6. Friedman, *The Human Way*, 75.
7. Andrew Harvey, *Son of Man* (New York: Jeremy P. Tarcher/Putnam, 1999), 7.
8. Geza Vermes, *The Religion of Jesus the Jew* (Minneapolis: Fortress Press, 1993), 14–15.
9. In Panikkar, *The Silence of God*, 167.
10. Ibid.
11. Dalai Lama, quoted in Das, *Buddha Is As Buddha Does*, xiv.
12. Ibid., 15.

13. Dalai Lama, quoted in "House of Compassion," www.edmundclt.org/news/renteam/page122.
14. Dalia Lama, *Ethics for a New Millennium*, 23.
15. Meister Eckhart, quoted in Raymond Bernard Blakney, *Meister Eckhart: A Modern Translation* (New York: Harper Torchbooks, 1957), 14.
16. Vermes, *The Religion of Jesus the Jew*, 2.
17. Friedman, *The Human Way*, 44–45.
18. Aloysius Pieris, SJ, in *Any Room for Christ in Asia?* ed. Leonardo Boff and Virgil Elizondo, *Concilium* (1993/2), 33.
19. Vermes, *The Religion of Jesus the Jew*, 215.
20. Harvey, *Son of Man*, 7.
21. Vermes, *The Religion of Jesus the Jew*, 46.
22. Ibid., 194.
23. Joseph Klausner, *Jesus of Nazareth: His Life, Times, and Teachings* (1925), 414.
24. Harold Bloom, *Jesus and Yahweh* (New York: Riverhead Books, 2005), 133.
25. Harvey, *Son of Man*, 73.
26. Ibid., 74.
27. Richard of St. Victor, quoted in Harvey, *Son of Man*, 126.
28. Harvey, *Son of Man*, 104.
29. Emmanuel Levinas, quoted in Jeffrey Bloechl, *Liturgy of the Neighbor* (Pittsburgh: Duquesne University Press, 2000), 54.
30. Emmanuel Levinas, *Otherwise Than Being or Beyond Essence*, 55.
31. Ibid., 149.
32. Cohen, "Introduction," in Levinas, *Humanism of the Other*, xxvii.
33. Levinas, *Otherwise Than Being or Beyond Essence*, 49.
34. Ibid., 149.
35. Ibid., 150.
36. Ibid., 147.
37. Cohen, "Introduction," in Levinas, *Humanism of the Other*, xxxiv.
38. Levinas, *Otherwise Than Being or Beyond Essence*, 138, xxv, 139.
39. Friedman, *The Human Way*, 96.
40. Levinas, *Otherwise Than Being or Beyond Essence*, 55–56.
41. Ibid., 138.
42. Dostoyevsky, in ibid., 146.
43. Levinas, in ibid., 154.
44. Cohen, "Foreword," in Friedman, *The Human Way*, xii.
45. Ibid., xix.
46. Ibid., xxviii.
47. Cohen, "Introduction," in Levinas, *Humanism of the Other*, xxxiv.
48. Harvey, *Son of Man*, 82.
49. Ibid., 22.
50. Ibid., 81.
51. Emmanuel Levinas, *Time and the Other*, trans. R. A. Cohen (Pittsburgh: Duquesne University Press, 1987), 114f.
52. Cohen, "Introduction," in Levinas, *Humanism of the Other*, xxxvi.

Index